MW00813630

BLACK INTELLECTUALS AND BLACK SOCIETY

Black Intellectuals and Black Society

MARTIN L. KILSON

FOREWORD BY
Cornel West

Columbia University Press
New York

Columbia University Press
Publishers Since 1893
New York   Chichester, West Sussex
cup.columbia.edu
Copyright © 2024 Columbia University Press

Library of Congress Cataloging-in-Publication Data
Names: Kilson, Martin, author.
Title: Black intellectuals and Black society / Martin L. Kilson.
Description: New York : Columbia University Press, [2024] |
Includes bibliographical references and index.
Identifiers: LCCN 2023052226 (print) | LCCN 2023052227 (ebook) |
ISBN 9780231215657 (hardback) | ISBN 9780231560900 (ebook)
Subjects: LCSH: African American intellectuals—Biography. |
African Americans—Intellectual life—20th century. |
United States—Intellectual life—20th century.
Classification: LCC E185.89.I56 K54 2024 (print) | LCC E185.89.I56 (ebook) |
DDC 973/.049607300922 [B]—dc23/eng/20231220
LC record available at https://lccn.loc.gov/2023052226
LC ebook record available at https://lccn.loc.gov/2023052227

Printed in the United States of America

Cover design: Milenda Nan Ok Lee

In memory of
Horace Mann Bond
John Aubrey Davis
St. Clair Drake

Contents

Acknowledgments

When Martin Kilson died in 2019, he left behind the manuscript that has become *Black Intellectuals and Black Society*. I wish to acknowledge several people who have contributed significantly to making the book a reality. Cornel West once again memorialized his former professor in the foreword. Julie Wolf once again disentangled some of Martin's prose in her preliminary copyedits. Ryan Perks completed copyediting for the Press. Stephen Wesley was a responsive colleague during the acquisitions process. Leslie Kriesel oversaw the production process. Finally, David Prout created the index. I am so very grateful to each of you for your contribution. I know how very pleased Martin Kilson would be by this book.

Marion D. de B. Kilson

Foreword

CORNEL WEST

Martin L. Kilson Jr. was the greatest political scientist of his generation, someone who focused on both Afro-Americans here and Africans abroad. He also was the first Black tenured professor in the history of Harvard University. Many of us cannot conceive of our intellectual vocation and scholarly work without Kilson's sterling example and genuine encouragement. In addition to myself, the highly acclaimed Fred Moton and the late Jerry Watts come to mind in this regard. There is no doubt that Kilson—alongside the great St. Clair Drake—is one of the two grand products and progeny of the golden age of the Black intelligentsia from the 1920s through the 1960s. This unsung, overlooked, and often downplayed generation of courageous and visionary Black intellectuals come alive in an unprecedented manner in this powerful and pioneering work.

Kilson highlights the "Afro-Americanization" of Negro colleges as a crucial institutional process, yet he never loses sight of the "perpetual interplay between formal ideas and Black equalitarianism struggle." He has a deep appreciation of organic intellectuals such as the "brilliant" Sojourner Truth, Nancy Ruffin, David Walker, Frederick Douglass, Richard Wright, James Baldwin, Horace Pippin, and Harold Cruse. Kilson's rich conception of the "broad-gauged social-class basis of the evolving twentieth-century African American intelligentsia" reveals how limiting and even impoverished the discourse on Black public intellectuals in our day has been. Kilson puts forward a subtle and sophisticated analysis that remains attuned to the intellectual and ideological dynamics of flesh-and-blood thinkers as well as the power and political dynamics of institutional and structural realities. His own immersion into these multidimensional dynamics and realities gives him a very special key to unlock new insights.

Black political thought has moved closer to the center of serious inquiry as a recognized academic discipline with the publication of the monumental text edited by Melvin L. Rogers and Jack Turner, *African American Political Thought: A Collected History* (University of Chicago, 2021), as well as the historic book edited by Brandon Terry and Tommie Shelby, *To Shape a New World: Essays on the Political Philosophy of Martin Luther King, Jr.* (Harvard University Press, 2018). Like Kilson's path-blazing work, both anthologies acknowledge the "impact of the Du Bois–Washington cleavage on the early Black intelligentsia"—the clash between "a firmly progressive but pragmatic skepticism" and "an accommodationist leadership." All three texts also lay bare the limitations of this Du Bois–Washington framework, which marginalizes Marcus Garvey's explosive Black Nationalism and "the great Black radical Ida B. Wells-Barnett's abolitionist anti-lynching movement." As Kilson quotes her courageous words in regard to Washington's compromising project, "This gospel of work is no new one for the Negro. It is the South's old slavery practice in a new dress."

Kilson then notes the strong words of the legendary Madam C. J. Walker at an event for Washington's own National Negro Business League hosted at her Hudson River estate, Villa Lewaro, in late August 1918: "My message to my people is this: Go live and conduct yourself so that you will be above the reproach of any one. But should but one prejudiced, irrational boast infringe upon your rights as men—resent the insults like men . . . and if death be the result—so be it. An honorable death is far better than the miserable existence imposed upon most of our people in the south."

For Kilson, the fundamental challenge of the golden age of the mid-century Black intelligentsia was "to smash the dual shackles of Bookerite accommodationist and fear of white racism." This effort required a maturing and ripening of "a variant of Du Boisian civil rights activism" and an attention to decolonization in Africa. What Kilson calls "narratives of Blackness or tales of Black equalitarianism struggle" here and abroad— "sparked by pioneer Black dancers like Pearl Primus, Donald McKayle, and Katherine Dunham" alongside a host of other artists and figures—fan and fuel this political activism. Kilson's text, so badly needed in our grim time of Black Lives Matter and Gilded Age excess, offers a highly illuminating and inspiring journey. His magnificent treatment of his mentor—the great Horace Mann Bond (beloved father of Julian Bond)—is one of the unique and beautiful moments in Afro-American letters. It is a singular combination of historical analysis, political inquiry, and personal tribute! The poignant triumph and tragedy of Bond's marvelous calling and courageous career of "Christian self-efficacy activism" (to use St. Clair Drake's apt words) are for the ages. Like Dante's homage to Virgil, Kilson gently guides us from the inferno of Jim Crow America (Alabama, Louisiana, and Georgia, including the first pre-Bookerite leader, William H. Councill, in Huntsville and the life-changing lynching of Jerome Wilson in Franklinton, Louisiana, in 1934)—to the false promise of the racist North. Bond's twelve years as president of the historic Lincoln University were groundbreaking—just as his political firing was pathetic (including a reneging on his salary and pension!). His commitment to decolonization in Africa was too much for his conservative white board. He responded by writing the definitive history of Lincoln University and cofounding (with John Aubrey Davis) the American Society for African Culture. Lincoln University graduates such as Nmandi Azikiwe of Nigeria and Kwame Nkrumah of Ghana played an important role in his new organization. Kilson's marvelous tribute to his lodestar, Horace Mann Bond—much like Du Bois's tribute to his own lodestar, Alexander Crummell, in *The Souls of Black Folk* (1903)—reveals Kilson's left-reformist humanism.

In our current environment, Horace Mann Bond would, I believe, recognize the need for a rebirth of Christian-humanist activism among the greed- and plutocracy-polluted corporatist stratum above all. I have in mind especially a rebirth of Christian-humanist activism on behalf of vanquishing the demeaning poverty that exists. If he were with us today, Bond's intellectual prowess would contribute boldly to this kind of Christian-humanist activist rebirth. This grand declaration reminds us of the precious legacy of Martin Luther King Jr. to which Bond, Kilson (in his distinctive, secular way), Preston Williams, Katie Cannon, and I are wedded! John Aubrey Davis—Kilson's other great mentor—indeed was "a rare breed." Davis's elite education at Williams College, the University of Wisconsin, and Columbia University was rare. His activism with the New Negro Alliance (including alongside Thurgood P. Marshall) was rare. His directorship of President Roosevelt's Fair Employment Practices Committee at the age of thirty-one was rare. His professorships at Howard University,

Lincoln University, and City College of New York were rare. And his cofounding of the American Society for African Culture was prophetic. Kilson's treatment of three towering figures—Ralph Bunche's early Marxist years, E. Franklin Frazier's scathing indictment of the Black bourgeoisie, and Harold Cruse's influential Black Nationalism—are now more relevant than ever. Contemporary discussions of Black Marxism, racial capitalism, abolitionism, Afro-pessimism, Afro-futurism, Black womanism, and Black Nationalism loom large. Yet Kilson's empirically based, analytically acute judgments are leaven in this loaf. Needless to say, Kilson's close readings of Bunche's prize-winning Marxist dissertation at Harvard on Togoland and Dahomey, of Frazier's famous critiques of the Black middle class, and of Cruse's fraught Black Nationalist project are absolutely brilliant. I was elated to see the chapter on the pioneering Adelaide Cromwell, and even more so to know that this chapter was written by the distinguished Harvard-trained anthropologist Marion D. de B. Kilson—Martin Kilson's brilliant wife and life companion. I can attest to the depth, breath, and scope of this magnificent marriage and partnership (as parents of such wonderful children and scholarly products)! Cromwell's unique trajectory from the acclaimed Dunbar High School in Washington, DC, to Smith College in 1936, to her groundbreaking Harvard doctoral dissertation on Black and white elite women in mid-twentieth-century Boston, and on to subsequent works on her historic family remains too often overlooked. Marion Kilson masterfully takes us step-by-step, text-by-text through Cromwell's rich corpus in a clear and succinct manner. From Cromwell's aunt Otelia Cromwell, the first Black student to attend and graduate from Smith College, in 1900, to Adelaide Cromwell's crucial years in Africa, including her major paper delivered at the Newark National Conference on Black Power in 1967, "What Is Africa to Us?," Martin Kilson ends this fabulous scholarly book with a fascinating typology of Black intellectuals—reform-leftist, ethno-activist, conservative, and establishmentarian—and examinations of the literary giant Ismael Reed as populist and myself as radical humanist. So Kilson's magisterial text begins with a heartfelt gratitude to his towering mentors and ends with a call to keep the grand Du Boisian tradition alive. Progressive Black intellectuals today have, I believe, a special obligation to scrutinize the new ranks among conservative and establishmentarian Black public intellectuals. It is a task we owe our forefathers and foremothers of the twentieth-century African American intelligentsia, who laid the foundations on which we function. May the rigorous cerebral and joyful visceral legacy of the great Martin L. Kilson Jr.—my dearest teacher, mentor, and lodestar—forever be one of the foundations on which we remain true to our calling, work, and witness!

BLACK INTELLECTUALS AND BLACK SOCIETY

Prologue

Probing the African American Intelligentsia

This work grew out of a long-standing desire on my part to pay homage to the second-generation cohort of twentieth-century African American intelligentsia personalities who staffed Negro colleges during what I view as the high-noon era of these institutions—that great five-decade era of the 1920s through the 1960s. My own undergraduate years at one of those institutions, Lincoln University in Pennsylvania, coincided with this period; I attended from 1949 to 1953. Many other prominent African American intellectuals of my age cohort attended Negro colleges during the same period. Among them were Larry Neal (screenwriter), Amiri Baraka (formerly LeRoi Jones, poet/playwright), Johnnetta Cole (anthropologist/college president), Florence Ladd (psychologist/college administrator), Toni Morrison (novelist/college professor), Alice Walker (novelist), Niara Sudarkasa (anthropologist/college president), David Levering Lewis (historian), Asa Davis (historian), John Blassingame (historian), C. Eric Lincoln (sociologist), Dennis Dickerson (historian/editor, *A.M.E. Church Review*), Preston Williams (theologian), James Cone (theologian), Clement Cottingham (political scientist), Wilbur Rich (political scientist), William Tatum (owner/editor *Amsterdam News*), Earl Graves (owner/editor, *Black Enterprise* magazine), Maynard Jackson (mayor), Andrew Young (civil rights leader/mayor), Julian Bond (civil rights leader/historian), James Lawson (civil rights leader), John Lewis (civil rights leader/congressman), and Martin Luther King Jr. (civil rights leader), to mention only a prominent few.

In general, African American professionals in my age cohort who attended any of these colleges during this period owe a special debt to their faculties, both African American and white American, who facilitated what I call the "Afro-Americanization" of Negro colleges, a topic brilliantly related in Raymond Wolters's *The New Negro on Campus: Black Colleges and Rebellion in the 1920s* (1975).[1] I also treat this topic in chapter 1 on Horace Mann Bond's intellectual odyssey. I myself owe a debt to a special group of second-generation African American intelligentsia personalities who shaped my intellectual formation while at Lincoln University, among them Horace Mann Bond (sociologist and president of Lincoln University), John Aubrey Davis (political scientist), Laurence Foster (anthropologist/sociologist), Joseph Newton Hill (English and drama studies), Henry Cornwell (psychologist), and Roscoe Lee Browne (English).

Unique Developmental Attributes of the Black Intelligentsia

This volume combines studies of the developmental dynamics of the twentieth-century African American intelligentsia *in aggregate* with studies of the intellectual odyssey (career and discourse) of representative African American intellectuals *in particular*. Our discussion here of the unique developmental attributes of the African American intelligentsia should commence with two definitional matters. One relates to the issue of "performing intelligentsia or intellectual functions." On this issue, I adhere to the definition of an "intellectual or intelligentsia personality" presented more than sixty years ago by the social theorist Seymour Martin Lipset, who defined an "intellectual personality" as someone who articulates ideas, values, moral/ethical positions, political choices, scientific hypotheses, and so forth for citizens in modern society to live by. Lipset wrote, "We shall here consider intellectuals to be all those who create, distribute, and apply *culture*—the symbolic world of man, including art, science, and religion. Within this group, two main levels may be discerned: the hard core, who are creators of culture—scholars, artists, philosophers, authors, some editors, and some journalists—performers in the various arts, most teachers, most reporters. A peripheral group are those who apply culture as part of their jobs—professionals such as physicians and lawyers."[2] This broad-gauged conception of the intellectual or intelligentsia role is, I believe, especially useful for understanding the unique facets of the development of the African American intelligentsia during the twentieth century.

The second definitional matter relates to the issue of the synonymous usage of the terms "African American intelligentsia" and "African American professional class or stratum," which I do in this volume. From the late nineteenth century onward, numerous African American individuals who became professionals (schoolteachers, nurses, doctors, dentists, morticians, people in the insurance business, bankers, and so on) found themselves articulating leadership responses to circumstances sparked by America's racist processes, laying out possible activist options (ethical, moral, educational, civic, political, etc.) for consideration.

In so doing, these African American individuals found themselves performing intellectual or intelligentsia functions, as it were, although prior to such experience their professional identities or training did not involve an intellectual or intelligentsia dimension. In functioning thus beyond their pro forma technical, professional boundaries, such professional-class African Americans were, I submit, simultaneously performing intellectual functions. Accordingly, throughout the twentieth century—in fact, commencing in the late nineteenth century—there was a *fluid interplay* between the African American professional class on the one hand and intellectual or intelligentsia personalities on the other, making them in operational and functional terms one and the same.

This situation had a corollary dynamic within the overall character of the evolving twentieth-century African American intelligentsia. It happened that from the embryonic dawn of the African American intelligentsia among Free Negro communities in the pre–Civil War era onward, there were very few social mechanisms that sustained rigid entry criteria for persons who put themselves forward to perform intellectual or intelligentsia functions. Put another way, the role of the intellectual among African Americans has never been a monopoly of persons with college-certified or formal knowledge skills (in education, law, medicine, the arts, and so forth). Thus, what was unique about the development of the twentieth-century African American intelligentsia (in contrast with that of white ethnic communities—for example, Irish Americans, Jewish Americans, and white Anglo-Saxon Protestants, or WASPs) was that the social class basis underlying the choice to characterize persons as "intellectuals or intelligentsia persons" was broad-gauged, which is to say, a fair number of individuals in the early development of the African American intelligentsia came directly from artisan, farmer, and working-class backgrounds. In short, performing intelligentsia functions among African Americans has historically involved numerous self-made intelligentsia personalities. In this connection, think of the Reverends J. W. C. Pennington and John Sella Martin, nineteenth-century abolitionists whose leadership was brought to light by the historian R. J. M. Blackett in *Beating Against the Barriers: The Lives of Six Nineteenth-Century Afro-Americans* (1986).[3] Think of other self-made nineteenth-century abolitionist leaders like David Walker, Lewis Hayden, Nancy Ruffin, and Frederick Douglass. Think of Sojourner Truth, the brilliant suffragette. Or think of self-made twentieth-century artists and writers, people like Horace Pippin, Richard Wright, James Baldwin, and Harold Cruse.

Given, then, the broad-gauged class basis of the evolving twentieth-century African American intelligentsia, major Black intellectualizing thrusts during the twentieth century were propelled by broad dynamics within Black popular society. From World War I onward, emergent Black working-class communities in the North, in which citizens were tormented daily by American racist behavior, spawned a variety of narratives of Blackness (tales of Black struggle), which, in turn, were translated eventually into overall Black intellectualizing thrusts. Such Black intellectualizing thrusts involved equalitarian ideas and orientations that spawned specific Black intellectuals' formation in a variety of areas; they involved civic activism by Black professional persons or groups on behalf of African Americans' equalitarian status; and they involved civil rights activism by Black professional persons on behalf of African Americans' equalitarian status.

Put another way, the developmental trajectory of the twentieth-century African American intelligentsia was something far more than a mediated process based on formal ideas or formal knowledge. Rather, it involved a multisided interplay between and intertwining of formal ideas on the one hand and Black equalitarian struggle on the other.

Black Intellectuals: Creatures of Formal Ideas and Black Equalitarian Struggle

The prominent generic characteristics of Black American intellectuals were shaped at any given point during the twentieth century by the multifaceted interrelationship between the American racial caste system and African American society in general. What was both structurally and behaviorally distinguishing about the developmental chemistry of Black intellectuals in the American nation-state was that in contrast with the experience of white American intellectuals, any given Black intellectual's modus operandi was closely connected with the aggregate attributes of his or her Black ethnic community in general.

From this perspective, then, the developmental character of the intellectualizing phenomenon of the evolving twentieth-century Black American intelligentsia personality is best understood in terms of *a perpetual interplay* between formal ideas and Black equalitarian struggle. This way of viewing the developmental chemistry of evolving twentieth-century Black intellectualizing patterns is suggested, I think, by the young W. E. B. Du Bois's seminal ethnography of post-emancipation-era Negro religious faith in his chapter "Of the Faith of the Fathers" in *The Souls of Black Folk*:

It is difficult to explain clearly the present critical stage of Negro religion. First, we must remember that living as the blacks do in close contact with a great modern nation, and sharing, although imperfectly, the soul-life of that nation, they must necessarily be affected more or less directly by all the religious and ethical forces that are today moving the United States. These questions and movements are, however, over-shadowed and dwarfed by the (to them) all-important question of their civil, political, and economic status. They must perpetually discuss the "Negro problem"—must live, move, and have their being in it, and interpret all else in its light or darkness. With this come, too, peculiar problems of their inner life—of the status of women, the maintenance of the home, the training of children, the accumulation of wealth, and the prevention of crime. All this must mean a time of intense ethical ferment, of religious heart-searching and intellectual unrest.[4]

However unique the realities of the Black community (what Du Bois dubbed the "Negro problem") have been in shaping the overall development of the Black intelligentsia, it is nevertheless important to recognize that when a minuscule educated, elite stratum made its initial appearance in post-emancipation African American society, the formal-knowledge or formal-ideas attributes of the fledgling Black intelligentsia were as important to its character as they were among the white American intelligentsia. The pioneering late nineteenth-century personalities who fashioned the organizational groundwork of the embryonic Black intelligentsia grappled fervently with these attributes, resulting in the founding of the American Negro Academy.

Formed in 1897 by seminal African American modern thinkers and professionals such as Alexander Crummell (a clergyman and philosopher), John Wesley Cromwell (an accountant and newspaper editor), Reverdy Ransom (a bishop in the African Methodist Episcopal Church and editor of its main organ, the *A.M.E. Church Review*, founded in 1884), Paul Laurence Dunbar (a poet), and Francis Grimké (a clergyman trained at Lincoln University and Princeton Theological Seminary), the American Negro Academy set out to cultivate a foundation of formal knowledge for the emergent African American intelligentsia. Crummell underlined this purpose in his inaugural address as the academy's first president, delivered in March 1897 under the title "Civilization: The Primal Needs of the [Negro] Race." That address had a profound impact on the young Du Bois, who included an intellectually elegant essay on the academy's leading figure titled "Of Alexander Crummell" in *The Souls of Black Folk*. In the first volume of his biography of Du Bois, David Levering Lewis remarks that Crummell's inaugural address "was a manifesto of high culture": "Crummell told the body that a race was civilized only when it produced 'letters, literature, science, philosophy, poetry, sculpture, architecture . . . all the arts.' "[5]

In this initial approach to fashioning the embryonic African American intelligentsia, I believe, like Du Bois, that the original participants in the American Negro Academy were correct, because in the national scheme of things, ultimate parity recognition for Black intellectuals depended significantly on African Americans' possession of a cadre of trained persons with vast knowledge, Black persons who could be viewed as full-fledged purveyors at the highest level of Western philosophical, classical, artistic, and scientific ideas.

Indeed, even before the founding of the American Negro Academy in 1897, it was evident that post-emancipation African Americans fully grasped the importance of furthering a highly educated and trained Black intelligentsia. For example, already by the 1870s and 1880s, talented first-generation higher-educated African Americans had carved out a solid foothold for themselves in the field of classical studies, a subject on which the Wayne State University historian Michelle Valerie Ronnick has published extensively. In her study *The First Three African American Members of the Philological Association* (2001), Ronnick relates the brilliant career of the classical studies scholar William Sanders Scarborough, an African American born in slavery who attended the nascent Atlanta University in the late 1860s and later gained an education in classical studies at Oberlin College, graduating in 1875.[6] His major published work, *First Lessons in Greek* (1870), was a phenomenal scholarly success treated in a fascinating article by Ronnick in the *A.M.E. Church Review* (October–December 2002). Scarborough was among the first three African Americans to achieve membership in the august American Philological Association, inducted at Harvard University in 1883. He was appointed vice president of Wilberforce University in 1897 and served as its president from 1908 to 1920.

In his seminal work *Black Intellectuals: Race and Responsibility in American Life* (1996), the University of California African American studies scholar William Banks underscores the important role of the American Negro Academy in propagating the significance to post-emancipation African American society of a cadre of higher-educated individuals who functioned at intellectual parity with the mainstream white intelligentsia. Banks maintains that Alexander Crummell and his associates in the academy correctly "concluded that an organization of highly educated African Americans could advance the interests of black people."[7] Accordingly, toward this goal of furthering a calibrated Black intelligentsia, the American Negro Academy's founding manifesto proposed the following:

1. To promote the publication of literary and scholarly works;
2. To aid youths of genius in the attainment of higher culture at home and abroad;
3. To gather into its Archives valuable data, historical or literary works of Negro authors;
4. To aid, by publications, vindication of the race from vicious assaults, in all the lines of learning and truth;
5. To publish, if possible, at least once a year an "Annual" of original articles upon various Literary, Historical, and Philosophical topics, of a racial nature, by selected members; and by these and diverse other means, to raise the standards of intellectual endeavor among American Negroes.[8]

The example of the American Negro Academy had a kind of multiplier effect, for during the late 1890s and the first two decades of the twentieth century, a variety of organizations mirroring its goals were founded by the African American upper stratum in cities such as Cleveland, Chicago, New York, Washington, DC, Atlanta, and Philadelphia. For example, a year after the academy's founding, Philadelphia's Black community witnessed the founding in 1898 of the American Negro Historical Society. Between 1900 and the outbreak of World War I, a plethora of similar, smaller societies emerged among upper-stratum Philadelphia Blacks, such as the Paul Laurence Dunbar Literary Society, the Phillis Wheatley Literary Society, the Pinn Memorial Literary Society, and the J. C. Price Literary Society. Roger Lane's seminal study on Black intelligentsia developments in late nineteenth- and early twentieth-century Philadelphia, *William Dorsey's Philadelphia and Ours: On the Past and Present Future of the Black City in America* (1991), relates the fascinating growth of such organizations among that city's Black professional stratum.[9]

Curiously enough, however, within a generation and a half of the founding of the American Negro Academy in 1897, it formally closed its doors in 1928. Similar closures of such Black intelligentsia associations in urban America also occurred in the late 1920s, including that of the Pinn Memorial Literary Society in Philadelphia (also in 1928), the most important of that city's Black intelligentsia organizations. The second most important Black intelligentsia organization in Philadelphia, the Negro Historical Society, had already been shuttered in 1923.[10] What was behind the decline of these knowledge-advancing associations among the Black intelligentsia during the 1920s?

Perhaps the primary reason was related to the expanding role of Black intelligentsia personalities in the leadership and faculties of Negro colleges. Prior to the 1920s and 1930s, the leadership and faculties of most Negro colleges rested in the hands of white individuals who were connected with white liberal religious organizations. Prominent among these white churches were the Presbyterian Church and the Methodist Episcopal Church, which founded the first two Negro colleges before the Civil War: Lincoln University in Pennsylvania in 1854, and Wilberforce University in Ohio in 1856. (The African Methodist Episcopal Church would assume full control of Wilberforce University by the start of the Civil War.) As recorded in the 1922 survey of higher education programs by the white Methodist Episcopal Church—*Methodist Adventures in Negro Education,* authored by Jay S. Stowell—other prominent Negro colleges launched by white liberal religious organizations included Clark University, Morgan State College, Bethune-Cookman College, Wiley College, Philander Smith College, Claflin College, Flint-Goodridge Hospital and Nurse Training School, Meharry Medical School, Bennett College, and Gammon Theological Seminary.[11]

However, what might be called the Afro-Americanization of Negro colleges in regard to leadership (presidents and broader administrative posts) and faculty posts didn't occur until the 1920s. This development, which is related in Raymond Wolters's important work *The New Negro on Campus: Black College Rebellions of the 1920s* (1975), entailed fundamental alterations to Negro colleges. Accordingly, it was especially the expanding role of the African American intelligentsia in executing the high-knowledge functions at Negro colleges from the 1920s onward that, in turn, led to a "brain drain" among the Black intelligentsia away from organizations like the American Negro Academy and Philadelphia's American Negro Historical Society.

There was, however, an additional developmental dynamic surrounding the decline of urban Black intelligentsia associations from the mid-1920s onward. That dynamic concerned the rapid growth during the World War I era onward of Black working-class populations in northern urban communities. These new communities were chiseled out of a racist-ravaged and oppressed southern Black agrarian proletariat, and their viable development in cities like Chicago, Cincinnati, Cleveland, Detroit, Baltimore, Philadelphia, and New York spawned new intellectualizing patterns, by which I mean Black intellectualizing patterns shaped not merely by high-knowledge or formal-ideas leadership processes, but by everyday social realities for African American communities—in short, racist-ravaged urban Black realities.

Impact of the Du Bois–Washington Cleavage on the Early Black Intelligentsia

Fortuitously for the new urban Black communities of the post–World War I era, the young W. E. B. Du Bois, while an avatar of the high-knowledge Black intellectualization modalities, was also an intuitively generic proponent of the unique needs of the new urban Black working-class communities. In *W. E. B. Du Bois: Biography of a Race* (1993), Lewis informs us that the young Du Bois was deeply enamored of Alexander Crummell and his blueprint for the post-emancipation African American. Indeed, Du Bois revered Crummell and his American Negro Academy circle. Lewis gives a marvelously affecting account of Du Bois's initial immersion in a Crummell-inspired Black intelligentsia circle at Wilberforce University in Xenia, Ohio, from the summer of 1894 to mid-1896, when Du Bois commenced research on his classic work, *The Philadelphia Negro: A Social Study* (1899).

At the same time, however, Du Bois was his own man. As compared to the typical Crummellian-inspired personalities among the Black intelligentsia inner circle at Wilberforce in the late 1890s, Du Bois was more skeptical and thus more inclined to populism in his grasp of the politics of equality for the African American within the American white supremacist national society; in other words, he was more circumspect than Crummell, his hero and mentor, toward full reliance upon high-knowledge modalities within the African American intelligentsia as a form of agency for Black people's freedom and equalitarian struggle.

Above all, for Du Bois, a rigidly marginalized and brutally denigrated ethnic community like that of post-emancipation African American society would be ill served if its intelligentsia exhibited too much respect for leadership orientations that skewed toward elitism. Du Bois believed instead that an effective American Negro intelligentsia must fashion a firmly progressive but pragmatic skepticism, a skepticism shaped especially by the everyday experience of a racist-ravaged Black popular society.

From this vantage point, then, Du Bois understood that the formative era in the emergence of modern urban Black communities—the robber baron capitalist era—was a special period for the formerly southern agrarian proletariat Black folk. For African Americans, Du Bois understood the dynamics of this era to be "a time of intense ethical ferment, of religious heart-searching and intellectual unrest." He wrote, "The worlds within and without the Veil of Color are changing, and changing rapidly, but not at the same rate, nor in the same way; and this must produce a peculiar wrenching of the soul, a peculiar sense of doubt and bewilderment. Such a double life . . . must give rise to double words and double ideals, and tempt the mind to pretense or to revolt, to hypocrisy or to radicalism."[12]

From this cogent reading of the racist condition of Black America at the turn of the twentieth century, Du Bois proceeded to define the preferred intellectual or leadership modality for the fledgling Black intelligentsia as one that should tilt *against* "pretense" and "hypocrisy" and *toward* "revolt" and "radicalism," but no doubt toward a liberal or democratic radicalism. This meant, in one of its dimensions, that an effective emergent Black intelligentsia for a gravely weak proletarian African American urban society must recognize the need to minimize and checkmate its own elitist proclivity toward status "pretense."

Du Bois was insistent that an effective Black intelligentsia in the early years of twentieth-century urban Black community development should especially recognize that what he called "ethical forces" jostling for dominance among white Americans (e.g., the "wealth gospel" of the robber baron era) were not yet spheres of viable African American participation, though of course Booker T. Washington's accommodationist outlook fantasized such participation. Above all, for Du Bois, the robber baron–skewed "ethical forces" were, for the early twentieth-century Black American, "overshadowed and dwarfed by the . . . all important question of their civil, political, and economic status" within America's racial caste system.[13]

Thus, in the formative era of early twentieth-century Black working-class communities in the urban North, Du Bois hypothesized two ideological strands, two Black leadership paradigms within the fledgling American Negro intelligentsia: "We have two great and hardly reconcilable streams of thought and ethical striving [among Negroes]," he observed in 1903. "The one type of Negro . . . is wedded to ideals remote, whimsical, perhaps impossible of realization; the other forgets that life is more than meat and the body more than raiment. . . . Today the two groups of Negroes . . . represent these divergent ethical tendencies, the first tending toward radicalism, the other toward hypocritical compromise."[14]

So Du Bois, nursing a kind of ideological dualism toward the embryonic Black leadership dynamics of the late nineteenth and early twentieth centuries, straddled both the outlook of the elitist-skewed American Negro Academy and the civil rights activism orientation, which skewed toward Black populism. At the same time, however, the political substance of Du Bois's ideological dualism tilted, from its infancy onward, toward the progressive side of the political spectrum, as keen analysts of Du Bois's politics have argued, including Manning Marable in *W. E. B. Du Bois: Black Radical Democrat* (1986).[15] Du Bois himself characterized the intelligentsia option he favored as "tend[ing] toward radicalism [not] toward hypocritical compromise."

Furthermore, it is important to recognize that had Du Bois not fashioned an instrument of his radical-leaning political tendency such as the Niagara Movement in 1905, which joined with the National Association for the Advancement of Colored People (NAACP) in 1909, the populist-oriented intelligentsia option he favored might well have been overwhelmed by Booker T. Washington's accommodationist ("hypocritical compromise") intelligentsia option. Indeed, in "Going Over Niagara: Du Bois and Washington," a brilliant chapter in the first volume of his biography of Du Bois, Lewis shows vividly just how close Du Bois's radical political option came to have been short-circuited by the maneuverings of the incredibly shrewd Washingtonian Tuskegee Machine between 1903 and 1908. These maneuverings were made on behalf of a pseudo-liberal Black intelligentsia paradigm, one that Washington's powerful white elite allies favored. The Wizard of Tuskegee, as the historian Louis Harlan dubbed Washington, was a master of the political sleight of hand, shrewdly calling his pseudo-liberal Black intelligentsia mechanism the Commission on Interracial Cooperation, on which Washington graciously offered Du Bois and his activist allies in the Niagara Movement representation.

Several intervening events, however, caused Du Bois to waver at the very moment he was about to swallow the Wizard of Tuskegee's fishhook, so to speak. Those intervening events were the vicious Atlanta race riot of 1906 and the resistance to Washington's Commission on Interracial Cooperation by Du Bois's most trusted confreres, especially Monroe Trotter, the militant editor of the Black weekly the *Boston Guardian*, and Mary White Ovington, a progressive white journalist. Accordingly, between 1908 and 1909, Du Bois steadily embraced the civil rights and militant outlook—the "toward radicalism" option—embodied in the Niagara Movement gatherings, eventually institutionalizing the civil rights activist orientation in the founding of the NAACP in 1909.[16]

Above all, as Lewis makes clear, it was especially "the Atlanta riot [that] spoke grim volumes about the extent to which the Bookerite bargain had become a fatal trap," thereby assisting Du Bois's decision to join Trotter and Ovington in opposition to Washington's Commission on Interracial Cooperation.[17] The Springfield, Illinois, race riot in August 1908 also functioned to reinforce Du Bois's tilt toward a mechanism premised on civil rights activism and embraced by the Black intelligentsia on the progressive side of the emergent African American political spectrum, as the historian Kevin Gaines points out in *Uplifting the Race: Black Leadership, Politics, and*

Culture in the Twentieth Century (1996). The 1908 gathering known as the National Negro Conference, which fashioned the "call" to found the NAACP a year later, was, observed Gaines, "called after a race riot in Springfield, Illinois. . . . The disturbance was touched off by an accusation of rape, and when a lynch mob was frustrated in its attempt to storm the jail, it vented its fury on two innocent black men and burned black homes and property. At the conference, [Jesse Max] Barber [editor of Atlanta's leading African American organ, *Voice of the Negro*] urged that full citizenship, the suffrage, and jury service were imperative necessities for African Americans."[18]

Black Intelligentsia's Dual Shackles: Accommodationist Compromise and Fear of Racism

At the core of Washington's accommodationist leadership methodology was a quest to gain from national white power structures financial resources for expanding the emergent Black middle-class stratum. In Washington's calculation, this goal required the surrender of full-fledged citizenship and human rights for the average African American. Such surrender would, in Washington's scheme of things, free the emergent Black intelligentsia to concern itself with what he called the "essential," not the "non-essential," features of life—namely, expanding each African American's personal wealth and social status in American society. As he put it in his 1899 book *The Future of the Race,*

> I believe the past and present teach but one lesson—to the Negro's [white] friends and to the Negro himself—that there is but one hope of solution; and that is for the Negro in every part of America to resolve from henceforth that he will throw aside every non-essential [citizenship and human rights] and cling only to the essential—that his pillar of fire by night and pillar of cloud by day shall be property, economy, education, and Christian character. To us just now these are the wheat, all else the chaff.[19]

Furthermore, in exchange for the monumental concession to white supremacy of Black citizens' human and political rights basic to Booker T. Washington's accommodationist schema was an implicit promise from the nation's white elites to open working-class job opportunities to African Americans. Washington and members of his Tuskegee Machine, however, never fashioned a mechanism with their white elite allies to mediate access to those opportunities, nor was there any timetable in Washington's accommodationist schema by which progress toward the realization of Black Americans' full-fledged citizenship and human rights would take place. The fact of the matter was, unfortunately, that Washington's schema was little more than a verbal bargain between Washington and key white elite allies that lacked moral or institutional force. As Gunnar Myrdal put it in his monumental study of American Blacks' status, *An American Dilemma: The Negro Problem and Modern Democracy* (1944), "Through thrift, skill, and industry the Negroes were gradually to improve so much that, at a later stage, the discussion again could be taken up concerning their rights." This was Washington's (leadership) philosophy.[20]

Indeed, in terms of Black Americans' overall interrelationship with the evolving twentieth-century American white supremacist system, Washington's accommodationist schema ensured a perpetual second-class status for the typical African American. Drawing from the analysis of Ralph J. Bunche, who produced for the Carnegie Corporation's *An American Dilemma* project an unpublished research monograph on "The Programs, Ideologies, Tactics of Negro Betterment and Interracial Organizations" (1940), Myrdal offered a shrewd characterization of the systemic implications of Washington's accommodationism in *An American Dilemma*:

> He [Washington] was *prepared to give up social and political equality*, even to soft-pedal the protest against inequalities in justice. He was also willing to flatter the Southern whites and be harsh toward Negroes—if the Negroes were only allowed to work undisturbed with their white friends for [vocational] education and business. But neither in education nor in business did he assault the basic inequalities. *In both fields he accepted the white doctrine of the Negroes' "place."* In education he pleaded for vocational training, which . . . certainly comforted the whites in their beliefs about what the Negroes were good for and where they would be held in the occupational hierarchy.[21]

Thus, at the very dawn of an emergent twentieth-century African American intelligentsia, its viable modern and equalitarian metamorphosis was rendered problematic by Washington's accommodationist leadership methodology.[22] This paradigm could have proceeded unchallenged by alternative Black American leadership thrusts from the late 1890s onward, but fortunately for future liberal and progressive African American intelligentsia patterns, this was not the case.

It can be too easily forgotten just how politically powerful the Bookerite accommodationist leadership juggernaut—fueled by ties to conservative white industrial and political elites—was in its quest to smash the civil rights activist strands among the early twentieth-century African American intelligentsia. The great Black radical journalist Ida B. Wells–Barnett testified to one aspect of the political crudeness of Washington's accommodationist leadership when she critiqued a distasteful joke that Washington told at a gathering of the Negro Chicago Women's Club in 1904. He recounted to the audience the conservative advice he typically gave to agrarian Negroes on how to husband pigs: "Yes, Mr. Washington, ebber sence you done tole us bout raising our own hogs, we niggers round her hab resolved to quit stealing hogs and gwinter raise our own." Enraged by Washington's tacky "humor," which was designed to make white people laugh at the expense of African Americans, Wells–Barnett penned a stinging response in one of the liberal organs of the period, *World Today* (April 1904). Washington's demeaning joke, she observed, was a slap in the face of "hundreds of Negroes who bought land [and] raised hogs . . . long before Booker T. Washington was out of school." She noted further that the famed Booker T. Washington's "gospel of work" was fraudulent, because the typical southern Negro understood the importance of work for several centuries under American slavocracy. Preaching the "gospel of work" to Negroes in the early twentieth century, she insisted, was just ideological dishonesty and trickery, an attempt to mask the refusal of the racist white power structures to provide opportunities for genuine social mobility to American Negroes. As Wells–Barnett put it, "This gospel of work is no new one for the Negro. It is the South's old slavery practice in a new dress. It is the only education the South gave the Negro for [the] two and a half centuries she had absolute control of his body and soul. The Negro knows that now, as then, the South is strongly opposed to his learning anything else but how to work."[23]

Furthermore, she was equally enraged at another instance of Washington's verbal subservience to the racist predilections of conservative whites in regard to the agrarian and working-class Black masses—namely, his evasive commentary on the horror of lynching. As reported by her brilliant biographer Linda McMurray, Wells-Barnett encapsulated Washington's weak stance as follows: "Give me some money to educate the Negro and when he is taught how to work, he will not commit the crime for which lynching is done." In response to Washington's characteristic caginess, Wells-Barnett remarked that he was ignoring the fact that "lynching is not evoked to punish crime but color, and not even industrial education [at the Tuskegee Institute] will change that."[24]

Interestingly enough, it is also almost forgotten today in our post–civil rights era that among the evolving African American professional stratum in the early 1900s, there was a broad understanding of a need to challenge Washington's accommodationist leadership juggernaut. One didn't have to be identified as a civil rights activist or radical Black professional to recognize this. Even among politically centrist Black professionals, there was recognition of the need to assist with civil rights activist political options on behalf of the African American masses. I have in mind especially a category of Black professional personalities active some five generations ago whom I classify as bourgeois-activist personalities (establishmentarian professionals who were occasionally civil rights activists). One individual who fits this definition is Charles Clifton Spaulding, who owned the North Carolina Mutual Insurance Company and who, as related in Walter Weare's *Black Business in the New South: A Social History of the North Carolina Mutual Life Insurance Company* (1993), frequently reached out to civil rights organizations from his successful base in business.

Perhaps the most storied professional figure of the early twentieth century who could be described as such and who seized opportunities to critique elements of Washington's leadership style was Madam C. J. Walker, the hair-preparation industrialist. Indeed, she did so on one occasion involving a gathering of Washington's National Negro Business League that was hosted at her Hudson River estate, Villa Lewaro, in late August 1918. Walker's address in part lambasted vigilante attacks against Black soldiers in towns surrounding army bases during World War I. In the days following Walker's address, a leading white member of the Tuskegee Institute's board of trustees—one Colonel William Jay Schieffelin—publicly chastised Walker for that section of her address. While such criticism from the inner circle of Washington's Tuskegee Machine would normally have quieted the typical African American professional personality of that era, this was not the case for Madam C. J. Walker. She replied to Schieffelin's criticism in the strongest language available to her, affirming the need for successful African Americans like herself to reject the Booker T. Washington leadership paradigm when human and civil rights were violated, or the citizenship rights of any Black person for that matter. (Incidentally, Washington's secretary, Emmett Scott, attended the 1918 Negro Business League gathering at Madam Walker's estate.) In Walker's biography, *On Her Own Ground: The Life and Times of Madam C. J. Walker* (2001), by her great-great-granddaughter A'Lelia Bundles, we learn of the entrepreneur's stinging reply to Colonel Schieffelin in a letter written in January 1919: "The Negro in the South," she reminded him, "had been denied the use of firearms . . . and has been no match for the fiends and brutes who have taken advantage of his helplessness." Having "bravely, fearlessly bled and died" to help defend America's honor, she believed the troops had every right to expect a patriot's reward:

> Now they will soon be returning. To what? Does any reasonable person imagine to the old order of things? To submit to being strung up, riddled with bullets, burned at the stake? No! A thousand times No! And what good friend, even of humanity, would wish it so? . . . They will come back to face like men, whatever is in store for them and like men to defend themselves, their families, their homes. . . . Please understand that this does not mean that I wish to encourage in any way a conflict between the races. Such a thing is farthest from my mind. . . . My message to my people is this: Go live and conduct yourself so that you will be above the reproach of any one. *But should but one prejudiced, irrational boast infringe upon [your] rights as men—resent the insults like men . . . and if death be the result—so be it. An honorable death is far better than the miserable existence imposed upon most of our people in the south.* . . . I have tried so very hard to make you see the thing thru the eyes of a Negro, which I realize is next to impossible. . . . Your talks [about my speeches] would do a far greater good if you would point out to the white people just what their duties to the Negro are.[25]

That, mind you, was the political centrist Madam C. J. Walker speaking! But never mind, for neither the Ida Wells-Barnett radical-type critique or the Madam C. J. Walker bourgeois-activist-type critique did much to alter the cagey conservatism of Booker T. Washington's accommodationist juggernaut in the early twentieth century. Between the 1890s and his death in 1915, Washington cynically used his strategic linkages to white resources to block civil rights activism by progressive Black American intelligentsia personalities like Wells-Barnett, Trotter, and Anna Julia Cooper. William Banks informs us in *Black Intellectuals: Race and Responsibility in American Life* (1996) of the ways in which Booker T. Washington maneuvered against civil rights activist challengers. On the one hand, he ostensibly feigned a compromise by offering "a carrot" to challengers, a tactic used often to seduce owners of Negro newspapers into his accommodationism: "Knowing the black press' potential to influence black community opinion, he worked to enlist editors for his accommodationist approach to social and political issues. Backed by wealthy whites, Washington skillfully dangled the lure of financial support before revenue-poor editors and rallied many of the nation's black newspapers, such as the *New York Age* and the *Chicago Defender* to his side."[26]

On the other hand, Washington didn't live by carrots alone. He wielded the "whip" as well, and often. Washington's "whip" against his challengers among civil rights activists and radicals included maneuvering financial crises for activist Negro newspapers, preventing start-up newspapers with an activist bent, and smashing the careers of activist editors. As Banks informs us, "Booker T. Washington's political and financial clout enabled him to squelch black papers that crossed him. J. Max Barber, the editor in 1904–05 of the [Atlanta] weekly *Voice of the Negro*, frequently printed material critical of Washington's accommodationist policies. Determined to silence Barber and his *Voice*, Washington secretly discouraged advertisers and later asked Barber's publishers to remove him as editor. Barber lost control of the paper and turned to a career in dentistry."[27]

Although this kind of personal exercise of the Bookerite accommodationist juggernaut ended with Washington's death in 1915, his autocratic legacy continued for at least two more decades, executed by numerous accommodationist-oriented Black professionals who occupied the inner circle of Washington's nationwide Tuskegee Machine. His legacy also had an ideological dimension. For example, even an incredibly courageous civil rights activist like Wells-Barnett exhibited in her formative phase a friendly tilt toward the successful vocational education regime at the Tuskegee Institute during the 1880s and 1890s. But after experiencing a vicious lynching of two Black businesspersons with whom she was acquainted, and having discovered Washington's unwillingness to publicly condemn the widespread practice, she entered what I call her maturation phase around 1904 and 1905, linking up with the Niagara Movement and the Du Boisian orientation toward civil rights activism.

Similarly, my probe of Horace Mann Bond's career in chapter 1 relates how he navigated between a formative-phase friendliness toward some aspects of Booker T. Washington's education regime at the Tuskegee Institute while also developing and practicing countervailing ideological tendencies over and against Washington's accommodationist legacy. Bond's early success in his late twenties as a young dean of faculty at Dillard University, launched by the Rockefeller Foundation in New Orleans in the 1930s, marked him as a kind of natural candidate for leadership co-optation on the Bookerite conservative-accommodationist side of the African American leadership spectrum. Fortunately for the future development of the progressive sector of the African American intelligentsia from the 1930s onward, however, Bond's quest for a maturation-phase intellectual identity enabled him to avert leadership co-optation along Bookerite accommodationist lines.

Interestingly enough, as had happened to Wells-Barnett a generation before, the maturation of Bond's progressive intellectual identity during this period grew out of his exposure to a vicious lynching of a Black youth in a rural Louisiana community where he and his wife, Julia Washington Bond, were researching as Rosenwald Foundation fellows in 1934 and 1935. Thus, in overcoming an early intellectual tilt toward the legacy of the Tuskegee Machine, Horace Mann Bond became a powerful example to others of his second-generation cohort of twentieth-century peers in the Black intelligentsia. Bond's successful maturation-phase quest demonstrated that the obsessively self-serving mode of Washington's conservative leadership co-optation was not a necessity for African Americans' professional careers. In setting this example, Bond influenced the intellectual identity of other talented African American intelligentsia personalities from the 1930s onward, helping to curb the ideological reach of Washington's accommodationist legacy by the 1940s.

Just as it was difficult during the formative phase of the twentieth-century African American intelligentsia for its members to challenge and checkmate the reactionary influence of Washington's accommodationism within their ranks, it was equally difficult to challenge and checkmate the broad fear of racism in the ranks of the African American intelligentsia. We owe an important part of our understanding of the issue of the fear of racism among the evolving twentieth-century Black intelligentsia—the fear, that is, of the authoritarian and violent patterns of white supremacy in shaping African American lives—to the reporting in the 1940s of the Pulitzer Prize–winning white journalist Ray Sprigle. Assisted by a strong tan on his pale skin, Sprigle traveled through the South posing as a fair-skinned Black man. It worked too. On the role that fear of racism played in the daily life of African Americans in the South by the 1940s—when 90 percent of African Americans resided in the South—Sprigle observed in his book *In the Land of Jim Crow* (1949) that "Fear walks beside the black man in the Southland, from his earliest boyhood to the bed in which he dies. And fear was the lesson that I learned first and the lesson that I learned best in my four-week lifetime as a Negro in the South."[28] In the everyday talk and manner of the typical African American in the South during his post–World War II sojourn, Ray Sprigle saw and heard fear—for self, for family, for surroundings.

In his pioneering study of the social system of white supremacist patterns in the rural South, *Growing Up in the Black Belt: Negro Youth in the Rural South* (1941), Charles Spurgeon Johnson, one of the first professional African American sociologists, uncovered the tenacious role of what he called "race etiquette" (authoritarian interpersonal rules) in mediating vis-à-vis African Americans in the South that sense of fear that "keeps them in their place." The "rigid" pattern he outlined was clearly the norm.

1. Negroes may never marry whites in any of the counties studied.
2. Negroes may never dance with whites in any of the counties studied.
3. Negroes may never eat with whites in . . . [most] of the counties studied.
4. Negroes may never play games with whites in any counties except Bolivar, Davidson, and Madison (Alabama).
5. Negroes must always use "Mr." and "Mrs." when addressing whites in all counties.
6. Negroes must give whites the right-of-way on the sidewalks. . . .
7. Negro men must take off their hats in banks, stores, and so forth.[29]

Further studies of white supremacist patterns of coercion and terror conducted in the 1940s substantiated Johnson's findings. Prominent among these additional studies of authoritarian racial-caste patterns in the South was Gunnar Myrdal's aforementioned *An American Dilemma*. Here, Myrdal characterized the fear-inducing dimensions of authoritarian racial-caste patterns as follows:

> Violence, terror, and intimidation have been, and still are, effectively used to disenfranchise Negroes in the South. Physical coercion is not so often practiced against the Negro, but the mere fact that it can be used with impunity and that it is devastating in its consequences *creates a psychic coercion that exists nearly everywhere in the South.* A Negro can seldom claim the protection of the police and the courts if a white man knocks him down, or if a mob burns his house or inflicts bodily injuries on him or on members of his family. If he defends himself against a minor violence, the loss of his job or other economic injury, and constant insult and loss of whatever legal rights he might have had. In such circumstances it is no wonder that the great majority of Negroes in the South make no attempt to vote and—if they make attempts that are rebuffed—seldom demand their rights under the Constitution.[30]

With some variation, the overall role of fear induced by coercive behavior and threatened terror by whites against Blacks was present in the experience of 10–20 percent of the population who settled urban Black communities outside the South between World War I and World War II. Studies of white police coercion patterns, judicial coercion patterns, and white vigilante coercion patterns outside the South have been produced by many scholars and analysts: Elliott Rudwick, Herbert Shapiro, Charles S. Johnson, and Leon Litwack, among others. Fear—both the deep form in the South and the attenuated form in the North—shaped much of that everyday quest for an equalitarian Black existence in American life.

It is important to keep in mind that, in a sense, this fear of racism haunted the everyday equalitarian quest of professional-stratum African Americans with consequences that were as devastating, if not more so, for this class's self-identity as they were among working-class Blacks. Candor regarding the cross-class internalization of fear of anti-Black racism among

African Americans was articulated by James Weldon Johnson in his auto-biography *Along This Way* (1933). He wrote of his time living in Europe, France especially, as his first experience of escaping a fear of racism. He observed,

> From the day I set foot in France [in 1905] I became aware of the working of a miracle within me. I became aware of a quick readjust-ment to life and environment. I recaptured for the first time since childhood the sense of being just a human being. . . . I was suddenly free: *free from a sense of impending discomfort, insecurity, danger*; free from the conflict within the Man–Negro dualism and the innumerable maneuvers in thought and behavior that it compels; free from the problem of the many obvious or subtle adjustments to a multitude of bans and taboos; free from the special scorn, special tolerance, spe-cial condescension, special commiseration; free to be merely a man.[31]

Of course, the antihumanitarian viciousness of the white supremacy that stoked American Americans' fear of racism was apparent to any white American who had the honesty to recognize it, as the literary scholar Lio-nel Trilling did. Writing in 1945 in a review of Richard Wright's auto-biography *Black Boy* for *The Nation*, Trilling was astonished at the racist reality Wright relates in the book. For Trilling, Wright's *Black Boy* was an earthshaking "document," "a precise and no doubt largely typical account of Negro life in Mississippi."[32]

As suggested above in regard to what I call the maturation phase in the intellectual careers of Ida Wells-Barnett and Horace Mann Bond, by the late 1930s onward, a rather broad-gauged maturation was occurring within the overall African American intelligentsia, evident in the fact that by World War II, the main body of the African American professional class and intelligentsia had elected not "to assimilate" to white supremacist dic-tates, and therefore at the same time chose not to follow the accommoda-tionist paradigm of Booker T. Washington.

Instead, by the 1940s, the postwar Black intelligentsia was participating in a variant of Du Boisian civil rights activism as leaders.[33] In doing so, they were prepared *to smash the dual shackles of Bookerite accommodationism and fear of white racism*. The ideological and intellectualizing groundwork was now prepared in the ranks of the African American intelligentsia for what evolved from the early 1950s onward as a militant civil rights movement, what popular media often dubbed a civil rights revolution.

Conclusion: Homage to the Du Boisian Leadership Legacy

When looking back over the twentieth century from today's vantage point, taking in the oppressive weight of American racism borne on Black folks' shoulders, the importance of the Du Boisian civil rights activist leadership paradigm as opposed to the Bookerite accommodationist paradigm cannot be overemphasized. The significance for African Americans of Du Bois's legacy can be found in the political ideas from which it was fashioned. Commencing with the Niagara Movement organized by Du Bois in 1905, the Du Boisian leadership paradigm promoted the view that the long, cruel, oppressive sojourn of Black folk in the political economy of the American slavocracy and of a white supremacist–delineated American democracy must be understood as an unpaid debt. The young Du Bois was thinking along these lines when, in *The Souls of Black Folk*, he reflected in the chapter titled "Of Our Spiritual Strivings" on the limitations of the post–Civil War American government's outreach to the needs of the Negro in freedom. The post-emancipation African American, he observed, "sought to analyze the burden he bore upon his back, that dead-weight of social degradation partially masked behind a half-named Negro problem. He felt his poverty; without a cent, without a home, without land, tools or savings. . . . To be poor is hard, but to be a poor race in a land of dollars is the very bottom of hardships."[34]

The rectification of this grave situation, Du Bois continued, required a determined form of affirmative assistance from the federal government. But such a public policy was not forthcoming. As Du Bois put it, "the vision of 'forty acres and a mule'—the righteous and reasonable ambition [among Negroes] to become a landholder, which the nation had all but categorically promised the freedmen—was destined in most cases to bitter disappointment."[35] Interestingly (and bitterly) enough, a generation before Du Bois penned *The Souls of Black Folk*, the leading Black abolitionist, Frederick Douglass, expressed in an address in Cincinnati in 1876 a similar perspective toward the needs of newly freed Blacks: "When the Russian serfs had their chains broken and were given their liberty, the government of Russia gave to those poor emancipated serfs a few acres of land on which they could live and earn their bread. But when you turned us loose . . . you turned us loose to the sky, to the storm, to the whirlwind, and worst of all, you turned us loose to our infuriated masters."[36]

Accordingly, it was along this ideological and political trajectory of the foregoing realpolitik-type understanding of the massive systemic weaknesses that characterized the status of the post-emancipation African American that Du Bois and his peers, first in the Niagara Movement and later in the NAACP, fashioned the civil rights activist leadership paradigm. And given the nearly century-long racial-caste marginalization and oppression of Black Americans from the demise of Reconstruction to the civil rights legislation of the 1960s, the citizenship and social advances achieved for Black Americans through the Du Boisian leadership paradigm were, I believe, far superior to what those advances would have been had the Washingtonian accommodationist leadership approach prevailed.

Thus, in this prologue I have endeavored to define and portray the Black intelligentsia's formative-phase developmental trajectory and the related Black intellectualization process as they both evolved out of the late nineteenth century into the twentieth. This development involved a unique interplay between formal-knowledge dynamics and Black equalitarian-struggle dynamics. This formative-phase development was also affected significantly by the prominence of Booker T. Washington's accommodationist leadership methodology within post-emancipation African American society. This was a leadership and intelligentsia methodology whose historical status was aptly characterized by the African American writer Ishmael Reed as akin to a "Black Vichy Regime."[37]

Owing to the cadre consisting of Black intelligentsia who embraced civil rights, following Du Bois, an effective intellectualizing challenge to Washington's accommodationism was mounted, defined during the formative-phase twentieth century by narratives of Blackness, of equalitarian struggle—that is, by tales of the everyday challenges against the American white supremacist edifice emanating from multilayered sectors of both southern agrarian Blacks and urban Black working-class communities.

By the way, as early as 1903 Du Bois was already cataloging for his generation "narratives of Blackness" in *The Souls of Black Folk*—in chapter 6, "Of the Training of Black Men"; in chapter 7, "Of the Black Belt"; in chapter 8, "Of the Quest of the Golden Fleece"; in chapter 9, "Of the Sons of

Master and Man"; in chapter 10, "Of the Faith of the Fathers"; and in chapter 14, "Of the Sorrow Songs." On rare occasions, these narratives of Black equalitarian struggle had their roots in heroic anti–white supremacy efforts by radical white Americans, as in the case of John Brown's raid on the federal arsenal at Harpers Ferry, Virginia (now West Virginia), in 1859. The Princeton University historian James McPherson makes this point, I suggest, when observing in an essay on John Brown's legacy that W. E. B. Du Bois's *John Brown* translated Brown's raid into a "narrative of Blackness."

> One of Brown's early biographers was the black intellectual and founder of the NAACP, W. E. B. Du Bois. On the fiftieth anniversary of Brown's execution, DuBois wrote: "Jesus Christ came not to bring peace but the sword. So did John Brown. Jesus Christ gave his life as a sacrifice for the lowly. So did John Brown." In 1906, the second annual meeting of Du Bois' Niagara Movement (forerunner of the NAACP) took place at Harpers Ferry. The delegates made a pilgrimage to "John Brown's Fort," the engine house where he made his last stand and which became a shrine for many African Americans. Black artists, poets, and musicians in the twentieth century celebrated Brown's heritage. For the militant black power movement in the 1960s, John Brown was, as one partisan said, "the only good white the country's ever had." Malcolm X told whites that "if you are for me—when I say *me* I mean us, our people—then you have to be willing to do as old John Brown did."[38]

Another fascinating instance of the unique African American intellectual formation process mediated through what I call narratives of Blackness or tales of Black equalitarian struggle can be seen in the well-informed obituary in the *New York Times* (April 19, 2005) on the passing of Joe Nash, the leading scholar of the African American modern dance tradition. The obituary observed that Joe Nash

> was the colorful griot, or community storyteller, for black dance in America and particularly New York. In this role, he often appeared in public in flowing robes and was a familiar honored elder at the Brooklyn Academy of Music's annual Dance Africa programs. He told vivid anecdotes not only about his colleagues' careers, but also

about his own as a dancer on Broadway, in modern dance troupes like the Charles Weidman company and in groups that featured choreography performed by black artists starting in the mid-1940s.

What is interesting about the foregoing instance of cross-generational transmission among African American intelligentsia personalities of narratives of Blackness is that the tales of Black equalitarian struggle relate not to the sphere of power but to the sphere of culture—to the African American modern dance tradition, from its nascent years in the early 1930s (sparked by pioneer Black dancers like Pearl Primus, Donald McKayle, and Katherine Dunham) to the peak period of the Alvin Ailey Dance Company.

Be that as it may, there is no doubt that narratives of Blackness influenced the intellectual formation or intellectual identity process of numerous African American intelligentsia personalities. As they functioned as agencies of intellectual formation or identity, the narratives of Blackness were transmitted (and still are today) within and between generations of African American intelligentsia personalities, from Ida Wells-Barnett to Anna Julia Cooper; from Monroe Trotter to Bishop Reverdy Ransom; from Francis Grimké to James Weldon Johnson; from Paul Laurence Dunbar to Langston Hughes; from Arna Bontemps to Sterling Brown; from Augusta Savage to Elizabeth Catlett; from Claude McKay to Richard Wright; from Paul Robeson to Lorraine Hansberry; from John Hope to John Hope Franklin; from Horace Mann Bond to St. Clair Drake; from A. Philip Randolph to Bayard Rustin; from Zora Neale Hurston to Alice Walker; from Nella Larsen to Toni Morrison; from Marian Anderson to Leontyne Price and Jessye Norman; from Mordecai Johnson to Benjamin Mays; from Howard Thurman to James Farmer and James Lawson; from Thurgood Marshall to Leon Higginbotham; from Mary McLeod Bethune to Marian Wright Edelman; from George Kelsey to Martin Luther King Jr., so forth and so on. A brilliant case study of the intellectual formation of narratives of Blackness (in this case, those mediated through Black religious modalities) as they were transmitted within and between generations of African American intelligentsia was published in *Church History* (June 2005) under the title "African American Religious Intellectuals and the Theological Foundations of the Civil Rights Movement, 1920–1955," by the Vanderbilt University historian Dennis Dickerson.

By the way, then, the metamorphoses of many evolving twentieth-century Black intelligentsia personalities was interconnected with the average

African American's struggle to prevail and advance in the face of the American white supremacist system. The analytical utility of this perspective on the development of the twentieth-century African American intelligentsia—on "the making of Black intellectuals"—has been philosophically underscored by the Harvard philosophy scholar Cornel West:

> A central preoccupation [among Black intellectuals] of black culture is that of confronting candidly the ontological wounds, psychic scars, and existential bruises of black people while fending off insanity and self-annihilation. Black culture consists of black modes of being-in-the-world obsessed with black sadness and sorrow, black agony and anguish, black heartache and heartbreak without fully succumbing to the numbing effects of such misery—to never allow such misery to have the last word.[39]

In the remainder of this volume, I take the reader on an analytical journey through the historical thickets of American racism out of which the multifaceted modern dynamics that defined the African American intelligentsia *in aggregate* and many thousands of African American intellectuals' formation—their identities—*in particular* evolved. In the process, special attention will be drawn to the professional careers and discourse of members of the intelligentsia influenced by the Du Boisian leadership legacy, to the varying intellectual styles represented among the African American intelligentsia, to the ideological and political patterns that have vied for prominence among the evolving twentieth-century African American intelligentsia in the development of the life chances of African Americans in general. I trust it will be a rewarding journey.

CHAPTER I

Horace Mann Bond

Black Intellectual in the Age of White Supremacy

H orace Mann Bond's career is viewed in this chapter as a representative instance of an intelligentsia personality metamorphosis within the evolving twentieth-century African American
society. Bond's intellectual identity was initially tilted toward Booker T.
Washington's education leadership perspective. But in 1935, while researching the status of education for Black children in rural Louisiana, Bond
witnessed a lynching. That brutal event was an epiphany for him, and it
shifted him fundamentally toward a pragmatic-activist or reform-leftist
intellectual orientation. His two college presidencies—the first at Fort Valley State College in Georgia and the second at Lincoln University in
Pennsylvania—provided platforms from which Bond commenced his intellectual odyssey, as both a prominent educator and a civil rights activist and
intellectual. Through an exegesis of two of his scholarly works—*Negro Education in Alabama* (1939) and *Education for Freedom: A History of Lincoln University* (1976)—as well as an analysis of his civil rights activist orientation,
I present in this chapter a portrait of Bond's intellectual odyssey in the age
of white supremacy.

Bond is an ideal figure through which to portray the intellectual journey of the first- and second-generation cohorts of twentieth-century African American intellectuals during the high-noon era of America's age of
white supremacy, from the early 1900s to the 1950s. Between the 1880s and

World War I, the first-generation cohort of civil rights leaders—among them W. E. B. Du Bois, the journalist Ida B. Wells-Barnett, the historian Carter G. Woodson, and the lawyer and writer James Weldon Johnson—established themselves in their professions. Upon entering Lincoln University as a freshman in 1919, Bond embarked upon his preparation to become a member of the second-generation cohort of African American intellectuals, joined in his professional preparatory phase during the 1920s and into the 1930s by a network of other talented Black Americans, including the sociologists E. Franklin Frazier, Charles S. Johnson, Ira de Augustine Reid, and his own brother, J. Max Bond; the political scientist Ralph Bunche; the anthropologist and psychologist Allison Davis; the economist Robert Weaver; the literary critic and poet Sterling Brown; the psychologists Henry Cornwell and Kenneth B. Clark; the historians John Hope Franklin and Benjamin Quarles; and Laurence Foster and St. Clair Drake, both anthropologists and sociologists.

Bond's Background in the Age of White Supremacy

Horace Mann Bond was born in 1904, one of five sons of James M. Bond, a clergyman who was born enslaved in 1863. The Reverend Bond's mother, Jane Arthur, was a servant to a Kentucky plantation family whose male head, Preston Bond, "acted in a not uncommon manner and undertook intimate relations with his [female] slaves. . . . Preston's Black and white children and their mothers formed a sort of extended family; all of the children called [Preston] Bond's wife 'Ma' and Jane 'Mammy.'"[1] Horace Mann Bond's mother, Jane Browne, was born in Virginia after the Civil War, to a Black mother and a white father. Bond's maternal grandmother married a Black stonecutter when Jane Browne was an infant, and the family moved to a small town in southern Pennsylvania. From there, Jane was sent by a wealthy white family to Oberlin College, a progressive white institution in Ohio with an abolitionist pedigree. Bond's father, James Max Bond, attended Berea College in Kentucky, another white college associated with the antislavery movement, and was pursuing studies in theology at Oberlin in the 1880s when he met and married Jane Browne.

All six Bond children attended college; three of them completed undergraduate and graduate degrees. Horace Mann Bond was the academic star among his siblings, displaying a precocious talent early in childhood, which resulted in admission to Lincoln University in Pennsylvania in 1919. Only fourteen, he was at least five years younger than most of his classmates. In his definitive biography of Bond, *Black Scholar: Horace Mann Bond, 1904–1972*, Wayne Urban notes that the young man imbibed a crucial leadership ethos from his father's decision at the end of World War I to leave the pastorship of a middle-class Black Congregational church in Atlanta to administer job-training programs for African American veterans of the recent war.

After graduating from Lincoln University in 1923, Bond enrolled as a graduate student in sociology and education at the University of Chicago the following year. He completed the course requirements toward the doctorate by the end of 1927, but before completing his dissertation, Bond returned south, where he undertook a series of teaching posts at Alabama State Teachers College in Montgomery in 1927, the Tuskegee Institute in 1929, and Fisk University from early 1930 to 1934. He became the first dean of faculty when Dillard University opened its doors with Rosenwald Fund financing in New Orleans during the 1934–1935 academic year. Five years later, in 1939, Bond attained his first college presidency at a Black college: Fort Valley Normal and Industrial School in Georgia, later Fort Valley State College. Those early years as a professional in the South brought the budding intellectual face-to-face with America's age of white supremacy—an authoritarian and Negrophobic social system that was candidly portrayed by the journalist John Gunther nearly three-quarters of a century ago in his classic travelogue *Inside U.S.A.* (1947):

> He is too proud to go to a Jim Crow theater; therefore, he can scarcely ever see a first-run movie or go to a concert. If he travels in a day coach, he is herded like an animal into a villainously decrepit wooden car. If he visits a friend in a suburb, he will find that the water, electricity, and gas may literally stop where the segregated quarter begins. He cannot as a rule try on a hat or a pair of gloves in a white store. . . . And at the bus terminal or similar point he will, of course, have to use the "colored" toilet . . . and drink from a separate water fountain. He is expected to give the right of way to whites on the sidewalk, and he will almost never see the picture of a fellow Negro in a [white] newspaper, unless of a criminal. His children must attend a segregated school; they could not possibly go to

a white swimming pool, bowling alley, dance hall or other place of recreation. When they grow up, no state university in the South will receive them.[2]

The Budding Scholar: *Negro Education in Alabama*

In 1936, Bond completed his doctoral dissertation, "Social and Economic Influences on the Public Education of Negroes in Alabama, 1865–1930," for which he received the University of Chicago's top dissertation prize in the social sciences. While still pursuing graduate courses at the University of Chicago, however, Bond undertook original research in the IQ testing field that resulted in a series of important articles critiquing the racist tilt he considered built into the early tests. Several scholars in the testing field have praised Bond's publications as pathbreaking scholarship.[3]

In the early 1930s, Bond, aided by his wife, Julia Washington Bond, conducted extensive research on the education of the children of formerly enslaved African Americans in the South, with special attention to Alabama. Julia Washington Bond was the daughter of Fisk University graduates and educators, herself earning a bachelor's in English from Fisk before continuing on to graduate studies at her husband's alma mater, the University of Chicago. One of Horace Mann Bond's first undertakings in this field had been as a coresearcher on a Rosenwald Fund project on elementary schooling among Black children in the South in 1931–1932. He worked with a white American named Clark Foreman who was pursuing doctoral studies at Columbia University. When the project was published, however, the volume, *Environmental Factors in Negro Elementary Education*, carried a writing credit only for Foreman.[4]

In 1934, Bond published his first book on his own. *Education of the Negro in the American Social Order* provided an overview of the opportunities in public and higher education—mainly at Black colleges—that were available to African Americans from the late nineteenth century through the first third of the twentieth century. It would become the standard work on the subject of Black education for the next two decades.[5] Five years later, the Association for the Study of Negro Life and History published Bond's revised doctoral dissertation under the title *Negro Education in Alabama: A Study in Cotton and Steel*.[6] A deep look at the core analytical themes in *Negro*

Education in Alabama will provide basic insights into Bond's broader intellectual identity growth during the formative phase of his career.

Advancing Negro Education During Reconstruction

Negro Education in Alabama is a deeply researched, analytically rigorous, and intellectually incisive exploration of the interplay of politics, economic dynamics, and racial-caste practices underlying the tortuous process of educational development of the children of formerly enslaved African Americans in post–Civil War Alabama. By the end of the Civil War, there were some 5,270,000 whites and 4,380,000 Blacks in Alabama, with most of the citizens of each race involved in farming, mainly of cotton. While the prominent white scholars in Reconstruction studies working before Bond's time had claimed that viable public education was established under the Confederacy as early as 1863, Bond's research disputed this. In his biography of Bond, Urban states unequivocally that *Negro Education in Alabama* properly credits Alabama's Reconstruction government with establishing common schools in the state.[7]

Of course, the inclusion of Black children in public education in Alabama had to await the defeat of the Confederacy in 1865. Following the war's end, the combined endeavors of the federal Freedmen's Bureau, a government agency funded by the U.S. Congress, and northern missionaries laid the groundwork for Black public education, which in turn was advanced by the Reconstruction state government promulgated in 1868—the Provisional Assembly of Alabama. "In most instances," Bond explains, "the Freedmen's Bureau assumed the responsibility of providing buildings in which schools could be conducted, while the mission societies selected and paid teachers. As of January 1, 1866, three schools aided by the Freedmen's Bureau were reported for Negro children in Southern Alabama. . . . These schools were reported to have fifteen Teachers and 817 students."[8]

Two operational features of the advancement of public education for Black children in Reconstruction Alabama were of particular interest to Bond. One was the development of teacher-training institutions; the other was the pedagogical character of public education provided to Blacks. The founding of normal schools or teacher-training institutions for Black and white teachers attracted Bond's attention partly because several Black politicians in Alabama's Reconstruction assembly spearheaded this development. One such politician was Peyton Finley, the sole Black person on the state board of education. Initially, annually funded normal schools were established by legislation in November 1871.

> [The legislation] provided that $4,500 should be divided among the four white schools, and $4,750 should be divided among the four Negro schools. The latter were to be located at Montgomery, Sparta, Marion, and Huntsville; two in the Black Belt [cotton areas with a large Black population], one in North Alabama, and one in South Alabama. The schools were to be controlled by a Board of Commissioners for each institution, numbering three persons. The Montgomery Board included Finley and two "Carpetbaggers." On the Marion Board were two Negroes, Porter King and John T. Harris. . . . Of the four white schools, three were placed in North Alabama, and the fourth in the "Wire-grass" section of Southwest Alabama. Not one was placed in the Black Belt.[9]

In regard to the pedagogical character public education provided Blacks in Reconstruction Alabama, Bond was particularly interested in the shift within a two-year period following the war from an initial use of religious texts to the proliferation of social studies and literary texts with a liberal orientation. As Bond put it, the first northern missionaries who went south after the war had pedagogical views and objectives that were "quite moderate." He quotes a member of the Freedmen's Bureau to explain what the phrase meant: "To make known the work of salvation—to gather and sustain Christian churches—to instruct the people in all that pertains to life and goodness." But following the adoption of the Thirteenth and Fourteenth Amendments to the United States Constitution, the pedagogical character of education programs influenced by northern missionaries in Reconstruction Alabama was altered fundamentally. According to Bond,

> With the passage of the Amendments giving Negroes the vote, the mission bodies immediately struck a new note. The schools were now to help realize the noble slogan, "Let Us Make Men!" The religious instruction stressed two years before was enlarged to include emphasis on "liberty, the ballot, and intellectual training." Those who would now be the "ideologists" of the work among Freedmen saw

clearly that change in political status signalized by enfranchisement created a new social objective for the Negro schools.[10]

In public schools managed by northern missionary bodies, this pedagogical transformation was especially prominent. "In Alabama," wrote Bond, "the personalities in control of the objectives and content of schools for Negroes were the officials of the American Missionary Association. They represented the strongest anti-slavery, 'equalitarian' sentiment of the Abolitionist North. . . . The textbooks used in the missionary schools were standard Northern books, containing anti-slavery poems by Whittier, Holmes, and others; a special textbook, *The Freedman's Book*, was widely used as a reader. The editor of this book, L. Maria Child, had been a vigorous anti-slavery worker for years before the Civil War."[11] Bond continued this discussion relating examples of other liberal-oriented texts used in Black schools, such as those by the white abolitionist Wendell Phillips, the Black abolitionist Frances Harper, and the aforementioned Child.

The financial management of education for Black children in Reconstruction Alabama was another central concern of Bond's research, owing partly to the way this topic had been treated by historians who had preceded him in Reconstruction studies. Major white historians, such as the virulently racist segregationist Columbia University historian William A. Dunning and his students, habitually claimed that Black Reconstruction regimes in the South had squandered state finances in the area of public education, virtually bankrupting Reconstruction administrations. This was one of the many critical characterizations of Alabama's Black Reconstruction regime presented by Walter Lynwood Fleming, one of Dunning's disciples and most prominent students, in his influential work *Civil War and Reconstruction in Alabama* (1905). By boldly challenging Fleming's thesis, Bond made what Urban calls "a major contribution to the field of Reconstruction History":

The work of Dunning and his students glorified the old South and defended white southerners and their treatment of freedmen after the Civil War. Bond attacked Fleming's view that the Reconstruction government of Alabama, heavily influenced, if not controlled, by blacks, saddled the state with an onerous debt of thirty million dollars; instead the debt was a result of political commitments made to various railroad interests, and the amount of genuine debt incurred under the Reconstruction government was comparable to that incurred by pre-Civil War and post-Reconstruction regimes.[12]

A year after the publication of Bond's *Negro Education in Alabama*, Howard K. Beale, a leading historian in Reconstruction studies, published the essay "Rewriting Southern History" in the *American Historical Review* (July 1940), in which he singled out the young Bond's work for special mention, embracing the main interpretive thrust of Bond's analysis. From this point on, *Negro Education in Alabama* was set on a path toward classic scholarly status. According to Urban, "By the 1950s, Bond's work along with the work of such historians as Roger Shugg, Vernon L. Wharton, Francis Simkins, and Robert H. Woody, had become known as the revisionist school of Reconstruction history. . . . By the 1960s, revisionist interpretations such as Bond's had gained the ascendancy."[13]

Negro Education Under Post-Reconstruction White Supremacy

Following the 1876 presidential election, the Reconstruction governments were undermined. The first blow came with the withdrawal of federal military authority from the South. The second blow was the rise of authoritarian white supremacist governance—the Jim Crow state—reinforced, multilayered vigilante violence against African American citizens in the South. By the middle of the 1880s, democratic voting rights and office-holding rights for African Americans in southern states had become negligible or nonexistent.

From about the midway point in *Negro Education in Alabama*, Bond turns to a skillful dissection of the new politics of race and education in post-Reconstruction Alabama. In a section titled "Political Changes Resulting from Economic Changes, 1865–1900," he unravels the evolving power politics of late nineteenth-century Alabama that resulted from what he views as the interplay between two declining forces and one rising force. The declining forces related to the smashing of the democratic politics of Reconstruction and the demise of the King Cotton economy of the Black Belt region in southwestern and south-central Alabama, once the center of statewide economic power for the previous half century or more. The rising force related to the vast investment of northern capital into both the railroad and steel industries in northern Alabama centered in Birmingham.

In regard to education policies affecting Alabama's Black population, the white supremacist–oriented governance of the post-Reconstruction era differed from Reconstruction's primarily democratic governance. For one thing, and above all, Black political participation was now undercut through both disenfranchisement laws and vigilante violence, in particular undoing Black decision-making roles in education policy like those that had been held by Peyton Finley on the Alabama State Board of Education. Furthermore, the post-Reconstruction education policies affecting Alabama's Black population evolved under a systemically bifurcated state political economy characterized by (1) an emergent but dominant railroad/steel political economy centered in Birmingham, and (2) a declining or residual cotton-growing political economy in southern Alabama's Black Belt.

Thus, in the second half of *Negro Education in Alabama*, Bond's treatment of the period from the 1890s to the 1930s focuses on this cleaved Black society. On the one hand, a majority-Black community resided in the residential cotton-growing Black Belt, where in 1925 Blacks owned some 48 percent of owner-operated farms, albeit small, hardscrabble ones; on the other hand, a minority-Black community had migrated northward to the mineral- and steel-producing region of Alabama centered in Birmingham.[14]

Interestingly enough, in regard to education policy affecting African Americans during this period, some advances occurred in general, though especially for Blacks who had migrated to Alabama's urban Industrial Belt. First, Bond provides an aggregate measure of education advances for Black people during those years. By 1930, the rural Black Belt reported "the highest rate of Negro illiteracy [30 percent]," and "the industrialized area . . . reports the lowest index of illiteracy [17 percent]," while statewide, the overall illiteracy rate for Blacks was 26.2 percent.[15]

Inasmuch as enrollment in high school could be taken as a measure of viable advancement for Blacks from the 1890s to the 1930s, Bond's discussion focused on this education level. Bond's research uncovers no serious evidence of viable education advancement for Alabama's Blacks within the first decade of the twentieth century. Only 724 Blacks were attending high school by 1912, with enrollment creeping upward to 1,418 by 1916; to 1,595 by 1920; and to 3,435 by 1926. By 1930, the total number of Alabama's Black children of high school age was 109,216, of whom only 6,365 were enrolled in high school. This amounted to only 5.8 percent of that age demographic. Compare that to the percentage of Alabama's white children of the same age who were attending high school by this time: 29.5 percent—six times greater than the corresponding Black population.[16]

Bond's research, however, revealed a nascent trend related to education toward what might be called interregional class-stratification patterns among Black Alabamans. This was apparent in regard to the overall high school enrollment for Black children by 1930, with some 3,128 of a total 6,365 statewide Black high school enrollment located in the Industrial Belt's Jefferson County, of which Birmingham is the county seat. In other words, Bond observed, "50.5 percent of all Negroes enrolled in the tenth, eleventh, and twelfth grades of public high schools in the State were to be found in one high school in Birmingham, the Industrial High School."[17]

At the same time, Bond's research revealed a dismal situation regarding high school enrollment for the majority of Alabama's Blacks who resided in the Black Belt counties. "The low status of high-school education for Negroes in the State," he wrote, "may be judged from the fact that Montgomery, the Capital city [located in the Black Belt], with a Negro population in excess of 30,000, maintained no public senior high school for Negroes in 1930."[18] Furthermore, he said, "In 1930 there were 22 counties where Negroes were in excess of 12.5% of the population, and in which Negroes of high-school age numbered 38,183, that had no four-year high school accessible. Nine counties with a Negro high school population of 22,705 had no four-year high school. These were Black Belt counties, in each of which Negroes were in excess of 51% of the total population."[19]

The Politics of Booker T. Washington and Negro Education in Alabama

What Bond considered most analytically fascinating in regard to the politics of Black education in Alabama between the 1890s and the 1930s was, I suggest, the special role carved out by the most prominent Black college in Alabama and its president: the Tuskegee Institute and Booker T. Washington. Accordingly, Bond dedicated a full chapter to this topic in *Negro Education in Alabama*. In chapter 14, "The Influence of Personalities on the Public Education of Negroes in Alabama," Bond deftly intertwines an analysis of Washington's byzantine political machinations involving northern white industrialists whose finances built Alabama's railroad/steel industrial complex with an analysis of his impact on education opportunities on the lives of Black Alabamans. Bond's chapter on Washington is, I think, the most acute and penetrating analysis of the defining forces in Washington's career to be found in the extensive literature on Booker T. Washington. I do not hesitate to say that it is without peer.

Here Bond lays bare for his readers the personality and systemic roots that produced the premier African American leader of the turn of the twentieth century. He does this in the first instance through a kind of indirect analytical portrayal of Washington by way of a diagnosis of a similarly politically canny Black leader from Alabama named William H. Councill. In fact, some white elite figures in Alabama considered Councill superior to Washington. John Temple Graves, an Alabama newspaper owner and publicist, described Councill in 1898 as "The wisest, and most thoughtful, and most eloquent Negro of his time—as discreet as Washington, a deeper thinker, and a more eloquent man. But for one hour of the Atlanta speech, Councill, of Huntsville, might stand today where Washington, of Tuskegee, stands—as the recognized leader of his race."[20]

Councill was the first Black person in Alabama to head a state institution to train Black teachers, Huntsville Agriculture and Mechanical College. In his diagnosis of the educator, Bond relates how his consummate political skills placed him neck and neck with Washington in Alabama's cynical white supremacist political culture. "Like Washington," Bond wrote, "[Councill] had begun his public life as a politician. The school that he headed at Huntsville had been established in 1874, under Reconstruction, by the same kind of political 'log rolling' which six years later was responsible for Tuskegee Institute. . . . The interests of Tuskegee and of the Huntsville school conflicted in numerous ways, and frequently gave rise to political maneuvering between Washington and Councill."[21]

Observing that it was a matter of mere historical accident that Washington and not Councill delivered the address at the 1895 Atlanta Industrial Exposition—an address that catapulted Washington over Councill, in the eyes of white elites, into the position of the nation's foremost Black educator and client-politician—Bond puts forth a penetrating characterization of Councill as a budding Reconstruction-era Black politician, keeping Councill's mirror image, Washington, keenly in mind:

Councill is important in interpreting Washington because his career exhibits in aggravated degree all of the opportunistic characteristics which some critics have ascribed to the more important man. This "discreet" man, "deep thinker," and "eloquent" orator [here Bond quotes the Alabama publicist Graves] was plainly an adroit and shrewd student of the foibles and prejudices of his white contemporaries, and bent his educational and public career to take best advantage of the susceptibilities of his masters. An accomplished orator, he used all the shibboleths dear to the hearts of romantic white persons. . . . [Councill's discourse] was a gospel of sweetness and light. . . . Councill like Washington, clearly discerned class differentiations among white persons, and staked his appeal for support on this basis. "When the old, gray-haired veterans who followed General Lee's tattered banners to Appomattox shall have passed away, the Negro's best friends shall have gone, for the Negro got more out of slavery than they did. . . ." He made a point of trying to have none but ex-Confederate officers on his trustee board.[22]

Bond suggests that the shrewd white-deferring traits manifest in Councill's political leadership were interchangeable with similar traits in Washington. And although both Councill and Washington were equally adept at appeasing upper-class whites in the white supremacist political culture of post-Reconstruction Alabama, Bond identified yet another cluster of political-cultural dynamics, what he termed "sub-surface forces"—a combination of white power-class individuals in Alabama politics and the railway/steel industrial complex (their patronage networks at the state and national level)—that ultimately elevated Washington over Councill:

Appraisals of Booker T. Washington may easily fall into the common error of attributing momentous social and economic changes to the impress of a great personality whose life was contemporary with those changes. Such great men, because they are identified in time with these changes, come to be regarded as essential causative factors *when more correctly their lives merely illumine, through their numerous contacts [power-class patrons], the slow and sub-surface movements of human events.*"[23]

In short, Bond argued that while Councill and Washington shared the successful Black client-politician's skills of political manipulation, Washington possessed an additional advantage that resulted in the prominence of his Black leadership paradigm—namely, that special ability to align the

Black client-politician's persona with the most politically effective prevailing power-class networks that dominated modern development in post-Reconstruction Alabama from the 1880s onward.

Evaluating Washington's Leadership:
Admixture of Self-Serving and Public Serving

At the core of Washington's leadership strategy as the most "influential personality" in Alabama and the South generally during the 1890s through World War I was what Bond called "a problem": "the social problem of race." For Washington, the "problem" was a delicate political juggling act, whereby he had to trade off perceivable benefits for a triad of diverse but interconnected constituencies. "The problem included three classes of people," Bond wrote, "the Negroes whom he hoped to educate and to aid in achieving progress; the Northern white people, whom he depended upon to finance the school; and the Southern white people, whose support was essential, first in order to permit such an institution as he envisioned to exist in the heart of the South, and second to make a success of the demonstration in better race relations which was his ultimate goal. 'I saw,' he said, 'that in order to succeed I must in some way secure the support and sympathy of each of them.'"[24]

It was the occasion of the 1895 Atlanta Industrial Exposition that Washington seized upon to test his political acumen at gaining that support and sympathy. As Bond relates in his brilliant diagnosis of Washington's famous address,

> Washington said afterward that he felt he "had in some way achieved" his object, which he described as "getting a hearing from the dominant class of the South." In composing the speech, he said he kept in mind that his audience would be composed largely "of the wealth and culture of the white South. . . ." An examination of the document shows Washington's mastery of the art of opposing shibboleth to shibboleth. "Social Equality" had been the stereotype by which the "dominant class" to which he now addressed himself had won the support of the poorer whites and overturned the Reconstruction governments.[25]

A subtle critique of his subject's rhetorical politics and wordsmithing can be detected throughout Bond's dissection of Washington's speech. One could say it is even contemptuous at a point. For instance, "Washington met the issue [of appeasing elite whites] with skillful phrases: 'The wisest among my race understand that the privileges that will come to us must be the result of severe and constant struggle rather than of artificial [civil rights activist] forcing. In all things that are purely social we can be as the fingers, yet one as the hands in all things essential to mutual progress.'"[26]

After such an unctuous and deferential bid by Washington to convince the white supremacist southern power class of the presumed loyalty of Black people in an evolving industrial South, Bond suggests that Washington proceeded to fall on both knees, as it were. In applying the icing on the cake to his accommodationist Atlanta Exposition address, Bond believes that Washington violated a fundamental respect for the honor of Black folks. This Washington did in what I will call a roguish intellectual manner that demeaned Black people, equating the African American personality with the then ubiquitous happy Negro of the Lost Cause: the prostrating, master-fearing, loyal slave of romantic southern white mythology.

> He invoked the shade of the traditional, paternalistic relationship so dear to . . . [whites'] romantic picture of the ante-bellum South. "As we have proved our loyalty to you in the past, in nursing your children, watching by the sick-bed of your mothers and fathers, and often following them with tear-dimmed eyes to their graves." Washington said the Exposition would introduce "a new era of industrial progress" to the South. The white people were advised to "cast down your bucket where you are," and not to "look [overseas] to the incoming of those of foreign birth and strange tongue and habits for the prosperity of the South." The Negroes were described as "the most patient, faithful, law-abiding, and unresentful people the world has seen," who could be depended upon to "buy your surplus land, make blossom the waste places in your fields, and run your factories." The Negro would continue to labor "without strikes or labor troubles."[27]

With regard to the roguish intellectual feature of Washington's leadership persona, it seems even Washington's slavish rhetorical disrespect for the honor of Black folks in the presence of white elites was not enough. Quite the contrary. The budding Black spokesman had even more insults to Black folks' honor to manipulate, reminding them, "We shall prosper in proportion as we learn to dignify and glorify common labor and put brains and skill into the common occupation of life"; that "there is as much dignity in tilling a field as in writing a poem."[28]

I should mention the sentence with which Bond concludes the paragraph quoted above: "Negroes must begin at the bottom and not at the top." The deadpan critical bite of Bond's summary here is palpable.

Bond had a particularly astute grasp of the underside of Washington's leadership paradigm, which is to say of the devious features of the interplay between the public-serving and self-serving dimensions of Washington's ascendancy as a leader among Black Americans. The long-run systemic consequences of his leadership methodology, accommodationism—ostensibly the means by which African Americans could succeed in turn-of-the-century America—seemed to translate most favorably for Washington's Tuskegee network and thus for Washington himself. To take a famous example, "Andrew Carnegie made numerous gifts to Tuskegee, including a personal donation of $600,000, the interest from which was set aside, at the request of the donor, to free Washington, during his lifetime, from any care or anxiety regarding his personal expenses."[29]

As Bond makes clear, Washington was a veritable master persuader among key elements in the national white power structure. Carnegie, Bond observed, remarked that Washington was "a modern Moses and Joshua combined," and indeed that "no truer, more self-sacrificing hero ever lived; a man compounded of all the virtues." Of course, to identify and underscore Washington's master-persuader skills during the highly exploitative and plutocratic robber baron era of American industrial capitalism was not, as such, to say something uniquely negative or reactionary about Washington. After all, everybody was doing it, so to speak. Master persuasion was a common entrepreneurial capitalist skill without which plutocratic success in the era was hard to come by. So I think this discussion of Washington's variant of master persuasion was informed by Bond's grasp of the historical or situational context surrounding it.

Indeed, what Bond is relating in regard to his careful tracking of Washington's money-gathering ties to white elites is, I think, something intrinsic about Washington's leadership persona; namely, Bond is intimating that Washington had near-religious faith in the white rich, and above all,

Washington wanted the masses of African Americans to embrace the self-same faith.[30]

Problematics of Washington's Strategy and Black Progress

In addition to his sharp insights into the intricate political chemistry that characterized the boundary between the private self-serving attribute and the public-serving attribute that defined Washington's leadership persona, Bond demonstrated an equally incisive understanding of the latter's adroit use of political propaganda:

> Washington and his colleagues were not hesitant in claiming substantial improvement in educational affairs for Negroes in the counties surrounding Tuskegee. In 1911 he claimed, as a result of the Tuskegee program, "a model public school system, supported in part by the [Macon] county board of education, and in part by the contributions of the people themselves." What had been done was an "actual experiment" to show "what a project system of Negro education can do in a country district toward solving the race problem." "We have," added Washington, "no race problem in Macon County; there is no friction between the races; agriculture is improving; the county is growing in wealth." His secretary, Emmett J. Scott, made the statement that "the better class of Negro farmers was greatly increased during the past thirty years, until at the present from 90 to 95 percent of the 3,800 Negro farmers in the county operate their own farms either as cash tenants or owners."[31]

Bond, however, was not seduced by the Washingtonian propaganda machine's smooth rendering of the Tuskegee Institute's good works among rural African Americans in Alabama's Black Belt. In 1939 he remarked, "The Tuskegee program aimed to 'create a settled class of Negro peasant proprietors,' i.e., owners of small self-sufficient farms. But Macon county was . . . [in the] 'shadow of the plantation' system which had been a more powerful resistant agent to educational, social, and economic progress than the school itself has been a catalytic one. Making the allowance for exaggerations made by Washington and others in justifying the too-early success of their program, the results after fifty years are somewhat unsatisfactory."[32]

Just one final thought on what an exegesis of Bond's *Negro Education in Alabama* tells us about his own initial intellectual identity pattern. At the time that Bond penned his penetrating portrait of Washington's leadership persona in the early 1930s, he was in a transitional state with regard to his own intellectual formation, from what I call his formative intellectual identity to a maturation-phase intellectual identity. The former was essentially a liberal-centrist phase while the latter became a reformist-leftist or pragmatic-activist phase.

I suggest that the reform-leftist phase was taking shape during 1937 and 1938 during Bond's fourth year as dean of faculty at Dillard University in New Orleans. This is confirmed in a passage in which he resolves his understanding of Washington's approach to an evolving Negro proletariat in urban Alabama, and thus by extension in the wider American society. Once again, notice Bond's undertone of critique and perhaps even contempt:

> Washington met the problem of unionization of Negro workers with silence, until just before his death [in 1915]. In 1904, when the effort to organize the Chicago Stockyards was defeated by the importation of Negro strikebreakers from the South, the officials of the union appealed to Washington "to use his influence to prevent Negroes from working in plants until the strike was settled, and to address a mass-meeting of colored citizens in Chicago on the subject 'Should Negroes become strikebreakers?'" Washington pled a previous engagement in stating his inability to address the mass-meeting, and never issued the appeal requested. In 1913 he published an article which by implication discouraged the unionization of Negro workers. Negroes generally, he said, looked to their employers as their friends and did not understand or like "an organization which seems to be founded on a sort of impersonal enmity to the man by whom he is employed."[33]

This clearly is not a flattering portrait of Washington's interface with the evolving twentieth-century Black working class in wartime. As already noted, Bond is presenting a critique of the roguish intellectual side of Washington's leadership persona. The rigorous critical-theory historical discourse through which Bond fashioned his critique of Washington and his accommodationist strategy provided the building blocks for Bond's eventual reform–leftist intellectual identity.

Bond's Formative Identity: From Washington and Du Bois to the Star Creek Epiphany

The ideological dimension of Horace Mann Bond's intellectual identity evolved through essentially two stages: a formative stage and a maturation stage. As mentioned earlier, talented African American intellectuals like the three foremost sociologists trained during the 1920s at the University of Chicago—chronologically, Charles S. Johnson, E. Franklin Frazier, and Horace Mann Bond—inevitably headed south with their professional scholarly skills to work in Negro colleges. It was also inevitable that they had to contend with the massive sway of Washington's legacy as an educationist and in political leadership.

Bond and his closest educationist colleague, Charles S. Johnson, fashioned their approach to Washington's legacy during the formative phases of their intellectual developments. They did so, however, along a cautiously critical trajectory. Bond especially came out of deep Black southern roots, which meant in part that his leadership orientation as an educator entailed the view of not getting too far ahead of the mass of southern rural African Americans.

While still a graduate student at the University of Chicago during the late 1920s and into the early 1930s, Bond wrote several articles in which he developed a pedagogical outlook for himself. In one never–published article, "William Edward Burghardt Du Bois: A Portrait in Race Leadership," Bond expressed a critical view of Du Bois's educationist outlook and of his civil rights activist leadership style. For Bond, Du Bois's northern elite–educated roots gave him an "alien Massachusetts soul" that stirred in him a radicalism or a progressivism not of hope but of "despair." This was an elitist–skewed radicalism, as Bond viewed it, as contrasted with what might be called a people's radicalism or a natural radicalism, one from the bottom up, something more akin to Bond's formative–phase ideological identity.[34]

Bond elaborated on his skepticism toward Du Bois in another article that was published in 1925, characterizing him as "rebellious" on the one hand but as a leader of "men of ability" on the other. Though clearly in awe of Du Bois intellectually, Bond appeared dubious of him politically, remarking that he was a professional figure "without sufficient personality . . . to attract the attention of a large mass of Negro followers."[35] As of the late 1920s, for the young graduate student, Bond's Tuskegee Institute educationist regime was not as shallow as its critics in Du Bois's circle argued, but was, rather, "a living, energetic leaven which slowly but surely was bringing forth a strong and organized ambition for [African American] progress."[36]

Genuine as Bond's tilt toward Tuskegee was in the late 1920s and early 1930s, new circumstances as a southern Black educationist and intellectual from 1934 onward would first modify and then radically alter his view. Bond was selected as the first dean of faculty at Dillard University in 1934, a position in which he surrounded himself with progressive young Black scholars like St. Clair Drake, Allison Davis, and the historian L. D. Reddick.[37] He also fashioned a broader network of progressive-thinking African American scholars located at other Black colleges—Charles S. Johnson at Fisk University in Tennessee, Gordon Hancock at Virginia Union in West Virginia, and J. Saunders Redding at the Hampton Institute in Virginia. According to Drake, intellectual interactions among this network of Bond's confreres during the late 1930s and into the 1940s focused on ways to advance the education regime at the typical agriculture/mechanical Negro college in the South beyond the Tuskegee model.[38] This meant altering Tuskegee's emphasis on hands-on job skills and enhancing intellectual efficacy among students attending such colleges, where the majority of working-class Black students were enrolled.

Bond assumed his first college presidency at Fort Valley Normal and Industrial School (later Fort Valley State College) in 1939. Following his arrival, his ideological tilt toward Du Bois became evident in both his own thought processes and in the curriculum he created. This evolved most importantly, I think, from a deeply transfiguring experience five years earlier that Bond and his wife, Julia Washington Bond, had had at Star Creek, Louisiana. With funding from the Rosenwald Fund Explorer Experiment, the Bonds had set out in the fall of 1934 to study the social system of Black education in Washington Parish, Louisiana. Their research focused on a Rosenwald Fund–financed public school, one of around a thousand such rural Black public schools that the great German Jewish philanthropist Julius Rosenwald had initiated going back to the early 1900s, a striking instance of early twentieth-century philanthropy. It was here, in Star Creek, that they witnessed a lynching in January 1935 that inspired an intellectual rebirth for Horace Mann Bond. Horace and Julia would submit the story of their transfiguration in a monograph-size report to the Rosenwald Fund in 1936. That report remained in manuscript form for sixty-one years, at which time it was published as *The Star Creek Papers*, coauthored by the Bonds and edited by Adam Fairclough of the University of North Carolina.[39]

Both the locale of the research project and the physical organization of its attendant fieldwork—which found the Bonds residing in a flimsy wooden village house that, like the others nearby, lacked water and electricity—thoroughly entrenched them in the kind of hardscrabble southern Negro milieu so vividly portrayed by Charles S. Johnson's studies on the rural South, such as *Shadow of the Plantation* (1934) and *Growing Up in the Black Belt* (1940). Like the majority of the African American rural poor in Louisiana in the 1930s, the couple started their day harvesting wood for the daily fire, pumping water for bathing, cooking, drinking, and washing clothes, and other tough housekeeping chores.

For two young intellectuals raised in the upper-middle-class homes of African American clergymen (Horace's father ran a Black Congregational church, and Julia's father pastored a Black Presbyterian church), such sharing of this threadbare agrarian existence must have been traumatic, calling forth a certain resilience on their part. Their rural Louisiana experience was also culturally, spiritually, and intellectually eye-opening. Horace Mann Bond was an avid letter writer, and he described the enrichment he and his wife derived from their sojourn from October 1933 until late January 1934 to many acquaintances, friends, colleagues, and mentors, including his former University of Chicago professor Robert Redfield, the African American journalist Fletcher Smith, the white journalist Frederick L. Allen, and the Rosenwald Fund official Edwin Embree.[40]

Furthermore, Horace and Julia spoke directly to the stimulation of their time in rural Louisiana during interviews conducted in the 1950s. Fairclough quotes from these interviews in his introduction to *The Star Creek Papers*. Star Creek, the Bonds observed, "proved one of the most valuable [experiences] of our entire lives." During the course of a typical day, Bond spent an hour or so gathering information from rural neighbors regarding agriculture practices such as the preparation of sugarcane and the slaughtering of pigs. The couple were also introduced to the local political scene that was available to rural African Americans in Louisiana at the time, especially as politics related to Black schools, as well as the broad dissatisfaction among the African American population toward the Black head teacher, whom some local Black leaders viewed as a "handkerchief-head Negro." "Professor," one resident told Bond, "he's just a cheap-grade teacher—about the best we knows about out here. He's in with these white folks. The white folks raised him. . . . He jus' a good ole nigger, ain't got much sense."[41]

As part of Bond's local political education, he also gained experience surrounding the bid by two local African Americans to secure funds for school desks from the Rosenwald Fund's white-controlled board. When the two spokespeople approached the white school board administrator, he clowned around with them in an attempt to avoid the seriousness of their visit, but they would have none of his evasiveness. As Bond observed, "They were dignified, self-assured, polite but not to be kidded."[42]

While settling into his first college administrator post at Dillard University in New Orleans, Bond reflected back on the four-month research experience, informing an African American journalist friend how much the Black community of Star Creek had captivated him: "My wife and I found ourselves liking the people there more than any we had ever known before. Honest, self-respecting, hard-working, they were my idea of what human beings ought to be."[43] This observation on the character of rural African Americans in 1935 Louisiana reflected Star Creek's transformational ideological impact on Bond. As it happens, just three short years before, in 1932, Bond's ruminations on rural Blacks as "shiftless [and] improvident" in a letter to the Rosenwald Fund had smacked of elitism.[44]

Although Bond's daily interactions with the Star Creek community clearly captured his imagination, a full ideological-cum-intellectual transfiguration would hinge upon another experience, one that would be emotionally riveting. It occurred in mid-January 1935 when the young researchers were brought face-to-face with the fury of white coercion and vigilante violence against Blacks in the rural South.

In July 1934, in Franklinton, Louisiana, a Black farm youth named Jerome Wilson had been involved in a dispute over cattle-dipping procedures between his family and the town's white sheriff, who mortally wounded Jerome's brother Moise during the altercation. Jerome, also shot, was said to have shot and killed the sheriff in the ensuing melee. Little over a week following the event, Jerome was found guilty of murder and jailed. Within six months, the Louisiana Supreme Court, having been petitioned by the National Association for the Advancement of Colored People (NAACP) and other allied groups, overturned Jerome Wilson's conviction on the grounds that he had not received a fair trial. On January 11, 1935, after the ruling, Wilson was dragged from his cell in the local jail and shot to death by a white lynch mob.

For some if not most rural Louisiana whites, Jerome Wilson did not warrant a jury trial, but instead the vigilante justice associated with lynching. The vile act of Wilson's lynching was ideologically shattering for Horace and Julia Bond, shifting fundamentally the groundwork of his formative-phase intellectual identity. While Bond did not yet fully see himself as a political activist, let alone a radical, he was nonetheless outraged at the lynching and the crisis it rained down on Wilson's family. As explained by Bond's biographer, Urban,

> Bond's anger at the lynching and its aftermath erupted in two letters he wrote to a black journalist [Fletcher Smith]. He noted that whites were chagrined mainly at black reaction to the lynching [not the lynching itself]. . . . Bond . . . recounted that white residents forced the family of the slain youth to leave town, whereupon Bond sought to find a farm elsewhere in the South for the family, as an alternative to the sure dissolution and despair they would face if they were to emigrate to a strange urban environment in a northern city. At the end of his stay in Franklinton, Bond spoke at a commencement exercise at the black school. Contending that both blacks and whites in Louisiana suffered under the legacy of slavery, he came dangerously close to open criticism of the white power structure.[45]

Furthermore, Urban informs us that Bond produced detailed notes from interviews and research around Franklinton with the intent to write a book on the oppressive side of Black life generally in the rural South. "He interviewed the father of the youth who had been lynched and used the interview as the basis of an article he submitted to *Harper's*. He also wished to combine the interview with his historical and observational studies of Blacks in Louisiana and the South into a book-length manuscript entitled 'Forty Acres and a Mule.' These publication plans, however, bore no fruit."[46]

From our post–civil rights revolution vantage point, Bond's forthright and inspired identification with poor Black folk who were violently trampled by white racists in rural Louisiana during the Depression era might not seem a particularly "big event" of civil rights activism. But in the Jim Crow years of the 1930s, it was indeed. Keep in mind that the typical middle-class Black American of the time—businessman, lawyer, physician, what have you—refrained from such forthright connecting of self with a smashed Black life. What Bond did at Star Creek was a rare example of courageous civil rights activism by a member of the Black intelligentsia at the time.

Indeed, Bond's civil rights activist outreach to these devastated Black lives in 1930s Louisiana signaled a generic ideological shift in his intellectual persona toward the civil rights activism of Du Bois, of whom Bond had been wary in the late 1920s. In turning toward the Du Boisian civil rights activist leadership paradigm, Bond was moving away from the sympathetic bent toward the Tuskegee experiment and its spokesman, Booker T. Washington, that had characterized his formative ideological phase.

When placed in historical perspective, Bond's mode of connecting his middle-class Black persona with the violated Black folk in the South was something of an anomaly in the 1930s; indeed, it was not until the rise of the militant civil rights movement in the late 1950s and 1960s that such an outlook would come to be entertained broadly by middle-class Black Americans. There was even evidence of a left-leaning activist mind-set emergent in Bond's forthright identification with Black lynching victims, as suggested in his correspondence with the Black American newspaper publisher W. P. Dabney in Cincinnati (April 2, 1935). Dabney had proposed that Bond might mobilize financial support from middle-class Blacks around the country for resettling Jerome Wilson's family; in response, Bond asked Dabney if he would be "willing to serve on a national committee, which would attempt to raise money for this purpose."[47] This suggestion from Bond was, I believe, an early instance of the national committee fundraising idea in the context of Black American civil rights activism, close on the heels of the famous 1932 Scottsboro Boys case, suggesting just how fertile Bond's budding reform-leftist orientation was at the time.

Thus, Bond was ahead of the civil rights activism curve among middle-class Black Americans in general with his outreach to beleaguered Blacks in rural Louisiana in early 1935. He stayed on during that year to lend a helping hand to these hard-hit families and to probe that cowardly vigilante violence against Black America. He used his own resources (money, energy, time, emotions, spirit) to relocate the family of the lynched youth,

Jerome Wilson, within the farming South, rather than have them endure relocation to the alien North. This reflected the birth of a deep humanist side to Bond, a feature of his intellectual persona that would broaden over the next decade.

In February 1935, when Bond left Star Creek to return to New Orleans and his academic work at Dillard University, his intellectual persona might be characterized as outwardly very polite and modest, but inwardly tough, intellectually brilliant, and above all cultivating a proactive Christian-humanist inner ethos. The latter, I suggest, became the driving force of Bond's intellectual metamorphosis in his maturation phase from the late 1930s onward.

Bond's Ideological Maturation: Shaping a Christian Self-Efficacy Activism

Bond left Dillard University in 1939 to assume his first college presidency, at Fort Valley Normal and Industrial School in Georgia. His goal here was twofold: to provide Fort Valley students, who were usually from working-class families, an excellent curriculum that provided not only rudimentary skills suitable for the sorts of middle-class jobs available to African Americans in the South's agriculture economy, but also one that was intellectually transforming and did not ignore the liberal arts. Biographer Urban vividly characterizes the dilemma underlying Bond's academic goals:

> Bond resisted attempts to make the college into [simply] a trade school. . . . Instead, he tried to use innovative ideas to make the school speak to the students' life problems and also to raise their [racial] expectation. He used the college's focus on teacher education as a base from which to enlarge its curriculum, including its range of academic subjects, to allow students to get the benefits of studies in the natural sciences, humanities, and social sciences in addition to their occupational focus on teaching. Yet he also stressed agriculture and home economics in an effort to help students survive and prosper [in the South's agrarian economy].[48]

St. Clair Drake, one of Bond's progressive confreres during his academic deanship at Dillard University, informed me in interviews in 1987 that he viewed Bond's academic regime as an early constituent feature of Bond's pragmatic activist identity. It was during this period that Bond experimented with what Drake termed "Christian self-efficacy activism."[49]

Bond fashioned the core ideas associated with Christian self-efficacy activism in a course he taught at Fort Valley State on the philosophy of Black education. Drawing on a letter Bond wrote to Edwin Embree at the Rosenwald Fund in January 1944, Urban suggests that what shaped the content of Bond's lectures on this subject was his discovery early in this presidency of "the positive outcomes that religion seemed to encourage in his young black students."

> He noticed that those at Fort Valley who were members of the "Sanctified," a local fundamentalist sect, refrained from alcohol and exhibited a strong personal discipline that carried over into their academic pursuits, for these religious enthusiasts were disproportionately represented among the better students in the college. . . . Bond described the special utility of faith for an oppressed people. Blacks, who were severely circumscribed in their present conditions, had a special faith in the future. . . . This special faith spilled over into the political arena. The principles enunciated in such phrases as "all men are created equal and are endowed by their Creator with certain inalienable rights" were attractive to religious blacks, fortifying their faith in a nation that refused to live up to them in practice. White recalcitrance on issues of racial equity could be interpreted by blacks as evidence that black citizens were the true Americans, while their white brethren were backsliders.[50]

The outlook of the Christian self-efficacy activism paradigm that was part of Bond's course held that the Old Testament book of Exodus, which depicts the enslavement of the Jews in Egypt and their eventual freedom from the pharaoh's oppression, exemplifies a supremely relatable story for Black Americans living under conditions of southern white supremacy. In prefatory material for the class, Bond wrote that "the Old Testament is the history of a minority race that has survived and flourished under endless oppression for three thousand years. Negroes ought to study the secret of their survival."[51] He saw it as essentially a template outlining for African Americans possible avenues out of the American racist system.

Interestingly enough, Urban intimates that something "conservative" characterized Bond's Jewish-Negro American analogy of historical oppression, providing "evidence for Marxists who saw religion as the people's opium, a narcotic that numbed their awareness that their condition might be ameliorated by social and political activism."[52] This reading of Bond's use of the analogy is, I think, mistaken. As I've already indicated, nearer to the truth of what Bond's use of Old Testament parallels represented is what Drake, in interviews in 1987, formulated as a progressive "Christian self-efficacy activism development" on Bond's part during his presidency at Fort Valley State.

Bond had, in fact, already arrived ideologically at the groundwork of a civil rights activist articulation in the context of his Star Creek epiphany in the early 1930s. This is suggested, I believe, by the graduation address he delivered at the Washington Parish Training School, the Black high school in the Star Creek district of Washington Parish, Louisiana, on May 5, 1935. At the heart of the speech was an implicit though palpable call that freedom be shared in the white supremacist South. In Bond's own words, he asked his graduating students to help the South "realize that there is enough freedom to go around" along racial lines, and if it were not shared soon, he suggested that the price to be paid would be one of social turmoil. But white Americans needed assistance to arrive at an orientation that embraced freedom and equalitarianism, he said; they must be challenged to travel "The Road to Freedom," as Bond put it in the title of his commencement address. "Young people," he said to the assembled students, "you stand tonight as a way-station on the road to freedom. Behind you are generations of people . . . who have fought the good fight." Finally, Bond observed that the struggles fought by generations past "on that road from slavery to freedom" must now be taken up by those who had obtained diplomas from Washington Parish Training School.[53]

Seven years later, outside of the classroom, he powerfully returned to his theme of the parallels between the lived experiences of Jews and African Americans in a public lecture at Gannon Theological Seminary in Atlanta on May 19, 1942. Using this Bible-based historical parallel in his discourse with Black graduate-level theology students, a genuine freedom-mobilization motif is implicit in the title of Bond's address, "Bring Forth the People Out of Egypt: The Mission of Minority Religious Leadership": "The years before us are filled with fear and foreboding. The Negro group that will be a Negro group for ages to come looks to you for rescue. There will be others and more to come along to help you; *I prophesy that when this War shall have shattered the idols of the Egypt in which we live, those walls will be thronged by hosts of young men and women of the Negro race who wish to help bring forth their people out of Egypt.*"[54]

Those "walls thronged by hosts of young men and women of the Negro race" conjured up by Bond in his Gannon address were clearly the walls of white supremacy in the South. Similarly, Bond's injunction to Gannon's theology students "to help bring forth their people out of Egypt" clearly referred to the South's white supremacist system. In short, Bond's allusions to the historical oppression of the Jewish people in the Old Testament were not some religious-escapist discourse, a use "of religion as the people's opium," to quote Urban again. Contrary to Urban's interpretation, I suggest that the allusion to the Old Testament Jewish historical experience was an example of a real-world application and consolidation of what Drake called Bond's Christian self-efficacy activism ideological orientation.

Moreover, in support of this perspective on Bond's Christian self-efficacy activism discourse, it should be noted that during the 1930s and 1940s, there was a partial variant of his ideological discourse evolving broadly among leading progressive-oriented African American educationists in religious studies at Black colleges. Those scholars included Mordecai Johnson, Howard Thurman, and William Stuart Nelson at Howard University; Benjamin Mays and George Kelsey at Morehouse College; African Methodist Episcopal bishop Reverdy Ransom at Wilberforce University; and Richard McKinney at Storer College. The incredibly important role these scholars played in fashioning a variant of Bond's Christian self-efficacy activism discourse in their teaching and writing is related in a brilliant article by the Vanderbilt University historian Dennis Dickerson titled "African American Religious Intellectuals and the Theological Foundations of the Civil Rights Movement 1930–55."[55] By the 1950s and throughout the 1960s, the intellectual beneficiaries of this development had fashioned the militant stage of the civil rights movement, among them Martin Luther King Jr., through the Montgomery bus boycott movement and the Southern Christian Leadership Conference; James Farmer through the Congress of Racial Equality; and James Lawson through the Fellowship of Reconciliation and later of the Student Nonviolent Coordinating Committee (SNCC).

The Christian-prophesy motif of Bond's Gannon Theological Seminary address was keenly prophetic, historically speaking. He foretold with uncanny accuracy the broad outlines of the civil rights movement's mobilization among the Black American masses that vanquished the edifice of systemic white supremacy. He spoke of the cutting-edge role in future Black militant mobilization against "the idols of Egypt in which we live" of African American youth, especially that of Black-college-educated "young men and women of the Negro race who wish to help bring forth their people out of Egypt." Interestingly enough, one generation after the Gannon Theological Seminary address, Bond's own Black-college-educated young adult children would play a leading role in advancing the 1960s civil rights movement, especially his son Julian Bond, a leading figure in the SNCC and later chair of the NAACP national board, and his daughter Jane Bond, a civil rights lawyer. Bond's great seminary address warrants elevation to iconic status among other great documents of the movement, even King's "Letter from Birmingham Jail." From Dillard to Fort Valley State to his Gannon address, Bond had used the Old Testament's story of the Hebrews' survival to package his Star Creek–influenced transition toward a pragmatic-activist or reform-leftist ideological identity.

Bond's Ideological Maturation: Shaping a Black Activist Identity

Bond's Gannon Theological Seminary address can be viewed as part of an ideology-transforming interlude, begun in 1938 and continuing through the first half of 1942, associated with his quest for a full-fledged progressive civil rights activism orientation. While Urban rejects my view of Bond's Christian self-efficacy activism, viewing it instead as a variant of pie-in-the-sky escapism, he nevertheless recognizes that Bond became "politically aroused about racial issues in other parts of the nation." To illustrate Bond's awakening, Urban shares an anecdote: "To a query from some black parents in Trenton, New Jersey, who were attempting to end segregation in the city's schools, . . . [Bond] responded with a vigorous and sophisticated defense of integrated schools."[56]

But this was only a minor feature of what I call Bond's ideology-transforming preparation for a civil rights activism identity. It was his participation in the founding convention of the Southern Conference for Human Welfare (SCHW) in Birmingham, Alabama, in November 1938 that launched his civil rights activism identity. As Linda Reed, the historian of SCHW, writes,

SCHW sought to help southern whites to understand that to remove limitations on its black citizens was to ensure the region greater prosperity. The southern-led SCHW, for its time, became the progressive movement [in the South]. . . . SCHW's recommendations challenged President Roosevelt, the Congress, and especially southern citizens to improve the region. SCHW singled out, for instance, the unequal facilities for white and black school children, unequal salaries of black and white teachers, and unequal incomes of black and white tenant farmers as examples of the inequity and wastefulness of a racially segregated society. Races that could not reap equal benefits for their labor could not live together harmoniously. . . . From 1938 to 1948, SCHW's major goal was the repeal of the poll tax. . . . The Southern Conference addressed issues of health problems, education, child labor, farm tenancy, civil rights, and constitutional rights in an attempt to rectify the south's wrongs.[57]

In addition to the content of the goals, the liberal and even progressive tilt of the SCHW was also apparent from both the initial officials of the organization and the makeup of white and Black professionals attending its founding convention. One of the elected officers was treasurer Clark Foreman. Bond's former Rosenwald cowriter and researcher—the white scholar who had received sole credit for work they had produced jointly—was now an official in the New Deal's Public Works Administration Power Division.[58] The admixture of liberal and progressive white professionals attending the SCHW's 1938 convention was equally pronounced among convention delegates—as Reed calls them, "a who's who of southern liberals."[59] What was even more important, perhaps, about the liberal and progressive tilt of delegates at SCHW's founding convention was the ideological makeup of the African American delegates.[60]

Bond's participation as a delegate was his inaugural organizational experience en route to a civil rights activist identity following his 1935 epiphany at Star Creek. Above all, perhaps, his presence at the convention afforded him contact with a broad range of Black intellectuals concerned with altering America's racial caste system. It was a kind of Black-progressive baptism for Bond. Those in attendance included activist liberals Charles Johnson, Atlanta University president Rufus Clement, and the formidable Cookman-Bethune College president Mary McLeod Bethune; antiwar pacifist Ira Reid; Marxist intellectual John P. Davis of the National Negro

Congress; and the working-class Communist union organizer Hosea Hudson.[61]

Following his experience at the convention, Bond embarked upon a multifaceted engagement with political and ideological issues affecting the racial-caste status of Blacks in American society. From 1941 into early 1942, a debate ensued among Black intellectuals around the obligation of an oppressed and pariah American ethnic community like Black Americans to fight as soldiers in defense of so-called American democracy. After all, Blacks enjoyed very little of democracy in America, either in terms of civil or human rights. In the early 1940s, Bond joined ranks with his intellectual confrere Charles S. Johnson, then head of the Department of Social Sciences at Fisk University, to articulate what would become an important perspective among Black leadership regarding America's role in fighting fascism in Europe: one, that white American racist practices notwithstanding, Black Americans were full American citizens and accordingly had an obligation to bear arms against German fascism; and two, by fighting in defense of the United States, Black Americans would be able to leverage their wartime sacrifice after the war to dismantle America's ingrained white supremacist patterns. In his September 1942 article "Should the Negro Care Who Wins the War?," published in the esteemed scholarly journal the *Annals of the American Academy of Political and Social Sciences*, Bond concluded that no other American ethnic community was better situated to translate the civil and human rights issues central to the fight against German fascism into fundamental postwar advances toward vanquishing American racism. Cognizant of a parallel between Nazi Germany's treatment of Jews and racist America's treatment of Blacks—rooted in his concept of a parallel between the historical oppression of Jews in the Old Testament and African Americans throughout this nation's existence—Bond argued that Black Americans and leadership *should* join forces with American society in World War II.

Prior to assuming the presidency of Fort Valley State College in the fall of 1939, Bond served as chair of the Department of Education at Fisk University, renewing his mentor-protégé relationship with Charles S. Johnson, which had begun in the early part of the decade. In 1942, Johnson, with Bond in tow, joined Gordon Hancock, a sociology professor and college dean at Virginia Union University, to organize a conference of notable Black scholars and civic leaders to discuss the need to advance Black Americans' interests in postwar America. Officially called the Southern

Conference on Race Relations, the event was held in Durham, North Carolina, on October 23, 1942, and "represented a wide spectrum of southern black opinion." Participants, including "diverse figures" such as Bond's fellow university president Benjamin E. Mays of Morehouse and Charles C. Spaulding, president of the North Carolina Mutual Life Insurance Company, were asked by Johnson to contribute "a list of the five most 'pressing needs of the Negroes of the South,'" which Johnson would use to establish the conference's agenda.[62]

Owing to Johnson's role as joint sponsor with Hancock in the Durham conference, Bond was given a place on the conference's reporting committee that Johnson chaired, and he was also afforded a hand in drafting the conference's official report, *A Basis for Interracial Cooperation and Development in the South: A Statement by Southern Negroes.* Just as Bond's participation in the SCHW in 1938 was a broad progressive baptismal experience for him, so, too, was his interaction here with Black intellectuals of civil rights activist and left-wing activist outlooks. Fellow members of the reporting committee—officially dubbed the "Editorial Committee"—fell readily into three categories: Johnson, Hancock, and Bond himself, along with Mays and Atlanta University's Clement, were in the civil rights liberal category; the publisher of the *Norfolk Journal Guide*, Plummer B. Young, Tuskegee's F. D. Patterson, and the Hampton Institute's William B. Cooper were in the "centrist liberal" category; and in the "leftist category" were New Orleans union leader Ernest Delpit and the Southern Negro Youth Conference's James E. Jackson, who by 1942 already had ties to Marxist intellectuals and would become an important Black Communist Party figure after World War II.

According to Johnson's biographers Patrick Gilpin and Marybeth Gasman, Johnson dictated the title of the Durham conference final report in the somewhat cautious language of "interracial cooperation," but that aside, the substance amounted to a call for the eventual end to prevailing racial-caste patterns in postwar America. What was absolutely crucial and politically groundbreaking about the 1942 Durham conference report—and thus the very conference itself—was the undeniably progressive thrust of its specific proposals for altering the racial caste system in the South and by extension in the country generally. Voting rights were paramount, as was the protection of civil rights for all African Americans. Specifically noted was the immediate need to curtail "abuses of police power by white officers of the law."[63]

Surprisingly, I think, the official report of the Durham conference had some Black critics among Black intellectuals of the radical Left like the journalist Roi Ottley, whose critique in his book *New World A-Coming* (1943) portrayed it as amounting to accommodationist proposals, a document from "Uncle Toms."[64] This was clearly an ignorant critique. A glance at the "Industry and Labor" section of the report, which advocates, for example, for full membership in labor unions and the right to collective bargaining, reveals the groundbreaking progressivism—indeed radicalism—of its proposals.[65]

Radical-leftist Black intellectuals' disdain notwithstanding, those who contributed to shaping the 1942 Durham conference proposals in the area of African Americans' civil and labor/economic rights helped plant the seeds for future growth of civil rights activism among a broader segment of middle- and working-class Blacks in the South. A perusal of the extensive literature on the history of the civil rights movement suggests that the 1942 Southern Conference on Race Relations and its groundbreaking proposals are not well-known.[66] But in truth, as a pioneering text for civil rights activism, the Durham conference's report, with its first step toward a civil rights activism initiative, became operationally manifest as a genuine political force in the post–World War II years.[67] Just as Bond's Gannon Theological Seminary lecture from earlier that year merits the stature of the most widely known civil rights–era texts, so, too, does the Durham conference report, also written, in part, by the prophetic pen of Bond.

Finally, Johnson, Hancock, and Bond also helped to initiate civil rights activism among a small segment of upper-middle-class white southerners. One such outcome was the Race Relations Conference, convened in June 1943 in Richmond, Virginia. Initiated by Ralph McGill, editor of the *Atlanta Constitution*, and Jessie Daniel Ames, who attempted to mobilize her fellow white liberals in the South behind a federal antilynching bill during the 1930s—a courageous endeavor in which she failed—the 1943 Richmond Race Relations Conference was a unique leadership event in the South during World War II, an interracial affair attended by civil rights–oriented liberal Black college presidents, including Bond himself, Clement, and Mays; Charlotte Hawkins Brown of the Palmer Institute in North Carolina; Albert Dent of Dillard University; and Mordecai Johnson of Howard University.

The conference also served as a stepping-stone to a permanent organization whose goal was to advance, however tentatively, the 1942 Durham conference's goal of reshaping the South's racial caste system in postwar America. The organization to emerge from the 1943 Richmond Race Relations Conference was the Southern Regional Council, formed at a second Richmond Race Relations Conference in January 1944. Bond participated in the affairs of the Southern Regional Council during 1944 and 1945; this would be the last of his southern-based civil rights activism. Thus, considering his work with the SCHW in 1938 and the Durham Southern Race Relations Conference in 1942, as well as its offshoot, the permanent Southern Regional Council, Bond helped to lay the foundation for a broad-based civil rights activism in the postwar South, and thus, too, in the nation generally. Reed, the historian of the southern conference movement of the 1930s and 1940s, enumerates some of the organizations that arose over the next decades, organizations that were heirs to those in which Bond played a critical part, among them the Union of Democratic Action in the North and the Congress of Racial Equality, both of which came to be during World War II; the Fellowship of Reconciliation; the Educational Fund; the SCLC and SNCC. "Each group," she writes, "had worked hard and paved the way to federal action in the 1960s."[68]

As World War II was winding down during the first six months of 1945, Bond's long-standing intellectual ties to Black people's affairs in the South—ties that shaped his identity as a civil rights activist—were also coming to an end. The board of trustees of Lincoln University in Pennsylvania—Bond's alma mater, from which he graduated at age of nineteen in 1923—selected him as its first African American president in early 1945. That fall, Bond entered his second Negro college presidency.

Bond and the Afro-Americanization
of Lincoln University

Horace Mann Bond brought to Lincoln University a penchant for intellectual and scholarly activism in the interest of dismantling racism in American life. However, in moving north in the fall of 1945, Bond faced a different situation from the rigidly legalized white supremacist patterns of the South he had worked under since the late 1920s. In the North, Bond encountered what might be called the other side of American racism, a pernicious and pervasive de facto racism that produced a unique variant of racial-caste patterns in American life. In the North, such Jim Crow practices as discrimination in housing and segregation in public schools and neighborhoods or in entertainment venues like cinemas and concert halls were enforced by custom rather than law. Even with these undeniable limitations, Black communities in the North, on balance, experienced more choice and maneuverability under de facto racism than under southern de jure racism.

There was something almost providential in the fortuitous match of Bond and Lincoln University as American society exited World War II. They needed each other, as it were, in a very basic way. Until Bond's ascent to the presidency in 1945, this first institution of higher education for Black Americans, founded in 1854 by white Presbyterian followers of the antislavery movement who favored the settlement or colonization of Free Negroes in Africa, had been governed by paternalistic-minded white Presbyterians who never recognized the importance of "Afro-Americanizing Lincoln University." For nearly a century, the university functioned under white rule. By emphasizing the "Afro-Americanizing" of Lincoln University, I mean to underscore the importance of two processes: (1) interlacing facets of the institution's academic program with the history, culture, and traditions of African Americans; and (2) advancing African American scholarly academic and administrative participation in the functioning of Lincoln University. By the time Bond arrived in 1945, only four African Americans had been appointed to faculty positions there—Joseph Newton Hill in English; John Aubrey Davis in political science; Laurence Foster in sociology; and Henry Cornwell in psychology. Furthermore, only one African American held an academic-administrative position by 1945—Hill as dean of college—and two African Americans had been appointed to the board of trustees.

Early in Bond's presidency, he set a progressive tone for the overall character of the university's Afro-Americanization. He cut a rare figure among presidents of Black colleges, inviting noted African American leftist intellectuals to speak on campus, such as W. E. B. Du Bois and the National Urban League's Ira Reid. A year before my own class of 1953 arrived at Lincoln University, Bond had brought Paul Robeson to campus as well. Robeson had spent several years of his childhood in the Lincoln University village community—a pre–Civil War Underground Railroad community—where his father pastored an African Methodist church before World War I.[69]

Another feature of the progressive tone Bond set in his early days at Lincoln University is also noteworthy. Joined by civil rights activist Black faculty members such as John Aubrey Davis in the Political Science Department, Bond participated in a court case to integrate segregated schools in southern Chester County, Pennsylvania, where Lincoln was located. Also, in the 1949–1950 academic year Bond joined with the student NAACP chapter, led by a senior named Jacques Wilmore, who would later join the Sociology Department, to picket and hold a sit-in at a segregated hotel in the neighboring town of Oxford, Pennsylvania. Located just a few miles north of the Maryland border, Oxford was known for its segregated institutions as well as the participation of some of its white citizens in a Ku Klux Klan chapter in neighboring Rising Sun, Maryland. Again, Bond distinguished himself among Black college presidents in the postwar era as an individual who dared to challenge racist practices through direct civil rights action. In doing so during the early part of his tenure at Lincoln University, he contributed to reshaping a progressive aura for what became the full-fledged Afro-Americanization of the school under his tutelage.

In his quest to Afro-Americanize Lincoln University, Bond inevitably ruffled feathers among the institution's white administrators, who governed along the lines of a father-knows-best principle. Such white paternalism was rooted in Lincoln University from its establishment by Presbyterians from the antislavery movement, and this legacy had both positive and negative dimensions to it. On the one hand, during the eighty years before the appointment of its first Black president, Lincoln produced skilled Black male professionals in myriad fields, among them the lawyer Archibald Grimké and his brother, the clergyman Francis Grimké; the medical scientist Hildrus Poindexter; the medical scientist and physician Toye Davis; the first African American Supreme Court justice, Thurgood Marshall; and the actor and poet Roscoe Lee Browne.

On the other hand, despite the production of such stellar members of the African American intelligentsia, the paternalistic legacy at Lincoln University, which held through the 1940s, was adamantly against biracial governance of the institution and thus against Afro-Americanization. This pattern stood out particularly during the 1920s, when a student protest movement at Black colleges in the South called for the full-fledged integration of administrations and faculty at these colleges.[70] This early student movement bypassed the Lincoln campus, where neither the white administration nor the Black students exhibited interest in Afro-Americanizing the university.

The appointment of Bond as president of Lincoln University in 1945 was indeed a precedent-setting event. But his appointment did not, in the first instance, alter the long-standing ethos that had informed governance and life at the institution for eighty years. Vestiges of paternalism plagued Bond's relationship with Lincoln's white faculty members, administrators, and trustees during the first five years of his presidency.

The arch perpetrator of this white paternalistic ethos at Lincoln University during Bond's early tenure was Harold Fetter Grim, an instructor of biology during Bond's undergraduate years and later dean of faculty, a popular and authoritative figure across campus. "Grim took in the affairs of Lincoln University an almost proprietary interest, one that intimately related to his long-term effort as benefactor of the black race," Urban writes. "Grim was not averse to lecturing Lincoln students and alumni on the appropriate ways for them to behave."[71]

Indeed, in the fall of 1947, Grim dispatched a letter to Lincoln alumni throughout the country informing them, in a tone more suited to school-children, that rowdy behavior at an upcoming Lincoln–Howard University football game in Philadelphia would present whites with a bad image of college-educated Blacks. The game was a major annual event for the two leading Black colleges. According to Urban, "He told alumni that they, along with their Howard counterparts, would be 'on trial' during the game and that their citizenship would be evaluated by [white] officials from the state of Pennsylvania as well as from Temple University and from Philadelphia."[72] The haughty letter "Provoked alumni . . . [who] protested Grim's letter to the president."

Such imperiousness was quite ordinary behavior on the part of Dean Grim, but in the fall of 1947, there was one new variable involved in the annual matchup: the presence at Lincoln University of its first Black president. To the surprise of Grim and his paternalistic circle at Lincoln, Bond met the dean's arrogance head-on. He penned a public letter in response to selected alumni who had protested Grim's exhortation, informing them in no uncertain terms "that the dean of the university spoke only for himself and that he had . . . been asked to clear all public statements about the university or to the university community with the president."[73]

Coming to the presidency of his alma mater after a decade of running Black colleges under white supremacist southern conditions, Bond had good reason to be sensitive to issues of race. No Black American educator of Bond's superior intellect and tough, pragmatic humanism could have refrained from responding forcefully to Grim's paternalistic posturing toward the alumni of a Black college in post–World War II America. No African American educator worth his salt could have tolerated Grim's public display of such shameless (and shameful) arrogance.

In just a few years, what I call Bond's tough, pragmatic humanist persona gained broad recognition among the young generation of faculty that he was recruiting to the Lincoln campus. Several white scholars associated with the Quaker pacifist movement made up one segment of the young generation of Bond-friendly faculty members, such as Thomas Jones, a historian of medieval and early modern Europe, and David Swift, a religious studies historian. Both Jones and Swift were Quaker social activists who joined early post–World War II Black civil rights activists like Bayard Rustin, James Farmer, and James Lawson in pioneering direct nonviolent protests against American racism. Another faculty member with Quaker ties recruited to Lincoln University under Bond was Dwight Whitney Morrow Jr., a scholar of American history who hailed from an elite WASP family. His father was the former Wall Street banker and United States ambassador to Mexico Dwight Whitney Morrow Sr.

A second segment of young faculty consisted of Black scholars also recruited by Bond. While there were only four Black faculty members at Lincoln when Bond arrived in 1945, by the end of the 1950–1951 academic year, many others had joined the faculty: Orrin Suthern II in music; Roscoe Lee Browne and H. Alfred Farrell in English; Abram Hill in drama; Walter Waring in French; Norman Townsend in chemistry; James Frankowsky in mathematics; Samuel Stevens in theology; Jacques Wilmore and James Young in sociology, both of whom were young followers of the antiwar organization Fellowship of Reconciliation; and the librarian Emery Wimbish. Bond recruited a similar cohort of Black administrators to the school, and he also appointed a Black secretary to the president, Grace Jackson Frankowsky, Lincoln's first Black secretarial staff person. Other Black appointments to the administration were James Bonner McRae as dean of students, Austin Scott as treasurer, Samuel Stevens as dean of school, Toye G. Davis as director of medical services, Manuel Rivero as director of athletics, and Robert Gardner as assistant director of athletics. Bond also appointed the university's first Jewish faculty members: Walter Fales in philosophy, Sayre Schatz in economics, and Martin Landau in political science.

As important as Afro-Americanizing the faculty and administration was to Bond, he cultivated and maintained an additional goal that would allow for the school's transformation during his tenure as president. He sought to identify Lincoln University with what might be called a freedom-expanding ethos, especially as it pertained to Black people's plight in America and colonial Africa. Bond's interest in the postwar civil rights activism of Black Americans extended back to what I call his Star Creek epiphany in 1935 and evolved through his formative civil rights activism experience with the Durham race relations movement in 1942 and going forward from there.

Bond's interest in postwar African decolonization movements stemmed from his deep knowledge of Lincoln University's special role in educating early twentieth-century African students who, upon returning home, launched various decolonial and nationalist organizations in such places as South Africa, Nigeria, and Ghana. As Bond's second five years at Lincoln University began, he worked to cultivate interest in these emerging movements among Lincoln's faculty and students. One of Bond's early initiatives in this regard was to establish an Institute of African Studies and a conference on new African political movements that commenced in the 1950 summer session. In the fall term of the 1950–1951 academic year, Bond added to the curriculum two new courses, one on African history and one on contemporary African developments.

Bond also launched a program to attract a significant number of African students to Lincoln University. Thanks to missionary groups associated with the school as far back as the 1890s, a typical Lincoln University freshman class at the turn of the century had several African students. By 1948, two African alumni, Nnamdi Azikiwe from Nigeria and Kwame Nkrumah from Ghana, occupied leadership positions in their home countries, a situation that significantly assisted Bond's initiative to recruit African students. From the fall of 1949 until the end of Bond's presidency, freshman classes generally had between 20 and 30 African students each, out of a total of 100 to 120 students on average.[74]

Interestingly enough, whereas Bond's initiatives to expand Lincoln students' awareness of civil rights issues was accepted by the university's board of trustees, they took a very different view toward his efforts to expand students' awareness of African decolonization movements. Those initiatives not only involved Bond's hosting of several conferences on African affairs on the campus, but also his making several visits to western and southern Africa to see firsthand the character of the continent's emergent anticolonial political awakening.

In 1958, during a week's visit to deliver a lecture on IQ testing as part of the Inglis Lecture Series at the Harvard School of Education, Bond mentioned to me that throughout the 1950s, he had heard unconfirmed rumors of dissatisfaction with his African interests among key members of Lincoln's white-dominated board of trustees. It happened that several key trustees still clung to a paternalistic view of their role in running a Black college, and something about Bond's pressing to advance awareness of postwar African decolonization movements fundamentally annoyed those members.

Bond's 1957 visit to West Africa to attend the inauguration of Prime Minister Kwame Nkrumah of Ghana, the first African head of state of a former African colony (and a Lincoln alumnus), tipped the smoldering antipathy toward Bond into full-blown opposition. No doubt a more fair-minded or pluralist-minded governing board of a school like Lincoln University, with a century-old role in the modern education of African Americans, would have welcomed participation by Lincoln University's first Black American president in the inauguration of Ghana's first African head of state. But such thinking from the governing board in 1957 was not to be. Quite the contrary. Thus, as Urban informs us, "It was while [Bond] was away on a trip to Ghana [in early 1957] that the Lincoln University Board of Trustees decided to seek his resignation."[75] Lincoln University's commencement in 1957 would be Horace Mann Bond's last.

Bond's History of Lincoln University as a Civic-Growth Agency

Horace Mann Bond was not only fired by the Lincoln University Board of Trustees in a rather back-stabbing manner; to add insult to injury, the board attempted to renege on salary and pension arrangements agreed upon as part of Bond's resignation. He had to initiate costly litigation to protect the terms of his contract.[76] This episode soured Bond's outlook toward an institution for which he cared deeply. Bond's widow, Julia

Washington Bond, confided to me that his years as Lincoln's president were the happiest and most intellectually rewarding of his professional career. His contributions to the Afro-Americanization of the university's academic and intellectual life during his twelve-year tenure as president were tremendous. Indeed, they were priceless. Bond never forgave the board of trustees for what he considered its cynical, paternalistic maneuvering against him. For the rest of his life—he passed in 1972—he refused several invitations from his beloved alma mater to return for an honorary degree. To my mind, it was understandable.

Be that as it may, Bond left behind one profound expression of his deep affection for the school: his brilliant, monumental *Education for Freedom: A History of Lincoln University.* He commenced this six-hundred-page work in 1947, spending many late nights and weekends—after his busy administrative workdays and workweeks—on the research required to write the history. I vividly recall seeing a light in President Bond's office on the second floor of the two-story administration building at midnight when I—the evening clerk manager of the campus canteen—took the canteen's money bag for deposit in the ground-level office of Professor McRae, dean of students. This happened night after night during my junior and senior years at Lincoln. Bond hoped to have a completed manuscript in time for the university's centennial anniversary celebration in June 1954, but he didn't meet this schedule. He eventually completed the manuscript after leaving Lincoln, but it remained unpublished at his death in 1972. Fortunately, thanks to the determination and dedication of a committee of Lincoln University faculty and staff, Princeton University Press published it posthumously in 1976. This committee also selected the book's very apt title.

Education for Freedom is not just another chronological account of a historic college's evolution but rather a conceptually informed work, and as such it is in the first ranks of histories of American higher education in general and of African American higher education in particular. One of the historical themes presented in *Education for Freedom* relates to the complex relationship that characterized the interplay between white administrators shaped by Presbyterian paternalistic missionary values and a Black student body in the age of white supremacy. Bond was fascinated with the dilemma faced by Lincoln University's white administrators and faculty, who officially represented the humanitarian-oriented gospel side of Christian activism but who still could not muster the capacity to challenge the de facto racist patterns in the North: Just what type of college-educated African American should a late nineteenth- and early twentieth-century white-managed Black college produce?

Bond's meticulous research into Lincoln University's post–Civil War metamorphosis revealed that when viewed from the vantage point of the mid-twentieth century, the men running Lincoln University fashioned an academic regime that afforded its students what might be called a "mental preparation for freedom." As I understand Bond's historical narrative and interpretation in *Education for Freedom*, the men who ran Lincoln University developed it as a civic-growth agency for the modern development of African American society. A scholastic stickler for what might be called the prehistory of history, Bond devoted the first half of his twenty-six-chapter work to issues involved in producing the foundational ethos of the eighteenth and nineteenth centuries to American slavery among a small sliver of middle-class and elite white Anglo-Saxon Protestant Christian families (Presbyterians, Quakers, Episcopalians, Methodists), focusing on developments in Pennsylvania. The humanitarian Christian values that were foundational to the antislavery movement were also foundational to the origins of Lincoln University and thus to what I call the civic-growth agency or civil-society-enhancement role of Lincoln University in the modern development of turn-of-the-twentieth-century Black American society.

Bond underscored the significance of the Christian humanitarian ethos early in *Education for Freedom* through a case study of the antislavery Philadelphia physician Benjamin Rush:

> On his return to America in 1769 [after medical school] he began the practice of medicine in Philadelphia. From this time to his death in 1813, he was involved in every movement designed to advance a humanitarian cause not only in Philadelphia and Pennsylvania, but everywhere in this country and in the world. . . . Our concern [in this book] is with the history of an idea, the idea of humanism. The idea of instant and vigorous response to any claim by the poor or oppressed for fair treatment; the idea that all men are the children of God, and thereby are brothers who owe each other the readiest and most generous response when a need becomes apparent. . . . More than most men of his time, Benjamin Rush epitomized this idea. He deserves here the most extended attention; for whatever good

Lincoln University has represented may be said to be the idea of good that this extraordinary man nourished, exemplified, and taught in the Philadelphia in which he practiced medicine from 1769 to 1813.[77]

In these observations on the humanitarian strain in Rush's career, Bond would appear to be writing under the influence of his epiphany at Star Creek, Louisiana, in 1935, that transforming experience that put the young scholar en route to his reform-leftist intellectual maturation, as discussed earlier in this chapter.[78]

In truth, Bond's thirteen chapters of the prehistory of Lincoln University analytically connect in a brilliant manner the past-present interface dynamic in the making of the institution. For example, in his fascinating discussion of the historical role of Rush, Bond wrote of the physician's relations with late eighteenth-century Free Negro clergymen Richard Allen and Absalom Jones, emphasizing Rush's role in facilitating their "African Church Movement" and especially his keen grasp of the significance of education in the development of Black people:

> The "Address" Rush presented to the annual convention of abolition societies held in Philadelphia in January 1795 stressed the necessity for continuing to work for "universal emancipation of the wretched Africans who are yet in bondage." He looked beyond emancipation to the problem of what was to be done for the enslaved to the problem of what was to be done for the freedmen thereafter. He found the answer to lie in education. . . . Fifty-eight years later, in 1853, a Presbyterian minister, John Miller Dickey, stood in the pulpit of the Oxford Presbyterian Church and set forth the design of a higher educational institution for youth of African descent.[79]

That institution became the Ashmun Institute in 1854. It was renamed Lincoln University after the Civil War.

To demonstrate the skillful leadership by Presbyterian personalities in shaping Lincoln University's historic role, Bond portrayed in the second half of the book the academic and governing role of a noble offspring of the antislavery white founders of Lincoln University, Dr. Isaac Norton Rendall. Lincoln's founding families, the Dickeys, the Ashmuns, and the Cressons, espoused the conservative ideals associated with the antislavery movement, such as African colonization. To Bond's mind, Rendall typified the best of the white Presbyterian founders of Lincoln University: he imagined a genuine liberal arts regime.

Educated at the College of New Jersey and Princeton University, Rendall served as president of Lincoln University from 1865 to 1905. For nearly a half century, he was, according to Bond, "a great educator who had a knack of making men from 'boys.'" Operationally Rendall functioned as "The patriarch of Lincoln University." Chapter 15 is, in fact, called "'Pap' Rendall, Patriarch." Rendall was highly knowledgeable in classical education and in Greek, Latin, and several other European languages.

Rendall was especially skillful at raising funds from white elites who were friendly to higher education for Black people, particularly Presbyterians, Quakers, Congregationalists, Methodists, and Episcopalians. In this function, Rendall encouraged the family of Mrs. Susan Dod Brown of Princeton, New Jersey (her father was a successful inventor and steam engine manufacturer), to build the Mary Dod Brown Memorial Chapel at Lincoln University during his presidency. Above all, perhaps, Bond depicted Rendall as respectful of the African American youth whom Lincoln University educated and worked persistently to ensure that high-achieving graduates of Lincoln gained admission to professional schools.

Upon entering the substantive history of Lincoln University throughout the rest of the book, Bond brought his readers into his core understanding of Lincoln University's historical purpose—to wit, the civic growth or civil-society enhancement of African Americans. To concretize this theme, Bond probed the careers of two prominent Lincoln University graduates. They were "The Grimké Boys," as chapter 17 of *Education for Freedom* is titled. The prominence of Archibald Henry Grimké (1849–1930) and Francis James Grimké (1850–1937) stemmed in part from their unique family background. Both were mulatto offspring of the white enslaver Henry Grimké, brother of Angelina Grimké Weld, the famous mid-nineteenth-century abolitionist and suffragette who openly acknowledged her brother's parentage of Archibald and Francis. Indeed, in 1868, she undertook financial responsibility for their Lincoln University education.

By probing the post–Lincoln University careers of the Grimké brothers, Bond related how their Lincoln education translated into an ongoing effort at civil society enhancement in service of the modern development of Black American society. Both of them pursued professional studies after Lincoln University. Francis initially attended for two years Lincoln

University's own law school and Howard University School of Law, later entering Princeton University Theological Seminary, which he completed in 1875. Archibald pursued law studies as one of the earliest Black Americans enrolled at Harvard Law School, graduating in 1874.

At the dawn of their professional careers, Archibald and Francis Grimké forged their college and professional school educations into tools to advance the modern development of Black American society, the first condition of which was to challenge the white supremacist oppression of Black people in American life. At the intellectual level, Archibald Grimké advanced antiracist thought and raised the consciousness of some educated white Americans by writing biographies of two major white abolitionists, William Lloyd Garrison and Charles Sumner. These were probably the first ever biographies of leading white American personalities penned by a Black American. He also launched an early civic action—oriented Black American magazine based in Boston, *The Hub*. Above all, Archibald Grimké fashioned for himself a civil rights activist political identity. He was one of the first late nineteenth-century Black professionals to break political ties with the Republican Party because of its cynical betrayal of Reconstruction policies in the South. This betrayal, after all, resulted in the massive disenfranchisement of Black citizens throughout the South and paved the way for the rise of authoritarian systemic political and judicial practices, reinforced by white vigilante violence, that dominated Black life in the South for nearly six generations, from the 1880s through the 1960s.

Education for Freedom follows Archibald Grimké's career as it relates to Lincoln University's historic interface with the fundamental dynamics of civic growth or civil society enhancement in twentieth-century African American society. The legal and public policy victories against American racism that were so painfully wrenched from the jaws of American white supremacy by the civil rights movement owe an enormous debt to the legacy bequeathed by Lincoln University and here represented by Archibald Grimké in his intellectual celebration of the abolitionist movement through writings on the lives of leading abolitionists; his participation with W. E. B. Du Bois, Monroe Trotter, and other early twentieth-century Black professionals in the founding of the Niagara Movement in 1905; his participation four years later in the formation of the National Association for the Advancement of Colored People and his role as an NAACP national officer for a decade; and his many years as a civil rights lawyer in the affairs of the Washington, DC, branch of the NAACP, including his leadership for a decade of that important branch. As Bond's portrait of "The Grimké Boys" intimated, Archibald Grimké's career as a pioneer in the enhancement of Black civil society and political leadership set an example for several generations of students who followed him at Lincoln University.[80]

Like his elder brother, Francis James Grimké also translated his Lincoln University training into endeavors that advanced civic growth or civil society capabilities of an evolving twentieth-century African American society. To use Bond's almost rapturous language and imagery, in doing this, "Francis J. Grimké . . . was a better Grimké, almost, than the best of the old Charleston family whose name Angelina [Grimké Weld] urged him, as a student at Lincoln, raise up from the dust of American slavocracy."[81] From the time he left the Princeton University Theological Seminary in 1875 until his death in 1937, Francis Grimké served as pastor of the Fifteenth Street Presbyterian Church in Washington, DC. The Reverend Grimké was such a brilliant Presbyterian preacher, generally speaking, that his sermons were admired by many outside of his Black congregation, appealing to the liberal branch of white Presbyterians as well.

Like Archibald, Francis Grimké typically leavened his civil rights activism with a sense of pragmatic restraint. This enabled both brothers to interact with the conservative accommodationist leadership style favored by African American professionals associated with Booker T. Washington and his Tuskegee Machine. Thus, in the Grimké brothers' view, Washington's success at sustaining an early Black college deserved their respect. "For many years," Bond wrote, "[Francis Grimké] was one of the few friends of Booker T. Washington among the [activist] Negro intellectuals; he admired the Negro who had shown, at Tuskegee, that a member of the race could build up and administer a large institution."[82]

However, by the early twentieth century—around 1905—when it became indisputably apparent that American racist patterns in regard to the political disenfranchisement of African Americans and the rising violence against their human rights were growing more rigid, Francis Grimké lost all patience for the accommodationist leadership methodology and "progressively more compromising attitude" embraced by Washington.[83] Both Francis and Archibald Grimké aligned with Du Bois and Trotter's Niagara Movement in 1905, pledging themselves to assist the subsequent development of a civil rights activist organization. This led them to publicly proclaim, in part, that they would not collaborate with any African American leader "who would compromise on the rights of the Negro, or whose utterances could be quoted in support of the position of those who denied the Negro such rights."[84] In choosing this civil rights activist option over Washington's, Francis and Archibald Grimké were in concert with other leading Black professional personalities like Ida Wells-Barnett, the anti-lynching crusader, and Jesse Barber, publisher of Atlanta's major Black newspaper *Voices of the Negro*.[85]

In relating the professional careers of Archibald and Francis Grimké as examples of Lincoln University's important contribution to the development of twentieth-century African American civil society, Bond's account contained an important subtext: their metamorphosis from an outlook that was friendly toward Booker T. Washington during their formative intellectual identity phase to one that grew averse to him during their mature intellectual identity phase. Why this subtext resonates so strongly in *Education for Freedom* is because Bond himself experienced, between the late 1920s and the mid-1930s, a similar intellectual metamorphosis, fashioning for himself from 1935 onward a civil rights activist and even reform-leftist intellectual identity. In short, in his probe of the Grimké brothers' professional and intellectual careers, Bond unveiled the mirror image of his own.

Thus, in his probe of the professional careers of two prominent late nineteenth-century graduates of Lincoln University—Archibald and Francis Grimké—Bond provided a keen understanding of his view of Lincoln University's historical role as a Black American institution of civic growth or civil society enhancement. For Bond, apart from the core function of advancing higher-education literacy, there was no more important systemic historical function that Black colleges could perform for formerly enslaved Black Americans. Their other critically important task, which Bond discussed at length in *Education for Freedom*'s final two chapters, was the recruitment of students from Africa, which would also enable the modern civic growth function for emergent nation-states in colonial African countries.

Forging Ties with African States: Bond's Africanist Endgame

In the fall term of 1953, Bond mounted a two-day conference at Lincoln University on African decolonization movements and the relationship of the United Nations, the United States, and Britain toward them. Several years later, Bond joined with Lincoln's former political science chairman, John Aubrey Davis, who had joined the Political Science Department at City University of New York in 1952, to search for a way to expand Bond's deep interest in African nationalist movements broadly among middle-class Black Americans. Their search ended in the spring term of 1956 when Bond, Davis, and several other Black American intellectuals attended the First World Congress of Black Writers and Artists, which was held in Paris. The group selected Bond as its spokesperson. The congress was convened by the major francophone African intellectual organization the Société africaine de culture (SAC) under the leadership of two leading Senegalese intellectuals, the poet and nationalist politician Léopold Sédar Senghor and the writer and publisher Alioune Diop, as well as a leading Martinican intellectual, the poet Aimé Césaire. Among the congress's final proposals was the granting of an organizational membership in the SAC to the Black American scholars attending the congress under the name of the American Society for African Culture (AMSAC).

Following the First World Congress of Black Writers and Artists and the delegation's return to the United States, Bond and Davis initiated discussions with a broad range of Black American intellectuals, and AMSAC was properly born in late 1956, incorporated with Bond as president and Davis as executive administrator. Bond's leading role in the founding of AMSAC had its origin in two cultural strands of his intellectual identity—namely, his race-sensitive commitment to equality for Black people under American white supremacist patterns, as well as to "African redemption," to use an old-fashioned term, which is to say to political freedom in colonial Africa. Bond's devotion to the civil rights of Black Americans and his deep African-redemption outlook shaped his eleven-year leadership of AMSAC.

Throughout the late 1950s and 1960s, AMSAC functioned as the premier institutional mechanism among African Americans that forged viable helping-hand linkages—intellectual and political—with emergent African states and their elites, enabled in part by Bond's personal friendship with two of Africa's leading national politicians, who were, like Bond himself, graduates of Lincoln University: Nmamdi Azikiwe of Nigeria and Kwame Nkrumah of Ghana. Furthermore, AMSAC's ties with various newly independent African states produced a kind of multiplier effect upon a broad range of African American professionals who, in turn, fashioned a variety of African-focused organizations, including the American Negro

Leadership Conference on Africa, Africare, and Operation Crossroads Africa. I will elaborate on each of these organizations, and particularly on the import of AMSAC, in chapter 2.

In terms of commitment to both Black American civil rights and "African redemption," what I call Bond's "Africanist endgame" was an effective way to close out his variegated and brilliant intellectual odyssey. Of the several ways one could sum up the core character of Horace Mann Bond's intellectual odyssey, the most apt would be, I think, to view it as a genuine humanitarian–intellectual quest.

A Concluding Note

Within the ideological spectrum of the twentieth-century humanitarian-intellectual paradigm, Horace Mann Bond is most properly classified as a radical humanist intellectual. But his mode of radical Christian humanism was forever open-ended, never taut or dogmatic. This was vividly apparent in Bond's great contribution to the history of African American higher education, *Education for Freedom: A History of Lincoln University.* In this work, Bond brilliantly delineated the ideological, social, and religious roots of the conservative branch of the antislavery movement, the Colonization Society, which launched Lincoln University (initially called Ashmun University) as the first institution for the higher education of Free Negroes before the Civil War. Its goal was Black American *colonization* in Africa, not Black American *education* as Bond perceived education.

Inasmuch as Bond's beloved Lincoln University was founded by the conservative wing of the antislavery movement, and Bond's intellectual identification was with the ideologically progressive wing, his historiographical quest in *Education for Freedom* was a difficult one—namely, how to portray Lincoln University's historical achievement in Black modern development under the tutelage of racially liberal white elite paternalism. The interpretative modality of Bond's discourse in *Education for Freedom* asserts that despite its conservative white elite paternalism, the Christian-humanist activism of the white Presbyterian leadership of Lincoln University from 1854 to the end of World War II possessed countervailing freedom-enhancing possibilities that were ultimately realized in the Black American civic-growth or civil-society-advancement role performed by five generations of Lincoln University graduates.

Furthermore, Bond's interpretive modality in *Education for Freedom* asserts implicitly that the same Christian-humanist ethos that informed the anti-slavery movement and launched Lincoln University also paved the way for the twentieth-century Black American civil rights movement. As the Reverend Dr. Martin Luther King Jr. well understood, these two evil-challenging movements marched in lockstep, as it were, under a freedom-enhancing banner across the freedom-denying landscape of American slavocracy and American white supremacist racism. It is, then, a core message of Bond's that without the Christian-humanist activism dynamic in nineteenth-century American history, the twentieth-century civil rights movement would have been inconceivable.

In our current environment, Horace Mann Bond, would, I believe, recognize the need for a rebirth of Christian-humanist activism at the middle and upper echelons of American society, among the greed- and plutocracy-polluted corporatist stratum above all. I have in mind especially a rebirth of Christian-humanist activism on behalf of vanquishing the demeaning poverty that exists among perhaps twenty million of our citizens. If he were with us today, Bond's intellectual prowess would contribute boldly to this kind of Christian-humanist activist rebirth.

CHAPTER II

John Aubrey Davis

Black Intellectual as Activist and Technocrat

J ohn Aubrey Davis was one of what we might call a rare breed. In the years surrounding World War II, only a handful of African Americans had obtained professional degrees at the doctoral level in political science; prominent among them were Ralph Bunche and Robert Brisbane, at Harvard University; Robert Martin, at University of Chicago; and Merze Tate, at Radcliffe College/Harvard University, one of an even vanishingly smaller number of women in the discipline. (Never mind political science: a very small cadre of African American professionals had obtained full-fledged graduate school training at all.) So when Davis enrolled in graduate school at the University of Wisconsin to study international politics and comparative politics, he was poised to join a unique professional subgroup within the evolving twentieth-century African American intelligentsia. In this chapter, I discuss the fascinating, far-ranging career of Dr. Davis, the man who was my first professor and mentor in political science.

John Aubrey Davis was raised in Washington, DC, in a middle-class African American household that was involved in civil rights activism. The three children—Allison, Elizabeth, and John—all attended college; John and his older brother, Allison, who would become a distinguished anthropology and psychology scholar and author of the landmark study *Deep South* (1940), graduated from Williams College, and Elizabeth from Wellesley College. This was a pattern that was quite rare for African

Americans in that high-noon era of Jim Crow America during the 1920s and 1930s, decades during which nearly every college-going African American—more than 95 percent, in fact—attended Negro colleges.

Upon completing the requirements for his master's degree by the summer of 1934, Davis returned to DC, where the new head of Howard University's Department of Political Science, the Harvard-trained political scientist Ralph Bunche, hired him as an instructor. It would be twelve years before Davis completed the graduate school requirements for his PhD, which he began working toward at Columbia University on a Rosenwald Foundation Fellowship in 1936. Davis described his major of American government and constitutional law in a letter to me as "a standard combination at Columbia [in that era]." For his minor in labor economics, he went "across department and against all advice about too tough a program." At the same time, Davis married a young African American librarian and English scholar named Mavis Wormley and embarked on a long academic association with Lincoln University, where he was appointed assistant professor in political science in 1935.

Davis submitted his doctoral dissertation in 1946. It probed the administrative structures, rules, procedures, and impact of the New Deal's social security policies, namely, the Social Security Act of 1935 and the Social Security Act of 1939. Davis's dissertation earned high distinctions, which led to its being published as part of Columbia University Press's coveted Studies in History, Economics, and Public Law series under the title *Regional Organization of the Social Security Administration: A Case Study* (1950). To my knowledge, the only other African American scholar to be published in this Columbia series was Ira de Augustine Reid, whose *Negro Immigrants* had appeared in 1939.

The foregoing constitutes the core features of John Aubrey Davis's academic background. As for his academic career, in 1953, after teaching at Lincoln University since 1935—with several years' leave of absence during World War II—Davis was wooed away to become one of several African American scholars to gain full professorships in the main colleges in New York City's college system, joining the faculty of City College. Hylan Lewis joined Queens College, and John Hope Franklin joined Brooklyn College.

This brief sketch gets us a couple of decades ahead in the story of Davis's intellectual and professional odyssey as a member of that small cadre of first-generation Black personalities in the field of political science. Now we will return to his core story.

The Role of Civil Rights Activism in Davis's Odyssey

Formation of the New Negro Alliance Movement, 1933

John Aubrey Davis was only several months out of Williams College with his bachelor's degree when he joined a street protest against a white-owned fast-food shop located in the heart of the Black community in Washington, DC. The protesters insisted that the Hamburger Grill, which had fired several Black workers and replaced them with white workers, rehire the African Americans; in the meantime, they asked residents of the local Black neighborhood to boycott the business. Davis's participation marked his first foray into civil rights activism. The historian Michele Pacifico describes the incident as follows:

> Monday morning, August 28, 1933. The Great Depression had reached all regions and levels of American society. In Washington, three African American employees of the white-owned Hamburger Grill on 12th and U streets, N.W. are fired and three whites hired in their places. The business is in a black neighborhood and depends entirely upon black patronage. Almost immediately after the three were fired, John Aubrey Davis, 21, a recent graduate of Williams College, organizes a group of young neighborhood men, most of whom frequent the grill, to picket the business. Their signs urge fellow community members to boycott the restaurant. The protest proves effective: the following day the Hamburger Grill closes. On Wednesday the three black workers are rehired, business returns to normal, and the informal group of neighbors savor their first victory in a battle to open up African-American economic opportunity.[1]

As Davis related to me in numerous conversations, his participation in the Hamburger Grill boycott in August 1933 awakened in him his first awareness of the broader political possibilities of street-level civil rights activism among African Americans. He pondered the possible political implications of the boycott against the store with a group of young Black professionals in Washington, DC, among whom were several lawyers, including Charles Hamilton Houston, the dean of Howard Law School; William Hastie and James Nabrit, faculty members at Howard Law School; and Bedford Lawson and Thurman Dodson, attorneys in private practice. Also involved was Doxey Wilkerson, a civil rights activist and professor of education at Howard. As a result of these discussions, by the late fall of 1933, Davis concluded that street-level civil rights activism could be translated into viable public policy mobilization against American racism. What was required, however, was an organized instrument to effect this outcome. Several of the lawyers in Davis's circle had gained insight into how they might proceed by exploring the linkage between trade union activism and public policy mobilization among white workers, a linkage that earlier had produced pro-labor legislation at both the state and federal levels, such as the Wagner Act in the 1920s that legalized the right to strike, and also several federal court decisions that advanced the rights of working-class Americans.

In the fall of 1933, Davis and his peers called the organizational instrument they formed the New Negro Alliance (NNA). In ideological terms, the movement adhered mainly to a pattern of civil rights activism that tilted more toward pragmatic than radical action; in other words, its policy goals were conceived along incremental lines. As Hastie observed in "The Way of the Alliance," an article published in *The New Alliance Year Book 1939*, the sociological character of the Black population in Depression-era Washington, DC, was hardly conducive to the application of overreaching activism:

> The colored population of Washington was divided into two socio-economic groups: one composed principally of salaried white-collar workers, a large number of them in public employment and the other composed principally of skilled and unskilled workers whose services were employed in the commercial domestic activities of a non-industrial city. . . . [So] when the New Negro Alliance was beginning its activities [in 1933] more than one-third of the Negroes in Washington were dependent upon some form of relief, while less than one-twentieth of the whites were similarly situated.[2]

There were, however, competing visions of political activism that diverged from the tilt toward pragmatic activism on the part of the NNA. One such competing vision that gained prominence in Black communities during the Depression was associated with Marcus Garvey's Universal Negro Improvement Association. This Black nationalist vision promoted what might be called a separatist Black communitarian activism. Hastie, Davis, and other members of the NNA rejected this as well as the Marxist vision, another variant of radical activism that was associated with the white leftist sector in American politics.

One of the notable figures among Washington's activist Black professionals during this period who embraced aspects of the Marxist vision was Ralph Bunche. As Charles P. Henry of the University of California notes in his brilliant biography *Ralph Bunche: Model Negro or American Other?* (1999), Bunche's variant of the Marxist perspective toward Black activism emphasized the political salience of an activism based on class rather than ideas of Black ethnicity. In other words, Bunche favored prior alliance with the white American working class and its trade unions as a precondition for effective Black American civil rights mobilization. Davis, Hastie, and most other members of the NNA, however, rejected Bunche's Marxist perspective, claiming that there was no serious evidence that white American workers were ready to challenge American racism; rather, they were among its core practitioners. As Davis put it in correspondence to me, "Bunche was never a member [of the NNA], only a critic. . . . Bunche attacked the NNA because he feared the division of the [American] labor movement on the basis of race; he saw the only good in the organization was that it taught public protest, solidarity, and direct action."[3] This issue is discussed later in this chapter.

Leadership Styles in the New Negro Alliance

There were some tactical differences among leading personalities in the NNA regarding their styles of civil rights activism. For instance, William Hastie, a lawyer and budding legal scholar, favored what might be called a kind of institutional activism, which meant a leadership-hierarchic mode of civil rights mobilization. Hastie described this orientation in an article in *The New Negro Alliance Year Book 1939*: "The neighborhood petition and, where necessary, the neighborhood boycott were the effective weapons of struggle. It was contemplated that in the course of many efforts of this sort, organization would be developed throughout the city. Such organization would permit an extension of programs with appropriate variation of tactics to the end that racial proscriptions and restrictions might be removed in public as well as in private employment."[4]

For Davis the budding political scientist, his leadership vision was one of distinctly populist activism. In a letter to me, Davis explained that in the early days of the NNA movement, he emphasized street-level political mobilization, reaching out to the grassroots through Black evangelical clergymen such as the Reverend Elder Michaux of the Apostolic Church of God in Washington:

> In 1933 I recruited personally at his home, 1700 Block of "C" St., N.W. Washington, D.C. The Rev. Elder Micheaux [*sic*] ("Happy Am I in My Redeemer"). He had a strong image where he had been successful in Newport News and Philadelphia. In 1933 the A&P opened an all-white store at 9th and "S" Streets, and I put up a picket line (including my sister—Wellesley '29). Micheaux supported us and took up money for us at his big rallies in Griffith Stadium. I addressed one of these. We had the camp meeting as well as the regular [Negro] church on our side. You may remember Micheaux's Radio Church of God in Philly.[5]

Furthermore, in the first historical probe of the NNA, presented by Michele Pacifico in *Washington History* magazine, similar emphasis was given to what I call John Aubrey Davis's street-level activist-mobilization methodology. When relating Davis's role in the founding events that shaped the NNA movement, Pacifico observes that

> The "Jobs for Negroes" campaigns, also known as "Don't Buy Where You Can't Work," relied on visible, even confrontational actions. They used negotiation, mass protests, and boycotts to force white businesses in black communities to employ African Americans, and to employ them in non-manual labor positions. Leaders exhorted black citizens . . . to boycott local businesses that refused to employ African Americans in clerical and managerial positions. They also worked to prevent black expenditures on goods and services in black neighborhoods where inequitable employment practices prevailed. The campaigns galvanized both poor and middle-class blacks to action.[6]

In short, as contrasted with Hastie's institutional activism, Davis's populist activism left a broad impact on the modus operandi of the NNA throughout its existence in the 1930s, especially in regard to a persistent endeavor by the alliance to expand the range of reforms demanded from both private and public employers in Washington, DC. This activist endeavor is revealed in *The New Negro Alliance Year Book 1939*, which shows a protest-oriented portrayal of the racial-caste patterns in Washington's social system as these related to public employment in that city's fire department. Namely, while Blacks made up 27 percent of the population, they held a mere 2 percent of the fire department jobs as of 1938. This amounted to 17 out of 871 fire department jobs (the same number that obtained in 1918), which meant that by 1938, African Americans experienced a deficit of 240 such positions. Similarly, while Washington's white population claimed 98 percent of the fire department payroll in 1938 ($2.1 million), Blacks claimed just 2 percent, which translated into a Black payroll deficit of nearly $600,000.

The Hastie's and Davis's contrasting mobilization styles in the operation of the NNA can be portrayed in yet another way. If Hastie's institutionalist activism can be viewed as a variant of bourgeois-establishmentarian mobilization, then Davis's populist activism can be viewed as bourgeois-progressive mobilization. The key difference between the political orientations of the two men was that Hastie exhibited more faith in middle-class individuals to function as activist mobilizers, while Davis was willing to reach beyond the Black middle-class ranks to working-class leadership sectors.

Here, then, was the populist dynamic at work in defining the young Davis's formative civil rights activism style. The roots of what I label his bourgeois-progressive activism reached back to his boyhood years around World War I and the 1920s, to his Black middle-class neighborhood on the northeast side of DuPont Circle in Washington, DC. The most activist district branch of the Washington NAACP was located there, and Davis's father played a leading role in it. Davis vividly recalled childhood memories of joining his parents in street demonstrations in support of an early antilynching bill in the United States Congress, one that stemmed from the courageous crusade pioneered by the African American journalist Ida Wells-Barnett. "My father," Davis remarked to me during a conversation, "used to carry me on his strong shoulders at those antilynching demonstrations."

One additional contrasting feature of Hastie's and Davis's mobilization styles should be mentioned. While Hastie's mode of bourgeois-establishmentarian mobilization often coalesced sympathetically with aspects of Booker T. Washington's accommodationist leadership strategy of forging ties with conservative white elite patrons, Davis's bourgeois-progressive activism was circumspect toward and sometimes disdainful of Washington's approach. For Davis, white capitalists in particular were, as we say today, part of the problem and not part of the solution. As a result, white business elements had to be made part of the solution through all manner of populist-skewed Black civil rights activism. In Davis's activist vision, there was even a kind of higher-order benefit for African Americans associated with progressive activism; namely, the fashioning of a sense of Black efficacy, of Black honor, if you will.

When, in 1933, Davis first entertained the idea of a formalized boycott movement directed at white businesses located in urban Black communities that hired few if any Blacks, he took this idea to his boyhood NAACP branch, assuming it had remained the activist-oriented branch of his parents' time. To his dismay, he discovered that the branch had gone establishmentarian, "completely dominated by the respectable, well-off, and stuff-shirt [Black] residents of the city," Davis told Pacifico.[7] That the branch would not, in Pacifico's words, "offer assistance to those struggling to obtain and keep jobs" was a position that simply "outraged Davis," who seethed "that [Washington NAACP] leaders were patronizing white businesses, especially chain stores, that did not employ any neighborhood African-Americans except in the most menial jobs. No one was acting to change these conditions."[8] It was this new establishmentarian aura of a once bourgeois-progressive NAACP branch in Washington, DC, that had initially radicalized Davis along Black-populist lines. Pacifico relates Davis's formative activism in the following terms:

> When events presented the opportunity that hot August day in 1933, Davis was prepared and launched the New Negro Alliance with the highly successful Hamburger Grill boycott. Davis gave the new organization its name. He used the words "New Negro" to separate it from the previous [leadership] generation of African-Americans whom he deemed too content and passive. Yet Davis did not embrace Alain Locke's "New Negro" movement of the 1920s, noting that

"Dr. Locke and the followers of his philosophy believed that racial prejudice would soon disappear before the altar of truth, art, and intellectual achievement."

Davis argued that the black people's problems in the 1930s could not be solved by saying—"I'm culturally worth something." He stressed that African-Americans had contributed to American cultural life since the time of the slave boats, but their situation had not improved. Overtly founded to win economic rights for African-American Washingtonians, the New Negro Alliance was an organization "with a new vision, a new thought and spirit, fearless in its undertakings and willing to sacrifice and fight for its own principles, even if it meant being thrown in jail," according to Davis. The New Negro Alliance would surpass the "New Negro" movement in its direct fight for economic progress.[9]

The Legacy of Davis's New Negro Alliance

There was perhaps a threefold legacy associated with the NNA. Despite justifiably singling out for the NNA a unique legacy in the history of civil rights activism, I should note here that it was not the first civil rights organization to champion "Don't Buy Where You Can't Work" campaigns. While there is some disagreement among scholars as to which city launched the first of these movements, there is little doubt that the Washington, DC–based New Negro Alliance was among the first. The NNA was upstaged in this regard by civil rights activists in Chicago during the summer of 1929. Davis provided me with a chronology of sorts for subsequent organizations. "We preceded the following: The Young People's Forum in Baltimore (Juanita Mitchell), The Clerk's Circle in Richmond, The Joint Committee on Harlem (Adam Clayton Powell and Rev. William Imes), started with the aid of [Davis's close friend] Belford Lawson, [Theodore] Berry's organization in Cincinnati, which was instigated by Belford Lawson (Berry was Belford's law partner at one time)."[10] Whatever place the NNA occupies on this time line, there is little doubt that in terms of a lasting institutional civil rights legacy stemming from the experience of "Don't Buy Where You Can't Work" activism, Davis and Hastie ran away with the prize.

When one conceptualizes the overall character of the NNA in the context of other middle-class-led Black activist organizations that existed by the 1930s, it can be said to have introduced new dimensions to the prevailing pattern of Black civil rights activism. While the NNA was neither explicitly Marxist nor Black Nationalist in orientation, it nevertheless blended leftist features and Black communitarian features. Furthermore, while the alliance's mode of activism functioned as a parallel pattern to the long-established NAACP activism in Washington, DC, it added at the same time something quite new to civil rights activism, something that might be dubbed a pragmatic-radical or reform-leftist thrust. Put another way, Davis and his activist Young Turk colleagues, among them Hastie, Nabrit, Lawson, and the educator and marketing professional Howard Naylor Fitzhugh, fashioned through the alliance what can be called a genuine style of bourgeois-progressive Black activism.

In this regard, then, the NNA was following the lead of A. Philip Randolph, who, during the World War I era with his Brotherhood of Sleeping Car Porters, had pioneered a viable mode of bourgeois-progressive or bourgeois-leftist activism. As such, the alliance's political mode differed from the bourgeois-establishmentarian activism pattern that, to his dismay, Davis recognized during the summer of 1933 among members of Washington, DC's NAACP branch. Above all, the NNA's bourgeois-progressive activism did not assume that there was an intrinsic capacity of laissez-faire capitalist American democracy to egalitarianize and liberate the oppressed and tormented racial-caste status of African Americans. Davis and his alliance colleagues believed that steady-state assertive civil rights mobilization among the ranks of Black popular society was required to achieve these ends, and also that something like what today we call affirmative action practices were required to achieve these goals.

It can also be argued that the alliance's bourgeois-progressive modality contributed to a sophisticated technocratic understanding of the need to link civil rights activism to effective public policy outcomes, a topic I treat in detail in this chapter. Although the NAACP also understood the issue of skillfully interfacing activism and public policy, the alliance's "Don't Buy Where You Can't Work" modality expanded political knowledge of this interfacing process. The NNA designed its picketing and boycott activism in a manner that translated into a systemically profound challenge to American racial-caste patterns. Here, then, was the very heart of a special politicizing dynamic that, over time, would characterize Davis in terms of what I call the Black intellectual as activist and technocrat.

The strategy of protest mobilization in urban neighborhoods employed by the NNA—calibrating any given protest action so as to increase the possibility that it would translate into a civil rights court case—meant that the alliance's inner circle had to be prepared with a range of intellectual knowledge and technocratic legal and administrative skills that would eventually be put to use in mounting such cases. Davis and his colleagues also needed a sophisticated grasp of the American political process. After all, these men practiced so-called long-run protest politics, which viewed boycott and picketing activism as stepping-stones to a more systematically conceived challenge against racist patterns in American life. In this conception, members of the NNA were pioneering a modality of civil rights activism that Houston, Marshall, and other Black lawyers associated with the NAACP Legal Defense Fund would institute on a national basis from the 1930s onward.

This, then, was what Davis and other young Black professionals focused on in assembling the New Negro Alliance movement during the 1930s in Washington, DC. I have thought for some time that the type of civil rights activism pursued by these young Black American professionals four generations ago warranted as deep a political and intellectual analysis as one could bring to it. I have decided to attempt such an analysis of the NNA movement by filtering it through a probe of the intellectual odyssey of one of its founding members, Professor John Aubrey Davis.

Organizational Dynamics of the New Negro Alliance

Black Intellectuals Challenge Racist Capitalism

It was in the summer of 1935, two years after the original demonstration around the Hamburger Grill, that Davis, Hastie, Fitzhugh, and other civil rights activists formally organized the New Negro Alliance as a mechanism to challenge permanently white businesses in Washington, DC, that were patronized by African Americans but either refused to employ them entirely or treated Black employees without parity in comparison to their white employees. Some ten task-based committees were created as the day-to-day operating units of the NNA, four of which were especially concerned with dovetailing the alliance's activist undertaking so as to maximize the public policy impact of the group's activism: the Civil Rights Committee, the Public Utilities Committee, the Legal Committee, and the Case Committee. George Johnson, law partner of Davis's closest friend, Belford Lawson, chaired the Civil Rights Committee; Doxey Wilkerson chaired the Public Utilities Committee; Thurman Dodson, another lawyer and colleague of Belford Lawson, chaired the Legal Committee; and Rolandus Cooper, a lawyer, chaired the Case Committee.

There was a kind of synergistic interaction among these functional committees of the NNA. For example, when the Public Utilities Committee identified utility companies that might be the object of an alliance boycott, it had to mobilize the other three around its concern before involving the executive officers or administrators. The Case Committee played a key role in this decision-making process, for its members developed the analysis as to whether a given business, if chosen as an object of an alliance boycott, would produce good dividends in terms of the public policy impact. The picketing and boycott weapon used by the alliance might not be initiated if the Case Committee decided to send a suspected business a preliminary request to hire Black employees and that request was agreed upon. For instance, a study of the activity of the Case Committee during 1938 contains the following report of a request the alliance sent to a Washington-area business to hire Black employees:

Case No. 163—Brown's Corner
Store—Seventh & T Streets N.W.

Case Committee: (Noting a part-time clerk only). We feel that your business being supported 100% by Negroes demands in all fairness to the policy you state that you subscribe to, a full-time clerk as well as a part-time clerk. Result: Suggestion accepted and complied with by proprietor.

In the following report, however, on another job request sent to a white business, a rather different outcome ensued. It happened that in two instances of job requests sent by the alliance, the white businesses refused even to enter into discussion.

Case No. 209—Capital Shoe Store. Case No. 297—Bonnett's Shoes

These stores have ignored three regular form letters, used by the Case Committee in its approach for a conference and also having ignored a registered letter, received as a last resort our Picket Line.[11]

The clear tone of pragmatism apparent in the foregoing instances of the alliance's dealings with white businesses in 1938 was, in fact, a central modus operandi basic to all of the organization's functioning. While Davis and other leading figures in the NNA were firm about their long-run goal of ending discriminatory practices by white businesses patronized by Blacks, they were not committed to a single method for achieving this goal; rather, they were fully experimental. For instance, the alliance made varying accommodations to the special circumstances of a given business where required, as illustrated in a report on negotiations with three businesses during 1938. The report observed that "All three [will] hire a week-end clerk to start and will increase by filling vacancies until majority of clerks are Negroes. These stores could not afford full week clerks."[12]

It is notable, however, that although quite attuned to the needs of specific businesses in their attempts to adjust to integrationist practices, the NNA never shirked from exercising a kind of normative surveillance in regard to the personal treatment accorded Black employees by white businesses. The alliance's leaders were firm about their progressive sense of interpersonal relations between whites and Blacks, and they were willing to pressure white businesses along these lines. This can be seen in the following report from the files of the alliance's Case Committee:

Case No. 303—Harry Kaufman Department Store

Case Committee: We respectfully wish to state that our Alliance definitely views the practice of having Negro clerks relieve the elevator operator and pressing articles for window display a vicious discriminatory policy unless all clerks, both white and Negro, are compelled to take regular turns at this work. We also take this opportunity to suggest that now is the opportune time to employ the promised third Negro clerk.

Result: Discontinuance of the discriminatory policy. No more non-clerical work. On account of Union affiliations which must be adjusted, a Negro Shipping Clerk (male) is to be employed by August 15th, 1939.[13]

Thus, in pressuring white businesses into both integrated hiring and fair interpersonal treatment of their Black employees, the NNA was clearly breaking new ground in the matter of civil rights activism. It should also be noted that the alliance broke new ground as well by demonstrating that a progressive Black activist organization could succeed at broad, militant mobilization among middle-class African Americans, for there was during the 1930s an assumption among progressive Black activists that working-class African Americans (trade union workers) were more welcoming to militant organizations. Davis was a veritable true believer in the activist potential of middle-class African Americans, a belief cultivated in him by his activist parents. His closest professional peer, Belford Lawson, shared this belief. In this matter, Davis and Lawson differed from other progressive Black intellectuals in the Washington community during the 1930s, especially Ralph Bunche and E. Franklin Frazier, social science faculty members at Howard University, whose progressive outlook tended toward Marxism. They were therefore inclined to look favorably upon trade-unionized working-class Blacks as soldiers of civil rights activism, while viewing middle-class Blacks as bourgeois and self-serving. Davis and Lawson were ahead of their leftist Black professional peers in their respect for the activist potential of middle-class Blacks, and Davis in particular initiated numerous linkages between the NNA and Washington's relatively sizable middle-class Black community during the 1930s. In correspondence to me, Davis noted that he established the New Negro Forum in 1935 as part of the NNA. The newly formed group met in the Berean Baptist Church at 11th and V Streets, NW. Among the featured speakers were Jiggs Donahue, one of three commissioners who ran the city, and John Sullivan, head of the American Federation of Government Employees.[14]

In general, then, a broad representation of Black professionals supported the civil rights activism of the NNA in Washington, DC. Middle-class volunteer associations broadly extended their resources to the alliance, such as the National Association of Negro College Women, a variety of Greek-letter fraternities and sororities, and Black civic associations of all sorts. Above all, nearly all of the leading Black churches in Washington participated in or were attentive to the alliance's activist agenda. The Black church's generally broad endorsement of the alliance was underscored in a report on its support base by James Nabrit for the alliance's annual yearbook, in which he mentioned by name several ministers and their congregations.[15]

Alliance Activism and the Courts

Between 1935 and 1940, it was typical for the alliance's use of the boycott to be met with court injunctions charging it with activity illegal to free commerce. Although the U.S. Congress's La Guardia–Norris Anti-injunction Act of March 1932 gave trade unions the right to use picketing and boycott tactics, it wasn't at all clear that federal courts would extend these rights to a pressure group whose members were not directly employed in the businesses being picketed or boycotted. Nevertheless, Davis informed me in discussions on the alliance's activist methodology that he, Hastie, and other figures within the NNA were aware that at some point a clash with the federal courts was likely.

As it happened, this clash did occur, but a decision from the courts as to how the La Guardia–Norris Act applied evolved slowly. During its first year and a half of operation, the alliance was met by court injunctions initiated by several Washington-area businesses that had been picketed and boycotted by the organization, but each time the federal courts refused to hear bids by the alliance to appeal the injunctions. This situation suddenly changed in late 1936, when the alliance mounted a broad-based boycott against a major Washington-area supermarket chain, the Sanitary Grocery Company. The Sanitary Grocery Company asked for and received from the U.S. Supreme Court an injunction that the alliance immediately appealed. The court granted its appeal, a decision that had a twofold political impact on Washington's African American community. First, the Supreme Court's granting of the appeal sparked a fissure between the upstart NNA and Washington's much older NAACP branch. Still smarting from the initial successes of the alliance's activism and not sure of the viability of its own civil rights methodology, the NAACP branch stayed out of the dispute. This decision proved politically disastrous for it, though, because quite a different response to the injunction was taking place at the grassroots level. Pacifico writes that the events surrounding the alliance's appeal of the injunction amounted to community-wide mobilization among Blacks in favor of the NNA:

> The black press publicized the story. It was a heady time for the young African-American legal team set up [separate from the NAACP branch] to fight this battle. If the New Negro Alliance could win the case, then all "Jobs-For-Negroes" picketers [nationwide] would have the force of law behind them.
>
> While the NAACP doubted that the Alliance could win its case and offered little support, the black community of the District of Columbia rallied behind the organization. The NNA declared Sunday, December 17, 1937, New Negro Alliance Day. Pastors invited NNA representatives to their churches to discuss NNA programs and the legal case, and to raise funds. Capping New Negro Alliance Day was an evening service with music and speeches at the John Wesley A.M.E. Zion Church at 14th and Corcoran Streets, N.W. John Aubrey Davis was the guest speaker with other presentations by Belford Lawson, Thurman L. Dodson, church pastor Reverend Stephen G. Spottswood, and John Zucker, the national representative of the Retail Clerk Association. The community turned out, donating a critical $500 toward the expenses of the Supreme Court case. . . . Belford Lawson and Thomas Dodson presented the Alliance's arguments, researched and prepared by William Hastie, Thurgood P. Marshall, Edward P. Lovett, Theodore M. Berry, and James M. Nabrit, Jr.[16]

Noteworthy in Pacifico's account is the fact that among the young activist lawyers who presented the NNA's case to the Supreme Court in 1937 was the litany of future leading figures in the African American legal profession in general, and especially key figures who directed the national-level NAACP desegregation cases in federal courts during the 1950s and 1960s. These early legal warhorses for the NNA evolved into major national civil rights figures, the most celebrated, of course, being Marshall himself, the head lawyer for the NAACP Legal Defense Fund in the 1950s who would later be appointed by President Lyndon Johnson as the first African American justice on the United States Supreme Court.

In returning to the 1937 case of *New Negro Alliance v. Sanitary Grocery Company*, the brief was argued before the U.S. Supreme Court on March 5,

1938. Its core thesis was that the alliance, in pressuring white businesses to employ Blacks in legal terms, played an equivalent role to that of trade unions in pressuring industrial firms on behalf of fair working conditions. Just as trade unions functioned as the key instrument for ensuring economic security and egalitarian social rights for their members, ensuring white workers especially against economic discrimination, the NNA's use of picketing and boycott strategies similarly functioned as a guarantee against racial-caste discriminatory practices committed by white businesses against African American citizens. Or, as the alliance's brief put it, the NNA was the "only defense [available] against a discriminatory policy which jeopardizes [Negroes'] economic security."[17] In this manner, then, the alliance's brief before the U.S. Supreme Court characterized its use of picketing and boycotts as the functional equivalent of a genuine labor dispute under the language and terms of the La Guardia–Norris Act of 1932.[18]

To the enormous surprise of Davis and other members of the NNA's inner circle, including the lawyers involved in the case's preparation and presentation, the U.S. Supreme Court, on March 28, 1938, ruled in their favor. In Pacifico's words, "In a six-two decision, the Supreme Court, led by Chief Justice Charles Evans Hughes, decided that 'those having a direct or indirect interest' in the employment of certain people should have the freedom to disseminate information and 'peacefully persuade others' to take action against such injustices." The climax of a four-year battle, the court's decision gave African Americans an effective method of fighting discriminatory hiring practices, a weapon they could lawfully use nationwide to combat discrimination in the workplace.[19] Elaborating on *New Negro Alliance v. Sanitary Grocery Company*, one of the NNA lawyers, Leon Ransom, proffered the following formulation:

Mr. Justice [Owen Josephus] Roberts read the history—making a decision which reversed the lower courts and dismissed the injunction. In the course of the decision, the Court pointed out that the employer-employee relation did not have to exist in order for a "labor dispute" to arise, and that an organization such as the Alliance, striving to obtain employment from employers who discriminated against them on account of race or color, could be a "person interested" in a labor dispute and so within the protection of the law prohibiting court interference.[20]

The immediate impact of the Supreme Court's ruling in *New Negro Alliance v. Sanitary Grocery Company* was an expansion of the alliance's activism agenda in the Washington area. "For the next three years, until 1941," writes Pacifico, "the Alliance used its newly won right to secure more jobs for black Washingtonians. In the wake of the Supreme Court decision, the struggle eased; white employers preferred compromise to boycotts and picket lines. . . . Old opponents such as Kaufman's Department Store and High's Ice Cream finally hired African-American clerks."[21]

At the same time, however, new developments at the national level set into motion a chain of events that eventually saw the dissolution of the NNA—America's entry into World War II in 1941 primary among them. The second important development related to World War II was the issuance on June 25, 1941, of Executive Order 8802. With the stroke of President Roosevelt's pen, Executive Order 8802 extended to the federal level the right to equal or fair employment that the young John Aubrey Davis and his peers in the NNA had spent nearly a decade seeking to apply simply to the District of Columbia. This federal policy set in motion a totally unforeseen series of events that would recalibrate the political activism to which the alliance's inner circle had grown accustomed between 1933 and 1940 from what I have called street-level political activism to technocratic-policy activism, now within public policy agencies of the federal government.

In formal policy terms, Executive Order 8802 created a government agency, the Fair Employment Practices Committee (FEPC), which was empowered to supervise a nationwide antidiscrimination program involving businesses in receipt of government contracts for the duration of World War II. In its preliminary form as a committee within the War Production Board and later the War Manpower Commission, the FEPC's first chairman was Mark Etheridge, a liberal white American and an editor of the Louisville *Courier-Journal*. Two chairmen during the formative phase of the FEPC found the agency's task immensely frustrating, owing to resistance from conservative and pro-racist forces among southern legislators in the United States Congress who were intent on blocking execution of the FEPC's mandate. As Davis informed me in correspondence,

[The FEPC] held one hearing in Atlanta against [the discriminatory practices of] companies in the Deep South. That lit up the Southern opposition in Congress. Then in 1942 . . . [the FEPC] scheduled hearings against Capitol Transit Co. in Washington, D.C. and the famous railroad hearing—the Southeastern Carriers hearings. Paul V. McNutt, head of the War Manpower Commission called off the [railroad] hearings, whereupon the Commission resigned including its executive director John Beecher, descendant of Harriet Beecher Stowe.[22]

While much indecision surrounded the chairmanship and the range of authority of the nascent FEPC in 1941 and 1942, what was important from the vantage point of African Americans was the selection of activist professionals associated with the NNA to function as key FEPC administrators. Although Davis himself and some other alliance peers didn't enter the administrative ranks of the FEPC until early 1943, several civil rights activists who were closely affiliated with the organization had gained administrative posts in its inaugural years. This was especially true of Robert Weaver. A Harvard-trained Black economist who had worked with the National Urban League during the 1930s, he was an early African American federal administrator in the New Deal at the time of his appointment to the staff of the War Production Board (later the War Manpower Commission) in 1941. Furthermore, through Weaver, another former official of the National Urban League branch in Baltimore during the 1930s, Clarence Mitchell, was appointed to the staff of the War Production Board as his assistant.

Thus, when Davis, only thirty-one years old, was appointed director of the Division of Review and Analysis in the FEPC in 1943, he began his transition from civil rights activist to federal policy technocrat. Put another way, Davis commenced the intricate interlocking within his intellect of the competing roles of the intellectual as activist and the intellectual as technocrat. For the next thirty-odd years of his professional career, Davis meshed these two strands of his persona with enormous skill and political finesse, as did a number of his peers in the NNA movement.

Linking Activism and Policy Making: John Aubrey Davis's Prelude to the FEPC

To gain an adequate understanding of Davis's initial experience with the intertwining strands of his intellectual persona, it is useful to characterize the formative academic-preparatory phase of his career, which began with graduate school in late 1933 and evolved intermittently through the 1930s to the mid-1940s. Davis took leave of his activist role in the NNA during the fall of 1933 to concentrate on his master's degree at the University of Wisconsin. He completed it in 1934 and returned to Washington, DC, to resume his work in civil rights activism in the NNA and to teach as an instructor in political science under Ralph Bunche in Howard University's Political Science Department. Davis also got his first government job following his return from Wisconsin, initially in the National Recovery Administration working for its director of research, Gustav Peck, and later in the Division of Negro Labor of the Bureau of Labor Statistics, where he "turned out reports on . . . U.S. labor union discrimination against black workers."[23]

In the fall of 1935, Davis became an assistant professor in political science at Lincoln University in Pennsylvania, and three years later he was awarded the most coveted fellowship available in the 1930s to African American scholars and intellectuals, a Rosenwald Foundation Fellowship. The award enabled him to pursue graduate study in political science at Columbia University. While shouldering heavy tasks as an administrator in the FEPC between 1943 and 1946, Davis found time to work on his doctoral dissertation, which probed the administrative arrangements, rules, procedures, and styles associated with the New Deal's Social Security policies, which were promulgated under the Social Security Act of 1935.

As the analytical work of a young African American scholar during the 1940s, Davis's doctoral dissertation on the Social Security system was unique in several respects. First, as already suggested, the topic was not one explicitly pertaining to African Americans, although of course as American citizens, Black people benefited significantly from the New Deal's policies. During this period, there were only a handful of Black scholars, both in Davis's discipline of political science and elsewhere, whose graduate studies were not related directly to Black concerns more narrowly defined. One such scholar was Otelia Cromwell, the aunt of Adelaide Cromwell, who studied Edwardian literature for her Yale University doctoral dissertation; another was the aforementioned Merze Tate, who studied European disarmament negotiations after World War I for her Harvard doctoral dissertation in the 1940s.

It should also be mentioned that there were two other preparatory events that outfitted Davis for his future role as an FEPC administrator. In early

1940, while pursuing doctoral research in New York City, Davis was asked by an influential group of Black professionals and politicians to go to Washington, DC, to lobby the White House to revise a proposed plan that Roosevelt had worked out with the executive secretary of the NAACP, Walter White, in regard to the status of African Americans in the U.S. armed forces. Among the group of influential Blacks who recruited Davis for this task were Arthur and Myra Logan, two prominent physicians; the artist Charles Alston; and Earl Brown, a prominent lawyer and member of the New York City Council. The group called itself the Citizens' Committee for Equal Rights in Defense, and as Davis related in correspondence to me, he was asked "to protest the condition of American Negroes in the armed forces and in the defense industry." Furthermore, he observed that

The matter was made urgent because Walter White had been to the White House and had had a session with the President and Eleanor. He had signed off on an agreement which was unacceptable, especially with regard to the status of Negroes in the armed forces. I was put in the position of running a protest against the White House but not against [Walter] White and the NAACP. We had a mass meeting at the Golden Gate Ballroom (next to the Savoy) where Adam Clayton Powell was the main speaker. We had a parade through Harlem headed by the Elks' band, for which Dr. Lowell C. Wormley [a prominent Black physician related to Davis's wife] advanced the money. The situation was made worse for the administration when Steve Early, the President's secretary, kneed a black policeman at the President's train. The White House appointed Hastie to be a civilian aide to the Secretary of War, transferred Weaver to the War Production Board [from adviser on Black labor in the Department of the Interior—Weaver's first federal job] to secure minority utilization in the war industry and appointed Col. Campbell C. Johnson [a Black army officer] as head of minority recruitment in the selective service system.[24]

After having successfully lobbied the White House into a more progressive stance on the status of African Americans in the armed forces, Davis was called upon again, two years later, to assist the governor's office in New York in fashioning a program that ensured against discrimination in wartime industries in New York State. In June 1942, Davis was appointed assistant director of the year-old New York State Committee Against Discrimination in Employment (NYSCADE), an agency promulgated by then New York governor Herbert H. Lehman, a longtime member of the NAACP board beginning in the Great Depression. Davis's task with NYSCADE was to supervise the production of a study that would provide hands-on knowledge and advice (methods) for realizing Governor Lehman's goal of maximizing job employment for African Americans in New York's war-related industries. In correspondence with me, Davis characterized NYSCADE as follows: "The committee was only a public relations outfit. Its chair [was] Frieda S. Miller, Secretary of Labor. . . . Andrew Doyle, the executive, was an old labor mediator with no schooling after high school, a really nice guy. He and I set up the investigating process, and he got a staff to do the investigating; whereupon the business and industry people on the committee complained loudly that they could not be expected to mix white and colored workers when schools, churches, YMCAs and the army could not."[25]

Be that as it may, by November 1942, Davis's investigatory staff had completed their study and the New York State War Council, the governor's wartime advisory body, had the findings of Davis's field investigators published and widely disseminated. Written by Davis and titled *How Management Can Integrate Negroes in War Industries*, the study was both an analysis of job integration in New York's war-related industries from the promulgation of Roosevelt's FEPC Executive Order 8802 in June 1941 and the fall of 1942 and a hands-on or how-to guide to the maximal achievement of job integration. Under Davis's keen and candid authorship, the study minced few words in rendering its advice. For instance, in the chapter "Introduction of the Negro Worker," Davis, writing under a subsection titled "Necessity for Firmness and a Real Desire to Integrate," observed that "All persons who have dealt with this problem including the personnel managers and government officials interviewed, agree that nothing is so important as a firm position in terms of management. Once this position has been stated in terms of Executive Order 8802 and the laws of the State of New York and a recalcitrant white worker still refuses to work with colored persons, management can only transfer the worker or ask for his resignation. This will seldom or never be necessary if the situation is clearly explained."[26]

Furthermore, in order to illustrate the importance of managerial firmness in regard to the introduction of Black workers in wartime factories,

Davis related the case of white women in an aircraft plant who had complained among themselves about interracial use of restrooms. Black female workers informed NYSCADE of their white counterparts' complaints, bringing the matter to the point of possible job action. The white women, however, had been firmly notified when the Black female employees first entered the aircraft plant that discriminatory behavior would not be tolerated during wartime. Davis's staff followed up with the white employees, conducting inquiries that revealed that what the Black workers had reported regarding the attitudes of white female workers was only partially true. From these interviews, it became clear that the proactive message regarding job-place integration in wartime industries had in fact penetrated the thinking of white workers, thus modifying their prejudiced proclivities. As Davis remarked in his study, "Preliminary investigation indicated that they [the white women workers] had no intention of really going through with their [job-action] threat because they knew it might jeopardize their own jobs."[27]

The upshot of Davis's sojourn with the NYSCADE was that it functioned as a kind of dress rehearsal for what he would experience from early 1943 to early 1946 as a Black federal technocrat in the Fair Employment Practices Committee. When Davis joined the policy staff of the FEPC, he was one of only two Black FEPC administrators with some previous exposure to the technocratic intricacies of administering governmental authority in the area of job discrimination. The other Black FEPC administrator was Robert Weaver, an economist who, prior to performing occasional administrative tasks under the FEPC, was the first Black American administrator on the staff of the War Manpower Commission, a position he acquired in early 1940, prior to the FEPC's creation.

Young Black Administrators Enter the FEPC

In the summer of 1943, the second chairman of the Fair Employment Practice Committee, Father Francis J. Haas, a Roman Catholic priest and an economist at Catholic University who succeeded Mark Etheridge in the position, asked Davis to assume the post of director of the FEPC's Division of Review and Analysis. With this appointment, Davis first encountered the issue of how to sustain the synergistic interaction between what I have called the two strands of his intellectual persona, the intellectual as activist and the intellectual as technocrat. Fortunately for Davis, this activist-technocrat synergy was shared by virtually all of the dozen or so Black professionals who gained key administrative posts in the running of the FEPC, professionals like George Crockett, a lawyer; George Johnson, a lawyer and former dean of Howard Law School; Clarence Mitchell, the first Black field administrator among the African American FEPC administrators; Elmer Henderson, a lawyer for the National Urban League; and Robert Weaver. The core issue they all encountered was plain enough: Would the day-to-day rule-management and rule-allocating tasks associated with guaranteeing job integration for Black workers in wartime industries—tasks that demanded considerable strategic-pragmatist bargaining—whittle away at and perhaps even nullify the civil rights activism that initially defined the intellectual persona of John Aubrey Davis and his Black peers in the FEPC?

However this dilemma was to be resolved for Davis and his colleagues, they received some measure of assistance from the fact that the processes that sparked the issuance of Roosevelt's Executive Order 8802 in 1941 were rooted in civil rights activism. Perhaps the best account that effectively evokes the primacy of civil rights activism in the FEPC's founding is Denton Watson's, presented in his brilliant biography of Clarence Mitchell:

> President Roosevelt's issuing of Executive Order 8802 on June 25, 1941, was the most celebrated act in the battle against discrimination in war industries. That date marked the launching of the modern civil rights movement. The struggle for the executive order was led by A. Philip Randolph, president of the International Brotherhood of Sleeping Car Porters. Walter White, since early 1940, had been mobilizing the NAACP branches to fight discrimination in the defense program, but Randolph became the driving force in the movement. The idea dated back to 1917–18, when the NAACP began calling for equal opportunity in employment. Randolph threatened to lead a march on Washington of ten thousand blacks (White increased the number to one hundred thousand) if Roosevelt did not issue the order barring discrimination in the armed services and defense industries. Roosevelt issued the order to stave off the march, which was to have been held on July 1. . . . Executive Order 8802 was a compromise that [left] untouched discrimination in the armed services, but Executive Order 8802 met Randolph's basic demands and created the Fair

Employment Practices Committee (FEPC) as an administering agency to implement the directive.[28]

Although Watson's portrayal of the birth of FEPC refers only to the goal of nondiscrimination in defense industries, Executive Order 8802 contained additional goals as well. In Davis's authoritative analysis in the *Annals of the American Academy of Political and Social Science* in 1946, he observed that in addition to outlawing discrimination practices in defense industries, "Executive Order 8802 . . . forbade discrimination in Government [jobs] on account of race, creed, color and national origins, or in vocational and training programs carried on by Federal agencies for defense purposes. The same prohibition was repeated in Executive Order 9346 on May 27, 1943 [which required agency heads to report violations of Order 8802 directly to the president's office]. These orders were issued under the powers of the President as bestowed by Congress and the Constitution."[29]

Of course, explicit public policy goals like those laid out in Executive Orders 8802 and 9346 are one thing—formalistically legal things, that is—while the actual realization of the purposes of such policy goals is something else altogether, which is to say that the day-to-day task of advancing Black employment under the FEPC proved to be problematic. The process involved some gains, yes, but gains that were often quite marginal. And there were numerous outright defeats as well. An important factor underlying the FEPC's difficulty was the fact that the committee was initially saddled with a type of dependent authority. Between June 1941 and July 1942, the FEPC operated as a unit of the Office of Production Management, lacking both its own office space and operational staff. As Watson, Mitchell's biographer, states, "[the FEPC] was required [between 1941 and 1942] to share staffs of the Negro Employment and Training Branch and the Minority Groups Branch [within the Office of Production Management]. The FEPC served [initially] as a board of appeal for those two units, which certified [discrimination] cases to it."[30]

But in the summer of 1942, the FEPC's status changed for the better. President Roosevelt transferred the FEPC to a new war-related agency, the War Manpower Commission, one of whose officials was the young African American civil rights–oriented economist Dr. Robert Weaver, who had already played a role in wartime and antidiscrimination policy in early 1940, making Weaver the first ever African American administrator of consequence involved with war-related policy in the Roosevelt administration.

As of July 1942, the FEPC gained bona fide parallel authority with the War Manpower Commission in regard to antidiscrimination policy, though the chain of command required FEPC staff to communicate through two War Manpower Commission officials, Weaver and Will Alexander, who was white. Above all, the new operational autonomy possessed by the FEPC was fleshed out through the appointment of several African American administrators who had been linked to Weaver through their civil rights activism in the National Urban League, the NAACP, and the NNA during the 1930s, among them Mitchell, Henderson, George Johnson, and Davis himself, who was appointed director of the Division of Review and Analysis.

Maneuvering the FEPC for Black Workers: Formative Phase

Following quite closely upon the FEPC having acquired a relatively viable administrative infrastructure of its own by the end of 1942, President Roosevelt issued an amending set of administrative rules and guidelines under a new Executive Order 9346 in May 1943. The new administrative arrangements included the authority to police discriminatory practices within federal government agencies. According to Professor Desmond King's authoritative study of the FEPC experiment, *Separate and Unequal: Black Americans and the U.S. Federal Government* (1997), Roosevelt's Executive Order 9346 directed federal agencies, under the authority of the FEPC, to "make a thorough examination of their personnel policies and practices to the end that they may be able to assure me [Roosevelt] that in the Federal Service the doors of employment are open to all loyal and qualified workers regardless of creed, race, or national origin."[31]

With these words, Roosevelt went a long way toward helping remove the glaring contradiction that had been allowed to persist under Executive Order 8802—namely, that of a federal government practicing discrimination in its own ranks while legally mandating the end of discrimination in war-related private industry. Thanks to an early 1943 memorandum from the third chairman of the FEPC, Malcolm Ross, Roosevelt had this issue clarified for him vividly and candidly. "Very early in its official life," observed Ross to Roosevelt, "the Committee came to the conclusion that its chances of success in securing cooperation from private employers would be lessened if the government's own employment practices were open to serious criticism."[32]

Even with a broadened authority to challenge discrimination in federal agencies, the FEPC's overall impact on ensuring government job-market access by African American workers during the course of World War II remained tenuous. This situation was recognized especially by the Black administrators in the FEPC, as Davis pointed out in his postmortem appraisal of FEPC in 1946 for the Annals of the American Academy of Political and Social Science. He observed, for example, that although the "FEPC has the power in government cases to report [discriminatory practices] to the President," it was important to recognize at the same time that "the President personally cannot be concerned with individual cases, and his assistants will not consider anything except general violations of the President's [executive] orders." Davis continued: "In government cases the . . . [FEPC] has never been allowed to hold public hearings as in the case of war industries, and thus the sanction of public opinion has not been open to it. As the enforcing agent of the national nondiscrimination policy, Government would perhaps be in an unfortunate position to have to expose its [own] failings to the public."[33]

Thus, Davis provided a rather unfavorable view of the federal government's policing of job discrimination in its own ranks. "Although government cases have formed 27 percent of its case load," he wrote, the "FEPC has felt constrained to resort to hearing[s] in only three government cases involving three agencies, as opposed to 27 industry hearings involving 102 companies and 38 unions."[34] Davis remarked further that nearly 80 percent of federal discrimination cases brought to the FEPC (2,043) were never acted upon for one reason or another. As he put it, "[only] 23 percent [of those cases] were settled satisfactorily; the rest were dismissed on merits, for lack of jurisdiction, or for insufficient evidence, or continued pending."[35]

Keep in mind, however, that for Davis and his Black peers, their dual commitment to both civil rights activism and pragmatic problem solving meant that they took a balanced perspective toward FEPC outcomes. Thus, while keenly aware of limitations in fulfilling the FEPC's job-advancement goals for Black Americans, the administrators were also appreciative of the degree of progress in wartime employment for Blacks that the FEPC facilitated.

This can be seen in one of Davis's tables summarizing federal and District of Columbia job data. Using data covering the pre-FEPC and post-FEPC years, he revealed that in the category of war agencies (the Army and Navy Departments) as of 1944, there were some 231,238 Black employees—12 percent—out of a total of 2 million employees. Black employment gains in Washington, DC–based federal jobs were also viewed favorably by Davis. As his baseline, Davis used data from a 1938 job survey that showed African Americans holding overwhelmingly custodial-type jobs in DC-based federal employment (some 90 percent of such jobs were held by Blacks) as compared to 9 percent of clerical-type jobs, and they held a mere 5 percent of professional jobs. But by the end of 1944, in DC-based federal jobs, "49 percent of all Negro employees were classified as Clerical-Administrative and Fiscal."[36] In other federal agencies—those organized outside the central cabinet or executive departments—Davis also identified an important measure of Black employment progress: "The March 1944 survey [for the FEPC] revealed that Negroes were 13.6 percent of all employees in the independent agencies. Comparatively good records were noted for the Federal Works Agency, the Federal Social Security Agency, the Veterans Administration, the General Accounting Office, the Government Printing Office, and the Tennessee Valley Authority."[37]

There was, however, one area of Black employment in federal jobs that moved Davis to the pessimistic side of the FEPC balance sheet. It happened that under the Civil Service Act of 1923, a twofold job classification was set forth for federal jobs: "classified" and "unclassified." "Classified" carried "the greatest security in Government," Davis and his colleagues noted in a January 1945 report on wartime FEPC, *The Wartime Employment of Negroes in the Federal Government*. This report found that only 7 percent of Black federal employees were "classified" in the category of high job security. This startled Davis and his FEPC colleagues, because as the war was in the process of ending by early 1945, they were cognizant of future federal job downsizing, which would more than likely result in extensive job dismissal among Black federal employees in particular. To avert such an outcome, Davis suggested that a new postwar federal agency be created that would have a special responsibility—what today we'd call an affirmative action responsibility—partly modeled on wartime FEPC procedures, to cushion the impact on Black federal employees of postwar downsizing: "For the time being, an independent permanent agency of Government is needed which can enforce anti-discrimination in [postwar]

Government by working with several agencies and by co-operating with the Civil Service Commission. The wartime experience of the Civil Service Commission and FEPC indicates that this can be a feasible arrangement."[38] Unfortunately, Harry Truman's administration did not adopt Davis's suggestion for a postwar policy targeting federal jobs for African Americans in this proactive manner. Instead, this would have to await the affirmative action policies of Lyndon Johnson's administration in the late 1960s and their further elaboration by liberal Republican policy makers in the administrations of Richard Nixon and Gerald Ford.

Maneuvering the FEPC for Black Workers: The Mature Phase

As Denton Watson makes clear in his biography of Clarence Mitchell, Mitchell went about his task as associate director of the Division of Field Operations with a keen sense of the FEPC's limited authority.[39] Likewise, Davis was similarly attuned to the FEPC's authoritative limitations, and he, like Mitchell, recognized their causes—namely, the rigidity of white supremacist patterns throughout American democracy. Accordingly, when looked back upon from the early twenty-first century, it is almost unbelievable that a small cadre of African American FEPC administrators and their liberal white peers could produce measurable advances in Black American employment in both war-related industries and federal jobs.

It is not easy to grasp from today's vantage point that facilitating and protecting job advances for African Americans during World War II in war-related industries, aided by federal programs for job training in those industries, was an enormous task owing to the tenacious character of the overall racial-caste marginalization of African Americans in American life during the 1940s. Furthermore, the American federal government was inconsistent about practicing the high-minded democratic values that it readily propagated in its contest against the totalitarian fascist states of Germany, Italy, and Japan. In particular, the Roosevelt White House and the Democratic Party–controlled Congress permitted congressmen and bureaucrats from southern states to exercise undue influence upon policies affecting the status of African Americans.

There were two key structural difficulties associated with the FEPC from the time of its debut in 1940. Functionally, the FEPC is best viewed in reference to the two "FEPC phases" identified by Watson. The "First FEPC Phase" as defined by Watson commenced when Roosevelt issued Executive Order 8802 in June 1941; the "Second FEPC Phase" in May 1943, with Executive Order 9346.[40] One key structural difficulty experienced in both phases of the FEPC related to its minuscule administrative staff, particularly in view of the agency's national purview. According to Davis's 1946 study in the *Annals of the American Academy of Political and Social Science*, during the first FEPC phase, from 1941 to the middle of 1943, the agency had only eight nonclerical professionals on staff. During the second FEPC phase, which lasted from mid-1943 to early 1946, the tiny staff had multiplied just over six times, so that by 1945 there were fifty-three persons in the agency concerned with operations.[41]

A second structural difficulty evolved from the small professional staff; namely, the immense scale of companies, trade unions, and complaints the FEPC confronted. Davis's study reported that the staff grappled with more than four thousand complaints during the combined first and second phases. These complaints, moreover, involved some 102 companies and 38 trade unions, with 27 FEPC hearings required to adjudicate them.[42]

Fortunately, there was throughout the combined phases of the FEPC what might be called a built-in countervailing ideological dynamic that enabled the committee's outnumbered staff to perform at an exceptionally high level, one related to the background in civil rights activism that was shared by the African American FEPC administrators. This was especially true of the five professional-rank Black administrators—namely, Mitchell, Davis, Henderson, George Johnson, and George Crockett. Furthermore, two other Black professionals performed numerous ad hoc administrative functions for the FEPC throughout its existence: Charles Houston, founder of the NAACP Legal Defense Fund and former dean of Howard University Law School, and the aforementioned Weaver, the former economist for the National Urban League whose role in the FEPC was performed through a post on the War Production Board that he gained in the early stages of Roosevelt's wartime administration. It should be mentioned parenthetically that, apart from Watson's seminal book on Mitchell's civil rights career, *Lion in the Lobby*, the only other study of the careers of the FEPC's Black administrators is Genna Rae McNeil's pathbreaking *Groundwork: Charles Hamilton Houston and the Struggle for Civil Rights* (1990).[43] The careers of Henderson, Crockett, Johnson, and perhaps above all Weaver cry out for study.

Apart from the structural weaknesses of the FEPC operation, another should be noted, one related to the broad and aggressive resistance the FEPC faced from numerous officials in federal agencies who favored the Jim Crow regime. One of the most notorious and, in the words of a liberal white FEPC official, "positively vile" instances of white federal administrators refusing to assist the FEPC in fulfilling its antidiscrimination mandate occurred in Alabama, in the federal wartime job-training program known as the National Training Program (NTP).[44] Weaver brought to Roosevelt's attention a white federal official's resistance to assisting Black participation in Alabama's obligations under the NTP. Roosevelt's White House staff in turn sent the matter to the FEPC for adjudication. The degree of African American exclusion from the wartime job-training program in Alabama was uncovered in an inquiry by a white FEPC official, John Beecher, who reported that "only 205 Negroes [were] enrolled in national defense training courses in the entire State." As for the booming city of Mobile, where shipbuilding reigned supreme, Beecher viewed it as a situation "where there is a great need, especially in the shipbuilding industry, for additional workmen and where there is a large local [Black] labor supply which is not being used in spite of that need."[45]

Within the boundaries of its own authority, the FEPC could only appeal to the head of the executive agency that supervised the NTP, the commissioner for the United States Office of Education, that "[Alabama] state officials in charge of defense training . . . have because of their race denied and are denying Negroes opportunities for adequate, equitable and necessary defense training financed by federal funds." The Office of Education, however, remained indifferent to its own obligations to ensure nondiscrimination in the NTP. This annoyed the FEPC staff to no end, causing it to produce a scathing condemnatory report on its dealings with the Office of Education. In that report, which Davis's FEPC Division of Review and Analysis produced, the FEPC took off the kid gloves: "[The Office of Education] (a) has acquiesced in and permitted the denial of adequate and equitable training for Negroes in Alabama, Georgia and Tennessee; (b) it has failed to require the officials in those states to provide in their training programs necessary and equitable facilities and opportunities for the training of Negroes; and (c) it has neglected to issue sufficient instructions and directions prohibiting discrimination by reason of race or color."[46]

Moreover, reminiscent of the days when Davis's New Negro Alliance reprimanded white businesses for unequal treatment of African American employees whom the NNA had had to pressure to hire in the first place, the FEPC took its complaint against the Office of Education one step further. It issued a compliance order, and this compliance order—probably written by Davis's colleague in the Division of Review and Analysis, George Johnson—minced no words. It demanded that the Office of Education "cease and desist from approving defense training plans which do not contain adequate provisions against discrimination." The FEPC order, as summarized by Desmond King, also told the Office of Education to "withhold funds for defense training [in the South] until discrimination against black workers was eliminated."[47] Of course, this was as far as the FEPC's own authority could take it in this face-off with an executive agency, for it could not itself activate the ultimate compliance lever in the hands of Roosevelt's office.

Even so, what the FEPC staff's dispute with the U.S. commissioner of education in the matter of job opportunities for Black workers in the South revealed was something quite fundamental—that the FEPC's African American administrators exhibited a special commitment to civil rights ideology and the realization of the FEPC's mandate, and that same commitment was equally exhibited by the FEPC's white administrators, Malcolm Ross, John Beecher, John Brophy, and Joy Davis, among others.

One final point on this issue: Desmond King concluded his account of the FEPC's face-off with the commissioner of education over equality for Black workers in the New Deal's job-training program by noting that such discrimination in federally funded job-training programs persisted well into the post-FEPC, postwar era. According to King, a study by the NAACP in 1960 titled *Negro Wage Earners and Apprenticeship* revealed massive discrimination against African American workers and concluded with a highly pessimistic projection: that it would take "Negroes 138 years, or until 2094 to secure equal participation in skilled craft training and employment."[48]

Of course, the fact that the FEPC faced fierce resistance from state governments, key federal departments and agencies in Washington, and the very war-related industries it sought to penetrate was a difficult situation in itself. But to this insult was added injury, so to speak, in the form of a fierce white supremacist reaction against the FEPC's antidiscrimination policies on the part of the white American working class and its trade unions, especially in the South.

This white working-class resistance was multilayered.[49] On one level, as viewed by the whites, Black workers were, in Denton Watson's keen formulation, "frozen in helper [job] categories. They earned more than apprentices, but if they wanted to advance to skilled mechanics, or master craftsmen, they had to start all over as apprentices, losing their seniority." On a second level, Watson identified "another form of conspiracy," this among boilermakers "in West Coast shipyards . . . that kept blacks as a class out of higher-paying skilled jobs." How? While white workers in ship-yards were organized in unions with closed-shop rules, Black workers "were relegated to auxiliary unions in which they paid full dues [like white workers] but had few of the rights of full-fledged members." On a third level, Watson relates how Clarence Mitchell—perhaps the key Black FEPC official as director of the Division of Field Operations—challenged a com-pany where "white workers refused to train twenty-seven blacks who were being upgraded." A mere twenty-seven African American workers! On yet another tier of white workers' resistance to fair job opportunities for Blacks during World War II, on May 25, 1943, white workers at the Pinto Island Shipyards in Alabama took their white supremacist venom one step further, articulating it violently. As Watson reported this white vicious-ness toward their Black compatriots, white workers at the Pinto Island Shipyards "attacked scores of black workers with iron pipes, wrenches, bricks, and clubs because twelve blacks had been upgraded to welders. The disruption lasted four days."[50]

It was mind-boggling that the upgrading of a mere dozen African Amer-ican shipyard workers to more technical positions provoked white workers to exact such barbarity against Blacks; that it lasted four days before satis-faction spread among white workers was equally unbelievable. The coun-try was, after all, at war with cruel, powerful, genocidal fascist states. But never mind. The anti-Black mayhem at the Pinto Island Shipyards in 1943 virtually shut down the plant, causing some twenty-six thousand workers to take leave during the four-day Negrophobic riots. The riots ended only when the White House ordered U.S. armed forces, along with the Ala-bama National Guard, to quell them.

Yet even this violence was not enough to satisfy the racist thirst of Ala-bama's white shipyard workers, to quell their animus toward the FEPC and its antidiscrimination mandate. Total gratification for Alabama's white shipyard workers was dependent on their mounting a full-fledged strike action—a kind of insult to injury two times over. Indeed, white workers' strikes associated with the FEPC's antidiscrimination mandate were almost everywhere during World War II: in Alabama at the Pinto Island Shipyards; in Philadelphia and Los Angeles among transit workers; in Baltimore among steelworkers; in Michigan among armament workers; and in other parts of the country as well. Strikes by white workers were, of course, a special mode of resistance to what the FEPC represented, because they could significantly damage the nation's war effort. Cognizant of the strikes' potential damage to that effort, Mitchell, who had already done major service by negotiating delicate settlements to several strikes at war-related industries, in late 1943 influenced the FEPC chairman, Malcolm Ross, to pressure Congress to design a set of rules and procedures for managing FEPC-related strikes by white workers. The FEPC's Division of Review and Analysis was called on for advice on such rules and procedures, and Davis had the task of producing a report for this purpose. According to Denton Watson, "John A. Davis recommended to Malcolm Ross that the agency [the FEPC] make a general statement of policy that it was opposed to strikes in industry that had a racial bias," with Davis reasoning that "[strikes were] a violation of public policy and of labor's pledge to the Government and [were] dangerous to the war effort." Finally, Davis underscored the special political-strategic value of the FEPC to the federal government's need to intervene in strikes that were racially inspired, observing that the "FEPC's value in racial strike situations lies in the fact that it has the confidence of the [nation's] Negro workers."[51] This reference by Davis to the FEPC's efficacy among Black workers had its origin in the skillful settlement by the agency's African American administrators of several thorny strikes initiated by Black workers owing to unequal pay and discriminatory work conditions that included threats of violence.

It was no doubt a matter of some intellectual irony for Davis, Elmer Henderson, George Johnson, and other Black FEPC administrators to experience the fierce resistance by white workers to the FEPC's quest to expand job training and job upgrading for Black workers around wartime America. During the period of early civil rights activism associated with several "Don't Buy Where You Can't Work" organizations during the 1930s, among them the New Negro Alliance in Washington, the Young People's Forum in Baltimore, the Joint Committee in Harlem, and the

Clerk's Circle in Richmond, a small group of Marxist-leaning Black intellectuals had argued that Black mobilization against job discrimination should wait upon the construction of an interracial coalition with white workers and their trade unions. Both Ralph Bunche and E. Franklin Frazier, scholars at Howard University during the 1930s, maintained this Marxist position, as probed in Jonathan Holloway's *Confronting the Veil: Abram Harris, E. Franklin Frazier, Ralph J. Bunche, 1919–1940* (2002).[52] This position held that class-based mobilization was more acceptable to and better understood by working-class white Americans, and thus Black ethnic- or race-based activism should give way to class-based activism. The experience of Black FEPC administrators, however, clearly demonstrated that working-class whites were fierce proponents of white supremacy.

The opposition of white workers to wartime job-integration practices was especially strident during the first FEPC phase (mid-1941 to mid-1943). But during the second FEPC phase (mid-1943 to early 1946), Black and white administrators in the FEPC succeeded in opening a fairly broad range of wartime private and public employment to Black Americans. This was, then, a clear measure of the mature phase of maneuvering the FEPC to serve Black workers, and thereby, too, to serve the wartime goals of the nation as a whole. From the perspective of John Aubrey Davis and his fellow participants in the NNA during the 1930s, the eventual success of wartime FEPC activities was a momentous achievement.

A Balance Sheet on John Aubrey Davis's FEPC Years

In terms of the overall outcome of the FEPC experiment in advancing Black employment in the spheres of wartime industries and federal agencies, that outcome was on balance quite positive. On this matter, there is no more authoritative account than that of Denton Watson.[53] Here is his well-considered appraisal of the FEPC:

> The FEPC was the most promising symbol of hope for equal economic opportunity that African Americans had ever had. . . . The best proof that the FEPC was opening doors of opportunity was the increase in the number of minorities employed in war industries, from less than 3 percent in early 1942 to more than 7 percent two years later, and 8 percent by the end of the war. Eighty percent of those

benefiting from Executive Order 8802 [and Executive Order 9346] were black; 14 percent were mostly Mexican Americans.[54]

Translated in aggregate terms, nearly 1 million Black employees were added to the United States' industrial workforce thanks to the FEPC. That figure represented more than 300,000 Black men and 600,000 Black women. Moreover, some 700,000 Blacks—mainly males—joined the armed forces from 1940 through 1944, and by June 1945 that figure reached 1 million.[55]

In addition to Watson's appraisal of the FEPC, John Aubrey Davis analyzed the FEPC's impact on African American employment during World War II in the *Annals of the American Academy of Political and Social Science*. Like Watson's, Davis's overall take was positive, so much so, in fact, that Davis proposed that a federal agency patterned after the FEPC be made permanent, empowered to "enforce anti-discrimination in Government."[56] Davis gave special attention to the impact of the FEPC experience on the general character of the African American political leadership stratum during wartime. In the pre-FEPC era, there was virtually no institutionalized authoritative status at the federal level for appointed African American officials. Instead, they functioned as clientage political appointments, officials who operated through another (read: white) official. In other words, such Black federal officials were limited to weak consultative or advisory roles, not given institutionalized line-administrative authority and policy-managing roles. As Davis explained it, Black Americans' pre-FEPC status as officials at the federal level "was characterized by numerous appointments as advisors on racial policy in many agencies which were carrying out economic and social programs." But that was all—advisory functions, not policy-managing and thereby policy-making functions.

The FEPC experience fundamentally altered this situation. Thanks to Executive Order 8802 in 1941, Davis observed, "Negroes participated as equals in policy formation and administration." This transformation, in turn, had a feedback effect on the several pre-FEPC advisory-type Black officials (for example, Mary McLeod Bethune, who advised on welfare and youth policies, and Robert Weaver, who advised on wartime manpower programs) by making "these [Black] advisers . . . more effective."[57] He pointed out in correspondence to me, however, that this metamorphosis in the authoritative status of Black federal officials took more than two years beyond the official rollout of the FEPC in 1941, a development that required a second FEPC directive or order from the president. Davis wrote to me in 1992, "The fact is that the thing that broke the back of discrimination in the Federal government was the President's [May 27, 1943] letter to the Department heads [mandating antidiscrimination in federal agencies] and the requirement that they report to the President on their progress. . . . This was the first 'affirmative action' to remedy [decades-long] discrimination."[58]

If Davis's appraisal in 1946 of the FEPC experience is juxtaposed with his civil rights activism as part of the New Negro Alliance in the 1930s, there was, I think, a kind of political-cultural symmetry between these two phases in his career, and also the career of his peers. Just as Davis and his peers achieved a unique intertwining of civil rights activism and pragmatic problem-solving attributes through the NNA in the 1930s, they similarly negotiated the FEPC agency during the 1940s in a manner that intermeshed civil rights activism and technocrat-pragmatic problem solving successfully.

Had Davis and his Black professional peers done no more than leave the 1930s NNA movement for future generations of African American professionals to learn from and build upon, they would have bequeathed a notable contribution. That they proceeded further and advanced upon their NNA legacy through their wartime FEPC experience, functioning as federal technocrats in the area of industrial and federal job advancement for African Americans, warrants a very precious and venerated rank for Davis and his Black professional peers in the hierarchy of the twentieth-century Black intelligentsia.[59]

A Black American and African Nexus: John Aubrey Davis's Endgame

Most intellectuals who could claim a professional role in the development of their ethnic group's leadership comparable to the role that John Aubrey Davis played from the 1930s to the 1950s would have taken a much-deserved vacation from additional leadership tasks. Not Davis. New and important postwar leadership tasks among African Americans had to be undertaken, and Davis assumed this responsibility.

In the late 1950s, Davis and Horace Mann Bond embarked upon an endeavor to revive a goal of the African American intelligentsia that extended back in time to one of its bedrock institutions, the American

Negro Academy, founded in 1897. In this post–World War II era, their goal was to design and execute a nexus between the fairly well-developed New World Negro (American) intelligentsia and its nascent Old World Negro (African) counterpart in newly independent African countries.

This is the story of the rise and fall of the American Society for African Culture, fashioned jointly by Davis and Bond.

Events Preparatory to the Founding of the
American Society for African Culture

The Lincoln University to which John Aubrey Davis returned in the fall of 1946 was quite different from the institution he had left in 1942 when he went to work for the New York State Committee Against Discrimination in Employment. That difference centered on the appointment of Horace Mann Bond as president of Lincoln University in 1945. As discussed in chapter 1, Bond undertook the expansive Afro-Americanization of Lincoln University at the outset of his presidency, which meant a broad cleansing of the practices and ethos associated with the paternalistic management style that had obtained among white Presbyterian clergy at Lincoln University from its founding before the Civil War.

I can't help but surmise that Davis likely would not have returned to his teaching post there had Bond not been appointed the university's president. It was, indeed, Bond's bid to Afro-Americanize Lincoln University that lured Davis back. Through the Afro-Americanization of the faculty and administrators and through the recruitment of a new breed of liberal-minded white faculty, Bond's presidency propelled a qualitative shift in the ideological character of the institution from its original establishmentarian identity toward a liberal and progressive one. Bond simultaneously fostered an interest among the younger generation of faculty—Black and white—in civil rights activism, focusing on segregation practices in southeastern Pennsylvania, where Lincoln was located, and in Africa's budding decolonization movements. It was a momentous shift for the university. Writing to me about his friendship with Bond, Davis had this to say:

> Horace and my relationship at Lincoln started out rocky. He was very prone to be niggardly on pay increases in a period of serious inflation. I warmed up to him when he suggested that he and I begin the

integration of Oxford [the racist-leaning mushroom-producing town bordering Lincoln University]. We went to the hotel [the only middle-class hotel around for miles] and were refused [drinks and a meal], starting a case that Jim Baker [a civil rights lawyer whom Davis had taught at Lincoln] won. He [Bond] worked hardest and was the most productive of the scholars I recruited for [the NAACP Legal Defense Fund's research on] Brown v. Topeka. We became mutual admirers and friends although he always called me Dr. Davis. [That formalism reflected a generic feature of Bond's public persona.][60]

In addition to expanding the number of African students at Lincoln and initiating courses on African history, Bond organized a Summer Institute of African Studies that focused on African political developments. Intrigued by this initiative, one that spoke to his earlier intellectual development, Davis joined the faculty as a lecturer in political science. A small group of African students would attend his courses, among them a student from Ghana (then Gold Coast) named Francis Nkrumah. In the postwar years, Nkrumah emerged as a leading nationalist politician in Ghana, readopting his birth name of Kwame Nkrumah and becoming the country's first prime minister and president following independence. By the late 1940s, the seeds that would lead to a Davis-Bond collaboration in the founding of the American Society for African Culture (AMSAC) in 1957 had been planted.

Before AMSAC grew and blossomed, however, Davis expanded his interest in African affairs further. Through his ties to Clarence Mitchell, who had set up the NAACP's lobbying office in Washington, Davis became involved in the NAACP's quest to expand Black foreign policy personnel in the U.S. Department of State. The NAACP secretary, Walter White, first articulated this goal in early 1951. By April of that year, Mitchell had organized a committee made up of representatives from several civil rights organizations. In a July 1952 letter to White, A. Philip Randolph elaborated on the outcomes of his group's tête-à-tête with top foreign policy officials in the Truman administration:

As a result of the meetings with Messrs. [former Director of Defense Mobilization Charles E.] Wilson and [Secretary of State Dean] Acheson, a subcommittee composed of my colleague Theodore E. Brown of the Brotherhood of Sleeping Car Porters, and Messrs. Elmer

Henderson of the American Council of Human Rights, and Clarence Mitchell of the Washington office of the National Association for the Advancement of Colored People continued to work with government officials on the details of our objectives. . . . A few weeks ago, Mr. E. W. Montague, the Director of Personnel for the Department informed Mr. Brown that as a result of the work of our subcommittee, Professor John Davis of Lincoln University has been appointed a part-time consultant in the Personnel Bureau. Professor Davis is expected to aid formulating hiring and recruiting policies in an effort to greater assure equality of opportunity to Negro applicants for positions in the domestic and foreign service of the State Department. . . . I understand that Dr. Davis expresses an interest in only serving as a part-time consultant because of other commitments. . . . It is hoped that as a result of Dr. Davis' appointment and the information already supplied by us to the Department of State that a new day may be approaching for all qualified Negroes who might desire to serve their country in the facilities of the Department of State.[61]

Perhaps somewhat surprisingly, White was as excited as Randolph was by Davis's appointment as a watchdog of sorts regarding the new integration thrusts in the Department of State. I say *surprising* because during the late 1930s, the Young Turk, street-level civil rights activist Davis and his peers in the NNA crossed swords on a number of occasions with one of the country's major NAACP branch offices, in Washington, DC. Between 1936 and 1938, Davis and the NNA had had a disagreement with the NAACP's national office over the issue of challenging in federal courts the job discrimination practices of the Sanitary Grocery Company, discussed in depth earlier in this chapter. White, however, did not hold a grudge, recognizing a good thing when he saw one: a federal appointment for an African American civil rights advocate. Thus, in a letter to the Department of State dated June 17, 1952, White remarked on Davis's "distinguished career as a university professor and public official" and referred to him as "one of the [Negro community's] pillars."[62]

Relative to what might be called the first-phase push by African American civil rights groups to open administrative positions for Blacks in America's foreign policy establishment, the appointment of a Black American in

1951 to help expand the Black cadre in this sphere was hardly a panacea. Davis himself was quite aware of this, understanding the need for a more politically assertive second-phase push. Meanwhile, there were some benefits associated with Davis's appointment and this initial step. First, a seemingly simple yet significant outcome was the production by the Department of State's Office of Personnel of a full accounting of the African Americans employed in foreign policy–related areas of the federal government. Made available in March 1953, within nine months of Davis's appointment, this census of Black personnel revealed that there were some 55 Blacks among a total of 8,231 foreign policy overseas personnel, and some 15 Blacks with upper-grade ranking (administrative positions) among a total of 8,700 domestic State Department personnel. Second, several key appointments—promotions, really—of Black foreign policy officers to the top ranks in the United States embassy staffs in Europe under the new Eisenhower administration were clearly facilitated by the events surrounding Davis's appointment. Third, Davis's experience as a State Department personnel consultant had the unanticipated consequence of strengthening his nascent interest in the emergent African decolonization movements of the 1950s.[63]

Forging the American Society for African Culture, 1956–1967

When John Aubrey Davis and Horace Mann Bond set out to forge relationships between Black American and African leadership intelligentsia in the mid-1950s, they were knowingly following in the footsteps of earlier Black American intellectuals who had trod the same path. Among their early twentieth-century forebears were W. E. B. Du Bois and his Pan-African Congress, which gathered in Paris in 1918 and elsewhere in Europe in the 1920s, and the Caribbean American Marcus Garvey's Universal Negro Improvement Association, which mounted a back-to-Africa movement in the 1920s and 1930s. There was also the Council on African Affairs, a post–World War II forerunner whose outreach to Africa bore quite directly on the kinds of events that Davis and Bond would encounter. The council included an important group of radical-leftist postwar African American intellectuals, as contrasted with the pragmatic-activist or reform-leftist mode with which Davis and Bond and their NAACP-linked circle were identified.

The first serious historical study of the Council on African Affairs was published by Professor Penny Von Eschen in 1997.[64] The agency's origins extended back to the 1930s, when a young African American YMCA administrator named Max Yergan, working in South Africa, founded it as a means of criticizing colonialism in Africa and especially mobilizing support among New World Black intellectuals for one of Africa's first modern political groups, the African National Congress. The inaugural set of Black American intellectuals attracted to the Council on African Affairs hailed from a broad ideological range and included the rather plainly liberal professional Mordecai Johnson, the first Black president of Howard University; the civil rights activist, clergyman, and politician Adam Clayton Powell Jr.; and more leftist-oriented Black intellectuals Paul Robeson, W. E. B. Du Bois, and Ralph Bunche. (Bunche was in the 1930s a Marxist-oriented leftist Black intellectual, a little-known feature of his early intellectual persona and one I discuss in chapter 3). Following upon the post–World War II Pan-African Congress that Du Bois convened in London in 1946, the Council on African Affairs emerged as the leading Black American organization concerned with ties with African nationalist groups and with the overall African decolonization struggle. The council's leading personalities like Du Bois and Robeson, however, were increasingly harassed by the anti-leftist and anticommunist thrusts emanating from the federal government from 1948. By 1952, Yergan, the founder of the council, had undergone an ideological transformation to the right-wing side of the political spectrum, and though Du Bois and Robeson assumed its day-to-day operation, along with Professor Alphaeus Hunton of Howard University, the Council on African Affairs faltered, partly because Du Bois and Robeson were restricted in their political freedom by intense government surveillance. By the mid-fifties, the situation had resulted in a political vacuum within the African American intellectual community in regard to its interactions with the growing African decolonization movements.

That vacuum, however, did not remain for long. Two political strands among the African American intelligentsia in the late 1950s—one of a primarily Black Nationalist orientation, the other of a pragmatic-activist or reform-leftist bent—attempted to fill it. Leading personalities among the Black Nationalist strand who were concerned with African decolonization included Dan Watts, an architect who founded the leading Black Nationalist magazine *Liberator*; Harold W. Cruse, a leftist journalist who published the most influential postwar book on Black intellectuals, *The Crisis of the Negro Intellectual*, in 1967, which I will explore in chapter 5; John Henrik Clarke, a historian who studied ancient African history; and Richard Moore, a follower of the Garvey movement in the 1920s who turned Marxist in the 1930s and shifted back to Black Nationalism after World War II. These men were quite skilled at gaining broad visibility for their activities.

Indeed, a major study of the activity of Black American intellectuals in support of African nationalist movements from the 1950s onward assumed—erroneously, I should add—that the Black Nationalist–oriented strand was the only sector among African American intellectuals concerned with African developments. Authored by the political scientist Martin Staniland, *American Intellectuals and African Nationalists, 1955–1970* (1991) traces the attitudes and politics of American groups concerned with African nationalist movements.[65] Staniland's research specifically on African American groups interested in African affairs, however, is quite shallow, focusing primarily on high-profile Black Nationalist personalities and organizations to gain an understanding of African American ties to evolving African nationalist developments. Nowhere in Staniland's book can one locate any evidence that African American intellectuals and political groups other than the Black Nationalists were fashioning ties with the emergent African decolonization movements of the late 1950s.

In particular, there is no mention in Staniland's book of African American intellectuals who were located on the pragmatic-activist or reform-leftist side of the political spectrum and who had ties with African decolonization developments, intellectuals like Bond and Davis; James W. Ivy, the editor of the NAACP journal *The Crisis*; Mercer Cook, a romance language scholar at Howard University; Adelaide Cromwell, a sociologist in African studies at Boston University; St. Clair Drake, an anthropologist in African studies; and William T. Fontaine, a philosophy scholar at the University of Pennsylvania. Perhaps an ever greater lacuna in Staniland's book is that it contained no mention whatever of the substantive experience and achievements of AMSAC in linking the African American intelligentsia with decolonization developments.

The idea to form AMSAC was initiated at the First World Congress of Black Writers and Artists, which was convened in Paris in September 1956 by a group of francophone Black intellectuals from African and Caribbean countries. They functioned through the Société africaine de culture in

Paris, which had performed the crucial task of rallying Black intellectuals from French colonies ever since the late 1940s through the publication of an anticolonial journal, *Présence africaine*. The organizers of the congress included Alioume Diop, the Senegalese writer and publisher of *Présence africaine*; Léopold Sédar Senghor, a Senegalese poet and the country's leading politician; Aimé Césaire of Martinique, the preeminent French West Indian writer at the time; Léon Damas, a major French Caribbean poet; Louis Achille, a writer and publisher from French Antilles; and Frantz Fanon, an essayist and psychiatrist from Martinique.[66]

Among this network of Black intellectuals residing in Paris in the 1950s was Richard Wright, a leading African American writer who had settled in Europe during the "Red Scare" that had consumed postwar American politics. Wright had already captivated francophone Black intellectuals through his brilliant novel *Native Son*, published in 1940, so Wright's place on the congress's planning committee came as no surprise. Wright in turn contacted Roy Wilkins, secretary of the NAACP, to help mobilize an African American delegation to the 1956 congress. In our correspondence, Davis adumbrated the course of events that produced the African American delegation to the First World Congress of Black Writers and Artists:

> In view of how AMSAC ended, I should indicate how it came about. I had been directing a study on the publicly expressed attitudes toward American race relations in the leading European and South American nations. It was financed by the Council on Race and Caste in World Affairs and was circulated when finished throughout government and private organizations [involved] in foreign affairs. Dick Wright wrote to Roy [Wilkins] in desperation because no American Negroes were coming to the September 1956 meeting of La Conférence Mondiale des Écrivains Noirs. Du Bois and Robeson had been deprived of passports by State. They were the first choice of the Paris Committee. Wilkins asked me if I could help in the situation. The NAACP had a long history of participating in and of stimulating conferences on Africa— . . . but its tradition and connections had lapsed. . . . I turned to the Council for money and proceeded to put the delegation together. Each person was my selection. When we formed the organization [AMSAC] in 1957, Horace was a natural to be president, for he and Mercer [Cook] had more hands-on experience with African leaders in the then recent time.[67]

As it happened, some six African American intellectuals comprised the American delegation that attended the First World Congress of Black Writers and Artists in Paris more than a half century ago. Bond and Davis were coheads of the American delegation, and they were joined by Cook, Fontaine, Ivy, and Wright himself.

The Davis-Bond Legacy Through AMSAC:
Outreach to African Affairs

Before AMSAC closed up shop in 1967 following the revelation that a contribution had come from a donor who had operated as a conduit for funds from the CIA, Horace Mann Bond and John Aubrey Davis, functioning as president and executive administrator, respectively, of AMSAC, had skillfully used the organization to realize its major goals: to disseminate information related to Africa among the African American intelligentsia; to foster close relationships between the African American intelligentsia and the emergent African political elites and African intellectuals; and to forge a viable Black American lobbying capability for foreign policy on African issues, thereby creating a platform upon which to fashion a skilled and viable cadre of African American foreign policy professionals, including policy analysts, cultural affairs specialists, development technocrats, embassy officials, and so forth.

The success of the first goal was made possible through the wide range of leading African American professionals and intellectuals who joined forces with AMSAC within several years of its formation, a process facilitated by the strategic location of AMSAC's headquarters in New York City, the "informal capital of the African American intelligentsia." The broad base of AMSAC's following among the Black intelligentsia ranged from leading Black clergy and academics to lawyers, doctors, and dentists, state and federal administrators, and a variety of creative artists.

The second goal—fashioning viable ties between the African American intelligentsia and emergent African leadership groups—was aided by a combination of historical patterns between Africans and African Americans on the one hand and the personal biographies of leading AMSAC personalities on the other. First, from the formative years of modern educational institutions for African Americans in post–Civil War America into the twentieth century, leading Negro colleges like Lincoln University, the Hampton

Institute, Howard University, Fisk University, and Morehouse College provided a small cadre of Africans with their initial experience with higher education. For example, the several African professionals who founded Africa's first anticolonial organization in South Africa early in the twentieth century, the African National Congress, were educated during the late nineteenth century at Lincoln, a development explored in Bond's *Education for Freedom: A History of Lincoln University.*

Second, key AMSAC personalities like Bond and Davis, Mercer Cook, and St. Clair Drake had cultivated friendships with African students who attended Negro colleges between the two world wars. Several students who attended Lincoln University in the 1920s and 1930s became leading political figures in new African states, such as Nnamdi Azikiwe, who founded Nigeria's major nationalist party, the National Council of Nigeria and the Cameroons, and who became Nigeria's first president in 1960; and the aforementioned Kwame Nkrumah, Ghana's first prime minister and later president. Drake, who attended the Second World Congress of Black Writers and Artists in 1959, was an undergraduate at the Hampton Institute during the early 1930s, where his roommate was Mbiyu Koinange, a Kenyan from the Kikuyu tribe who became a leading figure in that nation's post–World War II nationalist organization, the Kenya African National Union, functioning as the major adviser to leader Jomo Kenyatta. Further, Cook, through postwar research trips to France in the late 1940s and 1950s, forged close personal ties with Senghor and Diop, two key personalities in the Société africaine de culture behind the francophone African intellectual journal, *Présence africaine.*

What Davis and Bond considered their finest contribution through AMSAC was associated with what might be called the multiplier effect that emanated from the organization's effective dissemination of information on African nationalist developments among Black Americans and its mounting of a variety of intellectual events on African affairs among Black professional organizations. Such AMSAC initiatives sparked the Reverend James Robinson, a graduate of Lincoln University, to launch the student volunteer body Operation Crossroads Africa. Beginning in 1958, it dispatched thousands of American students in interracially structured groups to rural African areas, where they worked as teachers and multifaceted community developers. Similarly, in the early 1970s, another African outreach organization that was heavily influenced by AMSAC launched, Africare. Its founder, Payne Lucas, derived the idea for Africare from his association with the Reverend Robinson, and as Lucas constructed a mechanism through which Africare's goals of assisting African rural communities could be realized, he made broad use of African American churches. As Walter Carrington, the late ambassador to Senegal and Nigeria, observed, "Lucas began [his] relief effort center in the black [American] community. He tapped ordinary black Americans in a way they had not been solicited [for] an Africa-related cause since the days of [Marcus] Garvey. From all over the country, contributions to help African famine victims poured into Africare's headquarters in Washington."[68]

AMSAC operated for ten years, from 1957 to 1967. Had the Davis-Bond legacy stopped at stimulating broad African interest among the African American professional stratum, spawning major outreach organizations like Operation Crossroads Africa and Africare, this would have been a lasting contribution in its own right. But it did not stop there. It extended outward toward the full-fledged institutionalization of viable political linkages between Black Americans and African realities. At the foundation of these connections was the formation in 1962 of the American Leadership Conference on Africa, a mechanism composed of the major civil rights organizations in that period: Roy Wilkins's NAACP, Whitney Young's National Urban League, Martin Luther King Jr.'s Southern Christian Leadership Conference, and James Farmer's Congress on Racial Equality. In taking on the task of an embryonic Black American lobbying mechanism on behalf of African affairs, the American Negro Leadership Conference fulfilled a dream that Clarence Mitchell and Elmer Henderson first contemplated during the early 1950s when they were involved in pressuring the Truman and Eisenhower administrations to expand African American personnel in middle- and top-rank foreign policy posts.

Important as it was, however, the formation of the American Negro Leadership Conference was just a first step on the road to Black American foreign policy lobbying capability. It was the return of the White House to Democratic Party control under the Kennedy and Johnson administrations that proved to be the critical factor that enabled Black American leadership groups to consolidate their lobbying power. By the end of the 1960s—the decade when more than 90 percent of African countries ended nearly a century of European imperialist domination—African Americans gained a foothold throughout middle- and top-rank positions in the United States foreign policy establishment. Above all, the ambassadorial level was penetrated, especially in regard to the new African states. Mercer Cook, a founding member of AMSAC, was appointed by Kennedy to be U.S. ambassador to Senegal; under Johnson, he was appointed ambassador to Niger and Gambia. Franklin Williams, a former NAACP legal counsel and head of its West Coast legal office, served as U.S. ambassador under Johnson to Ghana. Clyde Ferguson, a former dean of Howard Law School and an international lawyer, was U.S. ambassador to Uganda during the Nixon administration. Wilbert J. LeMelle, a political science scholar and Ford Foundation aid official in East Africa, served as U.S. ambassador to Kenya under Jimmy Carter. Walter Carrington, the aforementioned civil rights lawyer and the founder of the NAACP chapter at Harvard and the youngest-ever member of the Massachusetts Commission Against Discrimination, served as U.S. ambassador to Senegal in the last year of the Carter administration, and was later ambassador to Nigeria under Bill Clinton; he served as both a national director in Africa and a regional director for the continent in the Peace Corps for a decade from its founding in 1961. Of course, such Black foreign policy officials were in the first instance responsible for pursuing American policy interests in African states, and these interests might well contain more negative outcomes for Africans than their surface or official characterization indicate. Even so, it can be hypothesized that, all things considered, African American foreign policy officials might be expected to manage U.S. policy interactions with African societies with a greater degree of sensitivity toward generic African needs and concerns.

To my knowledge, to date there is no scholarly study that has attempted to test the range of veracity contained in this hypothesis, though I would still consider it a first-level efficacious hypothesis.

The Davis-Bond Legacy Through AMSAC: African Policy Clout

Be that as it may, the era of the Kennedy and Johnson administrations also witnessed the growth for the first time of a full-fledged Black American political class, at the core of which were some five thousand elected Black officials nationwide by the late 1970s. The most politically powerful sector of the elected officials within this new African American political class were the members of the U.S. Congress, who numbered nearly thirty by the late 1970s and more than forty at the time of this writing (2007). One of these Black representatives was Detroit's Charles Diggs, who by 1969 had accumulated enough legislative seniority to become chair of the Foreign Affairs Subcommittee on Africa. From this vantage point, Diggs played a crucial role for more than a decade in closing down—partly through American foreign policy machinations—the last vestiges of European imperialist rule in Africa, especially in the white-racist colonial oligarchies of Angola, Mozambique, Southern Rhodesia (Zimbabwe), and above all in apartheid-riddled South Africa.

In his sustained quest to end colonial rule in these southern African countries, Diggs was aided by a skillful young African American civil rights lawyer, Randall Robinson, a graduate of Harvard Law School. In 1978, drawing on his activist leadership experience as a Harvard law student when he led the movement to end investments in South Africa, Robinson founded a new Black American lobbying organization, TransAfrica, to advance decolonization in South Africa and to assist new African states generally. TransAfrica's lobbying activity was aided by President Jimmy Carter's appointment of Andrew Young, a former civil rights aide to Martin Luther King's Southern Christian Leadership Conference, as a special U.S. ambassador to the United Nations. Young would of course go on to be elected mayor of Atlanta, serving from 1982 to 1990, succeeding Maynard Jackson to become the second African American to hold this position. (Since Jackson's election in 1974, everyone to hold the position of mayor of Atlanta has been African American.) A kind of division of labor evolved between Young's staff at the United Nations, especially his deputy Donald McHenry, on the one hand and Robinson's TransAfrica on the other. TransAfrica commenced pressuring the United States Congress in 1979 to impose strong economic sanctions on South Africa, while Young's staff secured through the United Nations a rigorous negotiation schema through which the Government of South Africa engaged in protracted discussions to end colonial oligarchic governance in South Africa. Of course, it was not until far more political upheaval transpired—including the cruel and vicious exercise of state coercion and violence against Black citizens and leaders in South Africa—before an end to apartheid was finally achieved in 1993. I believe that when historians arrive at a final reckoning of the forces that contributed to this most difficult of all African decolonization experiences, some aspect of the Davis-Bond AMSAC legacy will be mentioned.

AMSAC's legacy was also apparent in the politically skillful undertakings of the Reverend Leon Sullivan during the 1990s to institutionalize what AMSAC officials had in mind when the American Negro Leadership

Conference on Africa was formed in 1962. Beginning in April 1991, Sullivan fashioned a group of African American clergy and civil rights organizations into what he called the African/African-American Policy Summit. At the first summit in 1991—convened as all subsequent ones would be, on the African continent—government officials and leading professionals from twenty-four African states participated, including Nigeria, Kenya, Senegal, Zambia, Côte d'Ivoire, Zimbabwe, Tanzania, Ghana, Namibia, and Angola. Five such conferences were held from 1991 to 2003, a development that I suggest has lineage ties to the Davis-Bond AMSAC legacy.

One last thought on this particular subject. In the late 1950s, the dean of African American sociologists at the time, E. Franklin Frazier of Howard University, expressed some negative views toward endeavors by groups like the American Society for African Culture that sought to fashion connections with emergent African states and their elites. Interestingly enough, Davis and Bond gave Frazier the opportunity to present his views in a volume they organized announcing AMSAC's existence, *Africa Seen by American Negroes* (1958). Frazier titled his chapter "What Can the American Negro Contribute to the Social Development of Africa?" His answer: "Very little."[69]

This was quite an uninformed response to the question Frazier posed himself, one that had its origin in his polemical assault on the African American professional stratum in his famous book *Black Bourgeoisie* (1956), in which he claimed this class inhabited a "world of make believe."[70] (See chapter 5 for a full discussion of Frazier.) Davis used his introduction to *Africa Seen by American Negroes* to respond to Frazier's criticism, noting, correctly I think, that the historical record of New World Negroes' outreach to Africa was positive and productive by any serious accounting. The Boston University sociologist Adelaide Cromwell and I were contributors to *Africa Seen by American Negroes*, and a decade later, we coedited a volume documenting a century of outreach to Africa by the African American intelligentsia titled *Apropos of Africa: Sentiments of American Negro Leadership Toward Africa, 1850–1950s* (1969). Two years later, a Nigerian scholar, Okon Edet Uya, domiciled in America, edited a similar work, *Black Brotherhood: Afro-Americans and Africa* (1971). Some thirty years later, James H. Meriwether provided another broad-gauged perspective on the African American intelligentsia's interactions with Africa between the 1930s and 1960s, *Proudly We Can Be African: Black Americans and Africa, 1935–1961* (2002).[71]

Thus, contrary to Frazier's negative view toward AMSAC's founding, AMSAC's decade of activity demonstrated fulsomely that the late twentieth-century African American intelligentsia was up to the challenge of expanding upon the long tradition of Black intellectuals forging viable interactions with important modern African figures and organizations. Starting in the 1980s, when American elites linked to the conservative Republican Party fashioned a veritable hegemony over federal governance (save the one-term Jimmy Carter presidency in the late 1970s and the two-term Bill Clinton presidency in the 1990s), a variety of groups and individuals associated with the African American professional class emerged as the major source of foreign-policy lobbying capability on behalf of the development needs of African states. Most of these lobbying groups concerned with African development that had been led by white Americans, such as the American African Institute, had ceased operation by the late 1980s, making way for a variety of individuals and groups among the African American professional class to sustain this task. If there is a single organization among the African American intelligentsia during the Cold War years that can be identified as having significantly contributed to this outcome, that organization is, I believe, AMSAC. However, a probe of Cold War–era interactions between the African American intelligentsia and African decolonization developments by Kevin Gaines, titled *African Americans in Ghana: Black Expatriates and the Civil Rights Era* (2006), is rather equivocal in its appraisal of AMSAC's legacy, an equivocation I would dispute.[72]

Be that as it may, John Aubrey Davis and Horace Mann Bond fashioned a process of outreach to Africa among the African American intelligentsia through the agency of AMSAC from 1956 to 1967 that warrants, I think, the fullest respect from generations of the African American intelligentsia who follow them. I find it difficult to imagine any other response to their legacy.

Conclusion: The Post–Civil Rights Perspective on John Aubrey Davis's Career

John Aubrey Davis had a long life. He passed away in January 2002, in his ninetieth year. His professional career contains important lessons for the post–civil rights era African American intelligentsia.

The idea of an activist encounter with American racism was fundamental to Davis's career. Such an encounter challenges the American white supremacist edifice head-on, as it were, and refuses a quiescent response to the racist pariahization, marginalization, and oppression of the status of Black people in American life. Commencing his career shortly after his graduation from Williams College in 1933, Davis was part of a second-generation cohort of African Americans fortunate enough to attend college during the first third of the twentieth century. His peers did not have many everyday examples of Black professional persons who had fashioned an activist response to American racism. Instead, they saw numerous examples of African American professionals who had fashioned quite the opposite, which is to say who had subscribed to an accommodationist view of American racist practices, the sort that was given prominence from the 1880s into the first three decades of the twentieth century by Booker T. Washington and his Tuskegee Machine. This amounted to a Black middle-class conservatism that emphasized the self-advancement of one's own professional goals, benefits, and compensations, thereby ignoring the American racist barriers to the ordinary African Americans' citizenship and human rights.

Growing up as he did in a middle-class Black neighborhood in the early 1900s into the 1920s in Washington, DC, Davis saw many examples around him of the accommodationist demeanor of Black professionals who chose to put a special premium on their ability to maximize cashing in on whatever market value a racist American capitalist democracy was willing to attach to their middle-class attributes as businesspersons, pharmacists, lawyers, bookkeepers, doctors, dentists, schoolteachers, and so forth. The pervasive racist barriers endured daily by 90 percent of Black people who had nothing of value to cash in on appeared to be of little concern to the accommodationist-skewed middle class. These were largely decent, fair-minded Black American citizens, mind you, caring for their families and seeking to do the best by them in social-mobility terms. It just so happened, though, that by embracing accommodationism, their approach to American racism meant that broad sections of Black America's talented tenth remained unavailable for the enormous leadership task of challenging the American racist edifice.

Fortunately, however, during the second and third decades of the twentieth century, a growing segment of middle-class African Americans rejected accommodationism in favor of antiracist activism. Davis's family belonged to this segment, and they nurtured within him a thirst for such activism. After college, Davis, in turn, instilled in a small circle of his professional peers that desire to undertake an activist stance toward America racism. Above all, this attitude toward America's racist patterns provided Davis and his peers a way to withhold legitimacy from America's racist edifice. Accordingly, they were empowered, spiritually and intellectually, to create organizational weapons with which to challenge this nation's racist ramparts. The New Negro Alliance that Davis and his peers launched in the fall of 1933 was that weapon.

In addition to understanding the salience of what might be called the activist imperative to American racism, Davis and his colleagues also grasped the salience of what might be called the technocratic imperative. That is, they understood the need to possess a variety of technocratic skills through which the institutions of political, judicial, and economic power are managed and manipulated in the American system. They recognized that a developed quantum of technocratic skills was required to penetrate the institutions of political, judicial, and economic power on behalf of advancing the racist-ravaged life circumstances of the majority of African Americans in the interwar era. To this end, Davis seized upon every opportunity available to him to gain intellectual as well as hands-on experience in the workings of city, county, state, and federal bureaucracies, as did his circle of Black professional peers. This cohort was especially attentive to learning how to translate technocratic skills relating to the power structures in the American system into weapons for Black people's freedom quest.

It should be noted, however, that as crucial as the technocratic imperative was to Black people's quest for freedom during the formative phase of civil rights activism, possession of technocratic skills would not in itself produce the outcomes Davis and his peers sought. Something else was required, some degree of political alliance with liberal-minded white Americans who managed key power structures in the American system.

Fortunately for that second-generation cohort of pragmatic-activist African American professionals to which Davis belonged, there was a small cadre of such white professionals. The first important power-level test of their allyship occurred during their experiences with the Fair Employment Practice Committee under President Franklin Roosevelt. Davis and his peers recognized this opportunity and flocked to bureaucratic decision-making roles in the FEPC during World War II. Most of the committee's white chairs were basically liberal in outlook, the last and longest serving of whom, Malcolm Ross, was a progressive liberal.

Finally, an observation regarding the ideological contours of Davis and his peers in civil rights activism is in order. From the launching of the NNA in the fall of 1933 through the FEPC experience, Davis and his colleagues evinced a pragmatic-activist or reform-leftist ideological orientation, not a radical orientation. This mode of challenging American racism is classi-fied as assertive liberalism by Professor Jerry Watts in a keen probe of what he calls African American liberalism in his edited volume *Harold Cruse's The Crisis of the Negro Intellectual Reconsidered* (2004).[73] But the pragmatic-activist or reform-leftist type of civil rights activism mounted against the American racist edifice via the NNA and FEPC in the 1930s and 1940s differed from the radical-leftist activism practiced by some of the Black intelligentsia. This strand of the 1930s and 1940s was represented by per-sonalities like Paul Robeson, James Ford, and Benjamin Davis, and their activist encounter against American racism has been brilliantly explored by Gerald Horne in such works as *Black Liberation/Red Scare: Ben Davis and the Communist Party* (1994).[74] Whereas radical-leftist Black intellectuals like Ford and Benjamin Davis favored a revolutionary socialist reconstruction of the American system in order to vanquish America's racist edifice, John Aubrey Davis's circle of reform-leftist Black professionals believed that democratic processes in American society—despite their racial-caste inter-face with African Americans—made political space available for an effec-tive civil rights activism challenge and thus for rectification.

Interestingly enough, while this difference in ideological outlook and political strategy between the radical-leftist and reform-leftist strands was important, these two sectors of civil rights activism among the evolving twentieth-century African American intelligentsia shared many points of interaction between them, including close friendships. Today this kind of synergy among the radical-leftist and reform-leftist strands persists in the ranks of the African American intelligentsia, as reflected, for example, in the writings and political life of Cornel West, as he attests in *Race Matters* (1994) and *Democracy Matters: Winning the Fight Against Imperialism* (2004).

I want to reiterate, however, that what was particularly fundamental to the pragmatic-activist or reform-leftist orientation represented by Davis's circle was that whatever degree of political space America's democratic pro-cesses allowed the Black intelligentsia, that space was important for African American advancement only when a civil rights activism took advantage of it. The task, then, was to operationalize a politically effective Black civil rights activism agenda. To this end, Davis and his peers scoured the history of Black people's long freedom struggle for inspiration and guidelines for a viable Black civil rights activism. The Black historical inspiration and guidelines Davis's circle relied on reached back to slave rebellions against the American slavocracy; to the courage and political skills of Black abolitionists; to the first democratically elected Black officeholders in the Reconstruction era; and to late nineteenth- and early twentieth-century civil rights leaders like Alexander Crummell, Henry McNeal Turner, W. E. B. DuBois, Monroe Trotter, Archibald Grimké, Francis Grimké, Ida Wells-Barnett, Reverdy Ransom, James Weldon Johnson, and Mary McLeod Bethune. From the examples and experiences of such awesome predecessors, Davis and his peers fashioned their own civil rights activism identity and political methodology.

Above all, perhaps, teasing out facets of Davis's career from the vantage point of today's post–civil rights era teaches a contemporary African American intelligentsia one profoundly abiding lesson—namely, the lesson of human will, fortitude, courage, and intellectual discipline when facing the challenge to expand and deepen humanitarian goals in our flawed American democracy. It is especially important to underscore that John Aubrey Davis and his cohort practiced this lesson with a profound fidelity to the honor of Black people, a fidelity that subscribes to the view that Black people's equalitarian quest is not achieved until the plight of the weakest of our brethren is redeemed from racist and social oppression.

CHAPTER III

The Young Ralph Bunche and Africa

Between Marxism and Pragmatism

I was part of that small population of African Americans of the post–World War II era who attended college, some 95 percent of whom were attending Negro colleges when I entered Lincoln University in Pennsylvania as a freshman in 1949. My initial knowledge of Ralph Johnson Bunche as a prominent African American and international diplomat came from my alma mater. Horace Mann Bond, its first African American president, presented an honorary degree to Ralph Bunche at the university's 1948 commencement. My primary political science professor at Lincoln, John Aubrey Davis, had obtained his first teaching position as a lecturer in Howard University's Department of Political Science, headed by Bunche in 1934. At Lincoln, Davis had his students read several articles that Bunche, while still a graduate student at Harvard University, published on the political organization in Chicago's Negro election wards that sent Oscar De Priest to the United States House of Representatives in 1928. De Priest was the first African American elected to Congress in the twentieth century.

As one of about twenty African American graduate and professional school students at Harvard University from 1953 to 1959, I encountered Bunche personally several times, the first when Bunche addressed a graduate seminar during the 1956–1957 academic year on the workings of the United Nations trusteeship system. Professor of Government Rupert Emerson, who led the seminar, had been one of two Harvard Department of

Government professors (Emerson was an assistant professor at the time) who directed Bunche's doctoral dissertation. Completed in 1934, it won Harvard's top prize for political science dissertations that year.

In 1950, Emerson, a progressive WASP political scientist, entertained the idea of getting an African American political scientist appointed to teach at Harvard. To Emerson's surprise, his senior colleagues in the Department of Government agreed to a full-professorship appointment for his former student. Bunche, however, took a year to make his decision and, to Emerson's deep disappointment, elected to remain at the United Nations as director of the UN trusteeship system. I believe the international political order benefited immensely from Bunche's decision. A decade later, in 1961, Emerson facilitated an appointment for me as a research fellow in Harvard's Center for International Affairs, and in 1968 he facilitated my advancement to a full professorship in the Department of Government.

From my first discovery of Bunche's extensive scholarly writings, which occurred while I was a graduate student in the mid-1950s, I was struck by his seeming indifference to publishing his large body of brilliant social science scholarship. His superb 1934 Harvard doctoral dissertation, "French Administration in Togoland and Dahomey," perhaps the first fieldwork-researched political science analysis of colonial governance in Africa by an American graduate student, remains unpublished to this day.[1]

Be that as it may, another facet of Bunche's extensive and first-class social science research, however, did eventually see publication daylight. Based on his own fieldwork on the political status of African Americans, he produced two-thousand-odd pages of a manuscript called "Memoranda" for Gunnar Myrdal's *An American Dilemma: The Negro Problem and American Democracy* (1944), which was funded by the Carnegie Corporation. Fortunately, the Columbia University historian Dewey Grantham culled out and published roughly seven hundred pages of it under the title *Political Status of the Negro in the Age of FDR* (1973). Myrdal relied extensively on Bunche's material, often verbatim or close to it, in writing his monumental two-volume masterpiece.[2] Bunche's was a work of truly stunning analysis and stellar research.

Along with a small cadre of second-generation Black intellectuals from the mid-1920s into the 1940s, Bunche fashioned an intellectual outlook that was an admixture of leftist and pragmatist orientations. This chapter dissects the young Ralph Bunche's 1934 Harvard University PhD dissertation—a study of European colonial rule in Africa—as a way to trace the intellectual dynamics associated with Ralph Bunche's analytical application of a dual attachment to leftist and pragmatist orientations, and by extension that of other Black intellectuals of the era. To my knowledge, no one has heretofore plumbed Bunche's brilliant, prizewinning Harvard PhD dissertation for this purpose.

Ralph Bunche as a Black American Intellectual

In his formative phase, the young Ralph Bunche was a member of the second-generation cohort of African American intellectuals who gained professional training from the late 1920s into the early 1940s. The only African American in his graduating class, Bunche completed undergraduate studies in 1926 at the University of California, Los Angeles, as valedictorian. He spent the late 1920s pursuing graduate studies at Harvard University in political science and completed his PhD in 1934.

Bunche's ideology and politics were on the left-wing side of the American political spectrum, a topic that is explored in John Kirby's *Black Americans in the Roosevelt Era* (1980) and Charles Henry's *Ralph Bunche: Model Negro or American Other?* (1999). Bunche shared his left-of-center worldview with other Black intellectuals and professionals during the interwar years, among them the sociologist Ira Reid; the civil rights lawyer James Nabrit; the National Urban League economist Robert Weaver; the NAACP labor lawyer John P. Davis; the Dillard University anthropologist St. Clair Drake; the Lincoln University political scientist John Aubrey Davis; and the sociologist E. Franklin Frazier, all of whom were on the faculty of Howard University.

Bunche also shared another formative intellectual trait with his left-wing Black intellectual peers: they all stood on the broad shoulders of the radical democrat William Edward Burghardt Du Bois, the trailblazer of intellectual progressivism among the early twentieth-century African American intelligentsia. Influenced by the great Alexander Crummell, who helped found the American Negro Academy in 1897 and organize Wilberforce University in Ohio, Du Bois fashioned and propagated what I call a Black ethnic commitment for the period's Black intelligentsia. Writing in 1903 in *The Souls of Black Folk*, Du Bois observed that Black ethnic commitment among the evolving intelligentsia meant insisting "continually . . . that voting is necessary to modern manhood, that color discrimination is barbarism, and that black boys need education as well as white boys." For Du Bois, then, the African American intellectual committed to Black people needed to be engaged in facilitating the modern social system and development of citizenship rights of the Black working-class masses. Du Bois argued that members of the African American intelligentsia who failed to advance these goals were "shirk[ing] a heavy responsibility—a responsibility to themselves, a responsibility to the struggling masses, a responsibility to the darker races of men whose future depends so largely on this American [Negro] experiment."[3]

Furthermore, most members of Bunche's second-generation intellectual cohort shared what might be called an activist-pragmatic conception of their Black identity. Once more, it was Du Bois who offered an early and keen take on this notion. Also in *The Souls of Black Folk*, Du Bois formulated what came to be called a "double consciousness" for African Americans. This outlook candidly recognized that by the dawn of the twentieth century, New World Negroes had evolved an ethnic awareness that was fashioned out of both American cultural sources and the African heritage. As Du Bois puts it, "One ever feels this twoness—an American, a Negro; two souls, two thoughts, two unreconciled strivings; two warring ideals in one dark body."[4] To the core ingredients of the "two warring ideals in one dark body" Du Bois was evenly loyal, for he informed the African American intelligentsia that he would neither "Africanize America, for America had too much to teach the world and Africa," nor would he "bleach his Negro soul in a flood of Americanism, for . . . Negro blood has a message for the world."[5]

Thus, Du Bois taught the second-generation cohort of African American intellectuals that their Black-peoplehood consciousness was dialectically balanced, as it were, between a mainstream American commitment and a Black ethnic commitment. Now, not only did the vast majority of Bunche's peers adopt as part of their intellectual formation the Du Boisian double consciousness, they also translated this outlook along mainly civil rights activist and leftist political lines, which meant that they shunned the conservative accommodationist Black leadership paradigm fashioned between the 1880s and the early 1900s by Booker T. Washington at the Tuskegee Institute.

Yet Bunche tended to locate an independent turf for himself on the shoulders of Du Bois. As John Kirby and Charles Henry's work on Bunche's formative intellectual phase reveals, Bunche's leftist thinking exhibited a rather firm belief in a Marxist view of the Western working class as a multicultural radical force. Accordingly, in the 1930s, when a majority of Bunche's Black leftist peers were fashioning "Don't Buy Where You Can't Work" boycotts, which saw civil rights activists challenge white supremacist practices such as not hiring Blacks in white-owned businesses located in urban Black communities, Bunche steered clear. Instead, he entertained a kind of generic Marxist faith in the interracial radicalism of the white working class, preferring that Black civil rights activism be conducted in a manner that accommodated the white working class, despite the fact that there was no serious historical evidence that working-class white Americans had arrived at either a race-neutral or antiracist outlook that would have been a precondition for allying with Black civil rights activism.

As I discuss in chapter 2 on the intellectual career of John Aubrey Davis, Bunche's Black intellectual peers in Washington, DC, during the 1930s proceeded with forming perhaps the preeminent example of a "Don't Buy Where You Can't Work" boycott, the New Negro Alliance, organized in the summer of 1933. Its leading members included Davis and other Washington-based Black professionals. As Davis informed me in correspondence about the New Negro Alliance's relationship with Ralph Bunche in the mid-1930s, "Bunche was never a member [of the alliance], only a critic. . . . Bunche attacked the NNA because he feared the division of the [American] labor movement on the basis of race. He saw the only good in the organization was that it taught public protest, solidarity, and direction."[6]

Other Marxist-oriented leftist Black intellectuals of the 1930s adopted Bunche's moderately friendly but independent posture toward civil rights organizations based on Black community mobilization, such as E. Franklin Frazier and Abram Harris, each of whom kept organizational distance from the New Negro Alliance movement. What I view as the Bunche-Frazier-Harris contradictory kind of self-identified leftist Black intellectual perspective, one for the most part opposed to the mainstream civil rights activism of the period, is favorably portrayed in Jonathan Holloway's *Confronting the Veil: Abram Harris, Jr., E. Franklin Frazier, and Ralph Bunche, 1919–1941* (2002).

Bunche, Frazier, and Harris neither fashioned nor tested an alternative paradigm involving white working-class participation, and for very good reason: the dominant body of white working-class Americans in the era between the 1930s and 1940s clung to racist values and practices. The white working class made this brutally clear during those highly patriotic World War II years—highly patriotic for white people, anyway. As I discuss in chapter 2, the white working class violently and viciously attacked the courageous effort of Bunche's peers in the civil rights movement who became federal-level technocrats administering fair labor practices as part of President Roosevelt's Fair Employment Practices Committee at local levels in wartime industries in the North and South.

Although Bunche participated in the affairs of the National Negro Congress, the leading 1930s organization of left-wing Black intellectuals launched by A. Philip Randolph in 1935, during the late 1930s, as one of its prominent personalities, he also pursued another intellectual interest. Bunche spent two years broadening his academic and fieldwork knowledge of traditional African societies under European colonial systems, a project that involved study at the University of London and fieldwork research in East and South Africa.

As already noted, Bunche's interest in African societies commenced during his graduate school years when he pursued his doctoral dissertation on colonial governance in Africa. It is to an analytical exegesis of Bunche's Harvard doctoral dissertation that I now turn.

The Leftist-Pragmatist Persona of Bunche as Africanist

A fascinating intertwining of leftist and pragmatist elements in the intellectual mind-set of the young Ralph Bunche stands out in his writings on the nineteenth- and twentieth-century European colonial system in Africa. His main works on this subject were his 1934 Harvard doctoral dissertation, "French Administration in Togoland and Dahomey," and a small but very important book, *A World View of Race* (1936).

Bunche's leftist-pragmatist intellectual persona was rooted in the values and norms of the Enlightenment. Such values had laid the groundwork for the intellectual and economic revolutions from which was fashioned the modern European nation-state. Bunche considered this extraordinary metamorphosis out of Europe's feudalistic era a momentous opportunity for advancing humanitarian and equalitarian processes for the world at large, for all people regardless of race, religion, gender, and political origins.

Writing in the brilliant and analytically incisive *A World View of Race* just two years after completing his Harvard doctoral dissertation, Bunche embraces the Enlightenment legacy with these words:

> The concept of human equality and the doctrine of natural rights were cradled in the modern Western World. These ideals embodied the political promise of the future; indeed, they formed the warp and woof of the most modern political institutions. There was no limit to the promise which such doctrines held forth to peoples and classes which had been abused and oppressed for centuries. The "civilized" West of the nineteenth and twentieth centuries became a great testing ground for these principles which were counted upon to free the great masses of people from suffering and bondage.[7]

This respect for Enlightenment values and structures of progress was not, however, uncritical or one-dimensional. Quite the contrary. Bunche had a natural gift for the critical mind-set, and thus for realpolitik. If not fully present at Bunche's initial encounter with a new idea, policy, and system, this mind-set would nevertheless soon surface, governing his thinking and behavior. This, then, is what I mean when I refer to the pragmatist feature of his intellectual persona. Although he embraced the basic importance of the Enlightenment legacy, what might be called his gut-level sense of realpolitik regulated his fidelity to the European Enlightenment legacy.

Accordingly, for Bunche, real-world power dynamics required skepticism toward one's fidelity to the Enlightenment legacy. This I think is precisely what Bunche had in mind when he wrote the following:

> The practical history of our modern world . . . [indicates that] the ideal doctrine of the "equality of man" . . . has fallen upon hard times. True, we continue to pay lip service to the "sacred" concept of "natural rights of man" and its international corollary, the "rights of people." But the dominant peoples and powerful nations usually discover that such concepts cut sharply across their own economic and political interests. So, with those favored groups, who know well how to use them for their own profit, such doctrines come to assume a strange role.[8]

This theme of tension between ideals and power realities engaged Bunche throughout the 1930s. He entertained an especially strong preference for what might be called the cosmopolitan side of Enlightenment values, so much so, in fact, that writing in 1936 in *A World View of Race*, he even detects possible progressive patterns of class conflict evolving among oppressed groups influenced by "the principles of equality and humanitarianism advocated by [Marxian rulers in] the Soviet Union." Whatever their ideological roots—democratic or authoritarian—it seems that for Bunche, it was preferable that class patterns trump ethnic or racial conflict patterns when it came to politics:

> If the oppressed racial groups, as a result of the desperation and increasing understanding, should be attracted by the principles of equality and humanitarianism advocated by the Soviet Union (and it is both logical and likely that they will) then racial conflict will become intensified. In such case, however, racial conflict will be more directly identified with class conflict, and the oppressed racial groups may win the support of . . . previously prejudiced working-class groups within the dominant population.[9]

There was, then, a perpetual push and pull between the ideal and realpolitik elements in Bunche's metamorphosis, meaning that as a political actor he was ever shifting between leftist and bourgeois-pragmatist political contours. This dynamic pervaded, above all, Bunche's intellectual posture toward the European imperialistic mode of transferring a capitalist political economy to African societies.

Bunche's Cost-Benefit View of Colonial Capitalistic Rule

From the pages of Bunche's prize-wining Harvard PhD dissertation, we gain an understanding of the interplay of leftist/bourgeois-pragmatist patterns in his posture toward the impact of European colonial rule in nineteenth- and twentieth-century African societies. One might say that there were two stages in Bunche's interaction with the politics of modern colonial rule and the global implications of that politics: the first (lasting from the 1930s to the mid-1940s) saw him play the role of political analyst, while the second (stretching from the late 1940s through the 1960s) saw him assume the place of the crisis manager and diplomat.

Throughout the political-analyst stage, Bunche's perception of the metamorphosis of colonial rule in African societies vacillates between the price exacted by colonial rule (his leftist outlook) and the Western-type objective advantages transmitted by colonial rule (his bourgeois-pragmatist outlook). When characterizing colonial rule in *A World View of Race*, his most assertively leftist-skewed published work, Bunche is critically candid. He observes that the European imperialist process from the late nineteenth century onward crudely divided the globe between "advanced" and "backward" peoples, the latter being viewed as hopelessly underdeveloped and incapable of keeping in step with modernizing Western industrial societies. For Bunche, such theoretical classification of the world's peoples was mere deceit, an attempt, he wrote, "to mask [Europe's] cruelly selfish motives under high-sounding titles."[10]

Grasping that the rhetoric of power is seldom the reality of power, Bunche recognized that the essence of colonial rule in Africa was plain enough. "Powerful industrial nations have raped Africa under the false pretense of shouldering 'the white man's burden' . . . to convert [Africans] to the Christian religion and to expose them to the benefits of an advanced European culture," he writes. "[However,] . . . the backward peoples bitterly learn that the 'blessings' consist of brutal suppression, greedy economic exploitation of the natural and human resources of a country which is no longer their own, forced labor, the introduction of previously unknown diseases, vice and social degeneration."[11]

We can gain still another perspective on Bunche's interface with colonial rule in Africa if we ask, Why colonial rule in Africa in the first place? What I call the two mind-sets of Ralph Bunche—the leftist mind-set and pragmatist mind-set—responded in different yet overlapping ways to this query. In the 1930s, Bunche's leftist mind-set resorted to a rather conventional Marxist-Leninist wisdom to illuminate this query: "Imperialism is an international expression of capitalism. The rapid growth and expansion resulting from the development of industrialism and capitalism led the peoples of industrial countries to seek raw materials and new markets all over the world. This led to more general group contact and because of the base motives of the imperialism, to more widespread racial conflict . . . the accumulation of 'surplus capital' and the resultant demand for overseas investments, all [of which] tended to force European imperialist nations to invade completely the African continent."[12]

When Bunche frames his answer to the same query using the bourgeois-pragmatist mind-set, his response is more reflective; that is, less ideologically assured, evincing less operational close-endedness and thus entertaining some operational open-endedness toward colonial capitalist metamorphosis in Africa: "Perhaps its [colonial rule's] greatest significance is found in its possibilities as a fine proving ground in human relations—social, economic, and political. Here is one place in a troubled world where mistakes previously committed may be corrected, where, indeed, a new and better civilization may be cultivated, through the deliberate application of human intelligence and understanding."[13]

Thus, Bunche's bourgeois-pragmatist mind-set articulates the belief that, despite its wealth-expanding and power-enhancing purposes, the European colonial state in Africa might also entertain enough flexibility and creativity in form and ideas to permit institutional experimentation, in Bunche's words, to forge "a new and better civilization . . . through the deliberate application of human intelligence and understanding."

Furthermore, it is no surprise that Bunche resolved the seeming contradiction between his leftist and pragmatist perceptions of colonialism in Africa by applying rationality and knowledge to modern problem solving. After all, in the 1930s, Bunche, as an African American intellectual, was part of the second-generation cohort of the Black intelligentsia who were influenced by the Du Boisian activist leadership paradigm that was premised on a belief in the role of rational, social science thinking in resolving America's tenacious racist patterns.

Precisely, how do the fragile African people–serving dynamics within the colonial state—as contrasted with the dominant European wealth-appropriating and power-serving dynamics—carve out the ingredients of a quasi-equitable modernization beachhead? For American analysts of European colonial rule in Africa, including Bunche in his early years as well as Harvard's Raymond Leslie Buell and Rupert Emerson in the late 1920s and 1930s, the answer was not an obvious one. Emerson spent much of his intellectual career probing this issue, as evidenced by his monumental study *From Empire to Nation: The Rise of Self-Assertion of Asian and African Peoples* (1967). Of course, for Bunche especially, teasing out liberal potentialities within capitalist authoritarian colonial rule in Africa could not have been an easy matter.

Why? Partly because of the genuinely leftist bent of his intellectual formation and ties during the late 1920s and early 1930s, a topic addressed in two valuable works on Bunche: John Kirby's essay "Race, Class and Politics: Ralph Bunche and Black Protest" and Charles Henry's *Ralph Bunche: The Man and His Works* (both 1990). Above all perhaps, Bunche believed that for colonialism in Africa to tilt however haltingly toward liberal potentialities— toward a "momentous political moral transformation," to use his words— European colonial elites had to recognize the generic salience of Africans as human beings, thereby entertaining the parity of Europeans and Africans in the human equation. As Bunche formulated this issue in his dissertation in 1934, "After all, great though her natural resources are, the vital wealth of Africa is in the humanity that dwells within the sweltering continent. . . . The solution of the problem of the future of Africa is to be found in the determination of the eventual relationship that will prevail between the African and . . . [European] peoples."[14]

Shaping Accountable Colonial Rule Through an African Educated Elite

Regarding the issues of a 1930s leftist Black American intellectual arriving at a pragmatist outlook on the possibility of fashioning a liberal sphere within racist colonial rule in Africa, Bunche fashioned for himself an analytical perspective on how to remedy what his leftist mind-set viewed as the wealth- and power-grubbing character of colonialism. In dealing with this dilemma in his dissertation, I suggest that Bunche employed what might be called a twofold "systemic-remedial perspective."

Bunche's first systemic-remedial perspective focused on the role of the small educated African stratum—the budding Black African bourgeoisie, let's call it. Bunche's second systemic-remedial perspective focused on accountability processes within colonial governance, which is to say on the possibility of expanding participatory practices parallel to authoritarian rule, such as legislative councils in British African countries, local administrative districts known as "cantons" in French countries, and the role of international organizations in the post–World War I era, such as the League of Nations' so-called mandate system, which exercised limited supervisory authority over former German African colonies that were allocated to France and Britain at the Paris Peace Conference of 1919.

At the same time, however, Bunche's search for a pragmatist perspective toward colonial rule in Africa faced continual oversight from his leftist mind-set, suggesting that his systemic-remedial perspective was cautious but brave. Again, as he wrote in his dissertation, "Though the time when the West African will be able, in the words of the League [of Nations] Covenant, 'to stand alone in the strenuous conditions of the modern world,' is probably many generations removed from the present day, *he should be serving an apprenticeship in the art of self-rule under the tutelage of his immediate [colonial] rulers.* . . . It must be possible for him now to acquire the experience and develop the leadership essential to good government everywhere."[15]

As a leftist Black American intellectual, Bunche was quite certain that the governing precepts at the foundation of colonialism in Africa were both mistaken (as ideas out of the European Enlightenment tradition) and crisis-prone (as political blueprints). Asking himself, "By what devices is the African governed?," Bunche responded as follows in *A World View of Race*: "Two extremes of policy have been applied to him [the African]. The one, based entirely on greed, regarded him as essentially inferior, sub-human, without a soul, and fit only for slavery. The other, based entirely on sentiment, regarded him as a man and a brother, extended to him the equalitarian principles of the French Revolution and attempted to 'Europeanize' him overnight. Both were unscientific and devoted little attention to the needs and desires of the Africans."[16]

Not only were the formal governing precepts of colonial rule in Africa flawed, bereft of practicality because of either rank racist beliefs in the case of the British or because of phony romanticism in the case of the French; these major European colonial powers in Africa never even contemplated what might be called an endgame scenario. So Bunche, writing in 1936, chastised the major European colonial powers for what might be called power-class myopia: "England and France . . . [are] not thinking in terms of native independence or self-government for the West Africans."[17]

Young as he was, Bunche was politically astute, and he keenly understood that the importance of an endgame scenario under conditions of modern colonial governance (that is, authoritarianism exercised by Western democratic states) was that it presupposes steps and stages, however minuscule, through which a terminus point in authoritarian rule is reached. Anything less than this was, in Bunche's analytical scheme, a political recipe for systemic confusion ("policies . . . remain so vague as to the actual objectives aimed at"[18]) or systemic breakdown. For Bunche the pragmatist, the risks of systemic confusion clearly should be avoided. For one thing, they threatened the long-run interest of the global political economy, and they threatened, too, the prospects of bringing African societies viably into the global political economy. Nevertheless, for Bunche the leftist, the realization of a viable endgame scenario for colonial rule in Africa was at best problematic. As he put it in 1936, "the French and English alike are in Africa primarily for economic exploitation and not from motives of philanthropy. . . . Both powers intend to retain control of their respective possessions and their subject populations indefinitely."[19]

Whenever the European colonial rulers arrived at a systemic-remedial perspective owing to internal or global crises, however, Bunche believed that this would translate into some kind of endgame-scenario thinking on their part. In his understanding of global conditions that governed the endgame issue, Bunche was, I think, acutely perceptive. He recognized, for instance, that at the time he was conducting his fieldwork research in West Africa, the specter of fascism reigned in Europe, and the war that would be required to smash fascism involved serious systemic-remedial implications for European colonial rule in Africa.

Thus, in his analytical quest for an endgame option for colonial rule in Africa, Bunche's pragmatist outlook compelled him to contemplate achievable means to that end. For Bunche the pragmatist, such means must have at least one basic component. They must "exhibit a definite program for native development which will lead the native toward an ultimate specific political and social status. . . . The only sound objective of African colonial policies should be to prepare the Africans for membership in the community of the civilized world, not as individuals but as communities."[20] Accordingly, in this mode of endgame-scenario thinking in regard to future developmental trends under colonial rule in Africa, Bunche was both realistic and pragmatically utopian. While this was a seemingly contradictory position for Bunche to take, that was not the case. Why not? Because Bunche's dialectically sophisticated thought process persuaded him that power realism and power accountability can just as readily be reciprocal as they can be antithetical.

In Bunche's attempt to mediate analytically the colonial state's power-greed/power-accountability split consciousness—which is to say, in order that his quest for a serious endgame scenario for colonial rule in Africa were to make any operational sense at all—Bunche had to identify a reformist conveyor belt or agency within the colonial situation. Such a reformist agency appeared a mirage, but Bunche never settled for surface-level perception. It was, then, the embryonic stratum of educated Africans toward which Bunche turned his analytical telescope, perceiving it as a potential reformist agency in fulfilling colonial rule's endgame process.

Indeed, the fledgling African educated stratum could also fulfill its own modernization destiny, as it were, only through taking up Bunche's reformist conveyor belt function, a topic he discussed rather fully in *A World View of Race*.[21] It was through the hands-on fieldwork of his West African research that Bunche arrived at an understanding of the burgeoning African intelligentsia. In his dissertation, Bunche informed us that the group comprised "all notable members of the native community—chiefs, wealthy merchants, government clerks, members of [traditional] councils of elders, etc."[22]

Even with solid evidence of this growing elite, it was not clear why the colonial state itself facilitated this stratum. According to Bunche's analysis, there were several reasons for African elite formation by the colonial state. Although the core governance in the colonial situation was through European personalities, Africans were allowed a variety of sociopolitical tasks. And while Africans typically opposed the idea of colonialism, most nevertheless acquiesced to it, accepting the sociopolitical tasks afforded them by the system of European overrule. According to Bunche, the African's "immediate problem . . . is only to prepare himself to assume the meager share in his own administration delegated to him by the rules in the selection of which he has no voice."[23]

Furthermore, Bunche gave French colonial rulers the edge over the British in regard to facilitating a role for the emerging African educated sector in a systemic-remedial process under colonialism. "Beyond doubt," he observed, "the French know the native better, they come into closer contact with native life, while the British stand aloof."[24] Bunche articulated this favorable outlook on French colonial patterns even in his assertively leftist-skewed *A World View of Race*, characterizing—albeit rather naively, I think—the French racial openness as possessing "a measure of sincerity. There is no color line in France and none in her colonies, though individual instances of prejudice and discrimination may be encountered in both places." Bunche went on to present a vivid account of his sea voyage to West Africa in the early 1930s, underlining what he viewed as French racial openness compared to the rigid racist practices in American society:

The French attitude is strikingly evident on the boats of the French lines. . . . Here there is to be found a genial cordiality among the French and their elite associates of the darker races. . . . The genuine warmth of the association between these groups of upper-class black and white, the apparent lack of any race consciousness on the part of either, is quite startling when contrasted with similar groups on board the English and German vessels engaged in the same [Africa] service. On the latter most of the practice of segregation and aloofness common to the United States, its attitude toward its Negro population, are in evidence.[25]

Moreover, in numerous sections of his dissertation, Bunche discussed what he viewed as quite extensive efforts by French colonial rulers to cultivate access for a select cadre of Africans to governing posts. These posts included seats on municipal councils and such functional bodies as water commissions, school boards, and sanitation boards. Bunche also identified what he called "subaltern positions" in central government departments, representative positions in decision-making colonial assemblies—equivalent to what the British called legislative councils in their African territories—and even a few top-level positions in Paris relating to French colonial rule.[26]

Problematics of Systemic-Remedial Initiatives and Colonial Change

Although only a small measure of African elite formation was visible on the part of the colonial state in African countries during the interwar era, the pragmatist facet of Ralph Bunche's intellectual persona allowed him to entertain an endgame scenario for colonialism involving a critical role for an African educated elite. Nevertheless, throughout his writing on African affairs in the 1930s, Bunche was of several minds regarding the role of the African educated elite as an element in systemic-remedial change under colonialism. "The formation of the elite is at once the most cardinal and the most debatable point in the present French [African] policy," Bunche observed in 1934. The root of the quandary over the African educated elite for Bunche was simple enough: "The members of this elite above all others are to be bound to the French state and, through absorption of French culture, will become *assimiles* [assimilated]."[27]

Put another way, while on the one hand Bunche's pragmatist mind-set led him to recognize the systemic-remedial role that the embryonic African educated stratum could play under colonial rule, his leftist mind-set would not let him be uncritical about this important issue. Indeed, he speculated in his dissertation that "the presence of an elite group in the native community . . . may be a condition viciously inimitable to the best interests of the masses of the natives."[28]

Bunche's dilemma about the potential systemic-remedial role of the budding African educated elite became a testy issue for him in his dissertation. Referring to an anxiety on his part about "the elite native [becoming] black Frenchman," Bunche enters a curious discussion of a powerful and highly educated Senegalese man named Blais Diagne who had functioned as a provincial administrator in the colony and as an undersecretary for the colonies in Paris. Bunche was disdainful of what he viewed as Diagne's hedonistic display of the wealth and influence he derived from the French colonial connection—a pattern of the African elite, by the way, that has tragically plagued independent African nation-states for the past several decades. From the vantage point of his leftist mind-set, Bunche reflected harshly on Diagne's career: "It is a matter of serious doubt that the celebrated Senegalese Diagne now has much honest concern with things African extending beyond the African bric-a-brac of his elaborate and ornate Paris apartment."[29]

Somewhat unfairly, perhaps, Bunche resorted to a Black Communist magazine published in Paris in order to suggest that Diagne might in fact be politically illegitimate. Citing this magazine as his source, Bunche observed, "Already many of his native constituents have hurled the epithet 'traitor' at him."[30]

It was, then, the loss of an autonomous African modern elite—one defined along an African and not European cultural trajectory—that Bunche feared. He suspected—and rightly—that modern African elite autonomy, all things being equal, enhanced the chances of a viable redefinition of the colonial state in Africa. Here we see the crucial analytical role played by Bunche's leftist mind-set in pricking his awareness of the possible downside emanating from his recognition of the fact that colonial rule in Africa by the 1930s required systemic-remedial change toward an endgame scenario. Bunche's leftist mind-set aided his recognition of the issue of autonomy for the modern African elite for future African independent states, an issue we today in the postindependence era refer to as non-neocolonized African elites.

Bunche also identified another element likely to be involved in the future redefinition of the colonial state in Africa, what might be called a creeping dissidence. He glimpsed such dissidence among some educated Africans who, "endowed with the white man's training, are hungry for positions that carry the white man's dignity [benefits]."[31] Bunche also recognized that French colonial administrators suspected this tendency as well, noting their propensity to continually recast the colonial educational system in the hope of "avoiding the impending danger of the development of an intellectual proletariat in Africa."[32] This amounted to a crucial dilemma under colonial rule—namely, whetting the modernization appetites of educated Africans along one axis (skills, technology, administrative roles, etc.) but withholding fruition along the power-appropriating axis. It was this dilemma that Bunche felt might eventually assist systemic-remedial change under colonialism.

Precisely when such systemic-remedial change would take place, Bunche hesitated to speculate. Rather, his concern was with process, not events. So he turned his analytical antenna toward the process of the slowly evolving corporateness of the African educated stratum, a situation Bunche delineated when remarking that "the educated African is rapidly acquiring a zest for . . . political fetishes of the Western world."[33] Characterizing this incipient corporateness among educated Africans in language that anticipated that used by analysts of African affairs in the 1950s onward, Bunche observed that "sooner or later, as the educated class of natives increases in numbers, the French will be confronted with the difficult problem of the colonial administration of backward peoples, viz., *that there is no apparent peaceful means of transition to full self-control [governance].* This condition is already looming larger on the horizon in neighboring British Gold Coast."[34]

Bunche was also keenly perceptive about modernizing development patterns within the traditional societies of colonial Africa that would assist the corporateness of the developing African educated elite—assist, that is, their systemic efficacy. It was especially modernizing patterns within traditional African societies that could attenuate the deep-rooted fissiparous ethnic or tribal realities, for in Bunche's perceptive analytical vision, these traditional dynamics potentially threatened the quest for a viable modern African elite. Again, this was a topic Bunche discussed in his dissertation: "Tribal lines are being cut across as a result of improved means of communication and travel, and tribal authority has been broken down deliberately by the French. This may prove to be a blessing in disguise to the native, however, *for it will make it possible for him to ultimately present a united front in his demands for an increasing share in the control of his country.* This he could not do so long as tribal rivalries, jealousies, and isolation persisted."[35]

These analytical projections made by Bunche so early in his career were a sophisticated synthesis of the ideas of late nineteenth- and early twentieth-century analysts of modern capitalist development like Marx, Weber, and Schumpeter, all of whom Bunche had read. His insightful and prophetic formulations on the possible impact of modern colonial developments on future political patterns in African countries also shrewdly anticipated by a generation Karl Deutsch's famous social-mobilization thesis for explaining post–World War II nationalist movements in the non-Western world.[36]

Basic to Bunche's modern development projections for colonial African societies was a proposition formulated in his dissertation that "probably the greatest error [among Westerners] is the mistake of assuming ipso facto that the African and his problems are essentially different from the Western world. Basically the African is confronted by the same difficulties which any people in process of [capitalist economic] evolution encounter."[37] He slightly reshaped this formulation in *A World View of Race*, stating that "In truth the African is confronted with the same difficulties encountered by any people in process of [capitalist] social development."[38]

Convinced that "there is nothing particularly unique about either the African or his [modernization] problems," Bunche analyzed the stress and strain for African societies dominated by European capitalist nation-states squarely in what today we understand as a capitalist international comparative context. In so doing, Bunche was again anticipating a prominent post–World War II social science analysis of modern development in non-Western societies: Immanuel Wallerstein's world-system analysis of capitalism. "The African native today," Bunche wrote, "is comparable with the peasants and workmen of England and France a century ago, and with other workers and peasants today in less advanced countries of the modern world."[39]

A Concluding Note

At the end of what I call Ralph Bunche's endgame scenario analysis of colonial rule in Africa during the 1930s, he speculates brilliantly regarding potential sources of systemic political change. His conception of systemic political change in a colonial situation was dialectical. In Bunche's understanding, having thorough capitalist wealth- and power-expansion modalities, which were self-serving for Europeans in the first instance, whetted the modernization appetite of traditional, preliterate African societies, and the European colonial state set into motion dynamics that would redefine it. As he wrote in his dissertation, "The . . . [colonial state] cannot limit the experience and sophistication which inevitably come to the native along with the exploitative forces of Western civilization; these lead him to desire independence and self-assertion, making him 'troublesome' to the [colonial] administrators. . . . [Educated Africans] have news of the powerful weapons of effective resistance to abuses, employed by the oppressed in the Western world."[40]

Among the "powerful weapons . . . of resistance" referenced in his dissertation, Bunche mentions "the boycott" and "the general strike," both of which he suggested could be aggregated through "a strong movement of passive resistance . . . [that] could make the white man's presence in West Africa futile."[41] Of course, it was precisely this transnational flow of rebellious political ideas and methods in the post–World War II era following the vanquishing of Hitlerian fascism that proved fundamental to the continent-wide upheaval of the African nationalist movement.

Interestingly enough, although Bunche's endgame scenario analysis, written in the 1930s, clearly anticipated the postwar African nationalist upheaval, to my knowledge he never actually invoked the phrase "African nationalist movement" as such. The nearest Bunche gets to writing these words is in reference to what he called "Pan-African nationalists." This reference, however, was an unfriendly one, insofar as Bunche entertained a gut-level antipathy to this assertively race-conscious mode of educated African elite political mobilization against colonial rule. From Bunche's orientation as a leftist Black American intellectual in the 1930s, he opposed manipulating what he considered xenophobic cultural forces in order to either (1) redress global power imbalances or (2) protect existing imbalances. Writing about his perspective on so-called Pan-African nationalists in his 1936 volume *A World View of Race*, Bunche no doubt had in mind the Nazi use of anti-Semitism and race violence in Europe as well as Negrophobic patterns among white racists in the United Sates, such as the Ku Klux Klan.[42]

Accordingly, Bunche was downright contemptuous of the African leadership challenge to colonial rule that was associated with Pan-African nationalism. "There are those, like the Pan-African nationalists, who feel that the darker peoples of the world must band together and gird their black and yellow loins for the oncoming world conflict between the races. The stakes in this little fracas are supposed to be world supremacy."[43] Here, Bunche was articulating his belief that, in the context of culture- or race-based conflicts as between European colonial governments and the native societies they ruled in Africa, Asia, the Middle East, and elsewhere, culture-based political mobilization against colonialism should give way to political-issue-based or class-based mobilization. In this outlook, Bunche was expressing assumptions he shared with Western Marxists of the 1930s, that political-issue-based or class-based mobilization resulted in more genuinely modernist-systemic (rational) solutions or outcomes that avoided cultural, religious, and racial parochialisms in all of their potential xenophobic crudeness and meanness.

I believe, however, that Bunche's penchant for putting down culture- or race-based political mobilization against colonial rule was off the mark. He failed to recognize that for numerous weak, oppressed, and culturally despised non-Western societies dominated by European colonial power, the use of culture-based political mobilization was a historic first step toward more rational modes of political formation. The issue, then, was not that, say, the nationalist Congress Party in India during the interwar era manipulated traditionalist cultural modalities in order to stoke mass political mobilization against a century of British colonial rule. Rather, the issue was how effectively the Congress Party harnessed and disciplined such culture-based political mobilization in democratic and humanitarian directions.

Thus, Bunche grossly exaggerated his preference for political-issue-based rather than culture-based political mobilization under colonial rule. Such exaggeration can be seen in the above-mentioned quotation from Bunche: "Pan-African nationalists . . . feel that the darker peoples of the world must band together and gird their black and yellow loins for the oncoming world conflict between the races." Here Bunche distorted the political mobilization outlook of early African anticolonial organizations during the 1930s such as the National Congress of British West Africa or the African National Congress of South Africa. The Ghanaian (then Gold Coast) lawyer J. E. Casely Hayford, who headed the National Congress of British West Africa, and other fledgling African anticolonial leaders were opposed not to the intrinsic culture of Europe, but rather to the exploitative, oppressive, and racist governance by European colonialism. Like the Congress Party leadership in India, the leaders of the fledgling African anticolonial movement entertained the goal of advancing and transforming their European-dominated African societies into modern organized nation-states.

In short, the young Ralph Bunche failed to recognize that while there was a potential among the emergent African leadership for hyperxenophobic uses of Pan-Africanist mobilization (as it turned out, say, in the hands of President Robert Mugabe in Zimbabwe), there was also a potential for systemically progressive applications of Pan-Africanist mobilization. The latter was represented by the leadership of Ghana's first president, Kwame Nkrumah, and by South Africa's first African president, Nelson Mandela. Put another way, Bunche's endgame scenario analysis failed to grasp the valid non-xenophobic role of Pan-Africanist political mobilization in the African colonial situation. His preference for a kind of hyper-pragmatic rationalism on the part of the emergent educated African power contenders under colonial rule was a version of wide-eyed idealism, an idealism too far removed from the oppressive specificity of the European imperialist process in Africa.

Be that as it may, Bunche's particular critique of Pan-Africanist political mobilization under colonial rule was, on balance, a minor weakness in his probe of the generic character of the European colonial state in Africa. Bunche's Harvard dissertation was a remarkable analytical achievement, demonstrating his incredible talent for conceptually intertwining the leftist and pragmatist mind-sets that comprised his intellectual persona. His dissertation was a masterful contribution to the social science knowledge of the generic character of colonial rule in Africa.

Especially noteworthy is the fact that in his bold quest for what I call an endgame scenario analysis of European colonial rule, Bunche's analytical contribution exhibited prophetic dimensions. His analysis might be said to have espied key attributes of what became the postcolonial African polities in the late 1950s into the 1960s. Bunche's particular skeptical leftist outlook enabled him to detect potential governance dysfunctions on the part of future African governing elites in a postcolonial Africa, such as the manipulation of tribalist and racialist politicization modalities to mask crude power-oligarchic and wealth-oligarchic patterns.

It was with this issue in mind that Bunche drew attention to "the fact that for either a white or black man it is scarcely more pleasant to be exploited and oppressed by privileged members of one's own race than by members of some other race. . . . Race issues . . . tend to merge into class issues. . . . The titanic conflicts of the future will be the product of the uncompromising struggles between those who have and those who have not."[44]

CHAPTER IV

Harold Cruse Reconsidered

Anatomy of Black Intelligentsia and Black Nationalism

A contest between two core ideological orientations loomed large in the development of the twentieth-century African American intelligentsia. That contest pitted the integrationist orientation against the Black Nationalist orientation; in other words, a pro-acculturation and pro-systemic incorporation of African American perspectives toward American society against a Black-cultural separatist perspective. The governing conceptual and analytical thrusts presented by Harold Cruse in *The Crisis of the Negro Intellectual* are critical of the prominence of the integrationist orientation over the Black Nationalist outlook in the metamorphosis of the African American intelligentsia.[1]

This chapter presents a critical exegesis of Cruse's broad-ranging polemical assault in his 1967 tome on the mainline African American intelligentsia's preference for an integrationist civil rights activist challenge of the American racist edifice. Cruse's assault was not only framed along Black Nationalist ideological lines, but it was astutely couched in a radical rhetorical mode that lent it magnetic appeal among young college-going African Americans following the assassination of the Reverend Dr. Martin Luther King Jr. in the spring of 1968 into the 1970s.

What might be called the systemic setting of Cruse's book was the robber baron era in American society, the period of the late nineteenth and early twentieth centuries marked by an explosion in American industrialization. The era also saw the rise of an American "political culture of whiteness," a turn-of-the-century concept developed by social historians like David Roediger in *The Wages of Whiteness* (1992) and Noel Ignatiev in *How the Irish Became White* (1995).[2] During this period, bigotry in American life took on its most rigid and tormenting form as a regime of racist pariahization and marginalization against African Americans. As the historian John Higham demonstrates in his classic work *Strangers in the Land* (1955), bigotry, in its foundational form in late nineteenth-century America, evolved initially as a method of regulating relations among white American groups, particularly between lower-class immigrant Catholic groups and the already established so-called WASPs, or white Anglo-Saxon Protestants, those long-settled Americans of primarily northern European extraction.[3] During the first several decades of the twentieth century, this WASP-dominated bigotry against white ethnic groups (including but not exclusively Irish, Italian, Polish, and Jewish immigrants and their children) metamorphosed into a weapon deployed by *all* white American groups to diminish and demean the status of Black people in American society. The qualitative transformation in the character and structure of American bigotry, captured in the term "the political culture of whiteness," constituted an intricate web of white Americans' neurotically Negrophobic social and political institutional patterns that became accepted as cultural norms by most white Americans. The use of violence—via vigilante white citizens in the form of lynchings, anti-Black urban riots, and police brutality against Black citizens—to uphold an American political culture of whiteness occurred on a national scale, in the South and the North, from the 1880s into the World War II era.

In systemic terms, from the 1880s through the first half of the twentieth century, the political culture of whiteness generally prevented the viable political and institutional incorporation of African American citizens at parity with that of the aforementioned white ethnic groups. And when the sociopolitical incorporation of African Americans into the American social contract finally commenced by the middle of the 1960s, it required three things that the incorporation of these white ethnic groups had not:

1. A militant activist challenge of American racism by African Americans via the civil rights movement from the 1950s through the 1960s, a challenge that was violently resisted by white supremacist governments in the South as well as by vigilante white citizens.

2. Widespread urban riots on the part of the African American working class in both the North and the South during the late 1960s and into the 1970s.
3. Extensive public policy intervention by federal courts and the federal government generally.

African American responses to the long, cruel, cynical reign of an American political culture of whiteness were variegated, not one-dimensional. One sector of the African American intelligentsia—what would become the mainline sector—fashioned social and political responses that sought broad-gauged inclusion into mainstream American life and institutions at parity with white American groups. This strategy was popularly labeled *integration*, and it became the dominant Black leadership strategy as the twentieth-century African American intelligentsia matured.

From its onset, however, in the thinking of Black abolitionist figures from before the Civil War like Frederick Douglass, and in post-emancipation figures like W. E. B. Du Bois and Monroe Trotter, the integrationist strategy always confronted challenges from spokespersons for the Black separatist or Black Nationalist orientation. The Jamaican-born Marcus Garvey emerged as the preeminent spokesperson for the Black Nationalist strategy during the African American intelligentsia's formative phase in the early 1900s. Through Garvey's keen organizational skills—manifest in the Universal Negro Improvement Association (UNIA)—and his special talent for awakening the Black consciousness of many urban, working-class African Americans, the Black Nationalist strategy obtained a competitive status vis-à-vis the integrationist strategy during the interwar period. Although the majority of the institutional infrastructure of Black civil society (e.g., churches, mutual benefit associations, artisan and professional associations, trade unions, and women's organizations) were committed to the integrationist outlook as represented by mainline leadership groups like the NAACP, the National Urban League, the African Methodist Episcopal Church, and the National Baptist Convention denominations, the UNIA's variant of the Black Nationalist strategy made some operational inroads in these spheres of evolving twentieth-century African American life.

Accordingly, by the World War II era into the postwar years, organizations representing the integrationist outlook prevailed at the apex of the African American political leadership and overall intelligentsia ranking. It was, then, representatives of the integrationist strategy who initiated the heyday of the Black American civil rights movement from the early 1950s and throughout the 1960s.

To date, Harold Cruse's *The Crisis of the Negro Intellectual* remains the most influential published work probing integrationist and Black Nationalist orientations in the life cycle of the twentieth-century African American intelligentsia. Flavoring his narrative and analytical thrusts with a Black Nationalist feel, Cruse delineates the impact on the African American intelligentsia's ideological contours of the interplay of integrationist and Black Nationalist strands more evocatively—with more political emotive sway—than any other work in the period in which it was published. This chapter's exploration of *The Crisis of the Negro Intellectual* attempts to explain the appeal of Cruse's book on the one hand while unmasking its empirical, conceptual, and analytical flaws on the other.

Cruse and the Black Modernist Dilemma

Attributes of the Black Modernist Dilemma

A fascinating and curious dilemma characterized the evolutionary life cycle of the twentieth-century African American intelligentsia—namely, that despite the grassroots populist appeal of Black Nationalist thrusts among African Americans, the sociopolitical leadership organizations associated with the more mainstream integrationist strategy gained institutional prominence in the evolving twentieth-century African American society. When it came to the matter of connecting everyday African American realities with mainstream American processes of the time, the sector of the African American intelligentsia linked to leadership groups like the NAACP, the National Urban League, and the National Council of Negro Women were typically preferred by the average Black citizen to perform operational leadership tasks.

Put another way, while the cathartic leadership tasks faced by African American citizens were sometimes entrusted to proponents of Black Nationalism, operational leadership tasks were overwhelmingly entrusted to those members of the intelligentsia who were proponents of the integrationist orientation. It was this attitudinal bifurcation of the Black-ethnic mind-set among African Americans during the first half of the twentieth century that comprised the Black modernist dilemma.

I suggest that this issue of a split-minded African American attitude toward the integrationist and Black Nationalist leadership perspectives is a recurrent theme throughout the six-hundred-odd pages of *The Crisis of the Negro Intellectual*. For Cruse it was, I think, a disturbing dimension of the twentieth-century evolution of African American society that the Black Nationalist view of Black modernity did not vanquish the integrationist or acculturationist outlook. The Black modernist dilemma looms as an obsessive undertone in Cruse's book, amounting to gnawing disenchantment for the author. In fact, this is a basic conceptual way of understanding or defining the use of the term "crisis" in the title, because nowhere in his book does Cruse provide readers with an explicit definition of exactly what the crisis of the Negro intellectual is.

Be that as it may, Cruse's antipathy toward the Black integrationist outlook almost assumes the quality of a religious ethos. For Cruse, that segment of African American leadership favoring civil rights integrationist activism and mainstream-incorporation goals ought to be rejected and stripped of its Black-ethnic legitimacy. The kind of leadership style that leaned on the pragmatic adjustment to American institutions, the sort practiced by the NAACP and the National Urban League from 1909 onward, and that existed within a framework of civil rights activism against American racism was anathema to Cruse. In *The Crisis of the Negro Intellectual*, Cruse uses the term "interracialism" pejoratively in his discussion of this leadership perspective.

Explaining the Black Modernist Dilemma

Cruse often discusses events that relate to the Black modernist dilemma, but his discussion never goes far beyond the level of narrating events—that is, attitudes, actions, ideological leanings, and so forth—that suggest the kind of contradictions associated with it. His preferred mode of discourse on this matter involves rather polemical portraits of interracialist-oriented Black intellectuals, portraits calibrated in terms of one-dimensional psychologizing critique.

Among the intellectuals who are the target of Cruse's ire are LeRoi Jones (this portrayal will be considered in more detail later in this chapter), Lorraine Hansberry, John Killens, and Julian Mayfield. In Cruse's analytical schema and ideological vision, those progressive Black intellectuals of the post–World War II era, who locate themselves favorably vis-à-vis the liberal American interracialist orientation, represent a form of Black cultural perversion. For Cruse, this reeked of a psychological irrationality too dependent on, too welcoming of, whites. The appeal of the interracialist orientation to such a progressive Black intellectual amounts to a pathological psychic process, says Cruse—a kind of left-wing version of a generic Uncle Tom.

Dissecting Cruse's Black Nationalist Thinking

In *The Crisis of the Negro Intellectual*, the Black Nationalist orientation is Cruse's primary yardstick for appraising the leadership activity of mainline African American organizations and characterizing the activity and production of leading African American intellectuals. In overall design, the book delineates the interplay between the Black Nationalist and the integrationist strands in shaping the ideological contours of the evolving twentieth-century African American intelligentsia. Furthermore, Cruse's presentation is informed and calibrated throughout with a Black Nationalist–friendly aura.

Cruse's analysis proceeds along two trajectories. First, he presents case studies of key historical phases relating to the development of the African American intelligentsia; for example, the formative phase involving the rise of Black Manhattan or Harlem; the leftist or Marxist phase among Black creative artists and academics; the Garveyite Black nationalist phase; and the militant post–World War II civil rights phase.

The second of Cruse's discourses entails portraits of a variety of African American intellectuals whose activities, in Cruse's analytical schema, suffered from the seductions of interracialism. Among those who might be seen as, in Cruse's eyes, "ruined" Black intellectuals were Claude McKay, Richard Wright, Paul Robeson, James Baldwin, and the aforementioned Hansberry, Killens, Jones, and Mayfield.

The endgame of Cruse's analysis is, I think, plain enough: to cultivate favorable Black Nationalist perspectives with regard to the development of twentieth-century African American life in general and the development of the Black intelligentsia in particular. He arrives at this goal through critical discourse on the mainline African American civil rights integrationist leadership sector, as well as on the activities of African American intellectuals associated with the integrationist or, to use Cruse's term, the interracialist leadership perspective.

While Cruse's intention is reasonable enough, the key issue remains the historical validity, analytical effectiveness, and intellectual viability of Cruse's execution of his discourse. My overall reconsideration of Cruse's discourse proceeds along the lines of these evaluative criteria. We must first, however, sort out the particulars of Cruse's affinity for the Black Nationalist perspective.

Basic Elements of Cruse's Discourse: A Naive Psychologism

Cruse's discourse on the interplay of the Black Nationalist and civil rights integrationist orientations in shaping the contours of twentieth-century African American leadership is not expressed systematically. Instead, he presents a variety of predilections, propositions, and events relating to the face-offs between Black Nationalists and civil rights integrationists in a scattershot manner. They appear somewhat haphazard, depending on what set of ideas relating to the Black Nationalist perspective Cruse is seeking to affirm or what group of mainline African American leadership figures and intellectuals Cruse is seeking to debunk.

Perhaps the best starting point for understanding Cruse's discourse is found halfway through *The Crisis of the Negro Intellectual*, where he offers critiques of different integrationist-minded Black intellectuals, one of whom was the aforementioned poet and playwright LeRoi Jones (later Amiri Baraka). For Cruse, Jones is something of a bête noire among interracialist African American intellectuals during the 1960s. It happened that Jones had fashioned for himself what might be called a Janus-faced ideological identity as a radical Black intellectual, one that combined a Black Nationalist demeanor with an interracialist orientation. Among the numerous errors of Jones's political ways, Cruse posits, was his ambivalence "toward Black nationalism of the traditional kind. He was dubious at first about what he called Harlem Black Nats (nationalists). His first Harlem organization, 'On Guard for Freedom Committee,' was an interracial group."[4] For Cruse, this situation amounted to a kind of Black-oppositionary contradiction.

Cruse believed in an ideological symmetry between a progressive Black intellectual's identity and that intellectual's political alliances. But when such an ideological symmetry was absent, it was akin to a Black-oppositionary flaw, a situation bordering on an interracialism disease. Accordingly, when seeking an explanation for the young Jones's succumbing to the intellectual pathology of interracialism, Cruse offered the following observation:

> Negro intellectuals have been sold a bill of goods on interracialism by white Communists and white liberals. As a result of this, a peculiar form of what might be called the psychology of political interracialism (for want of a better term) has been inculcated in the Negro's mind. Even before the average Negro attempts to undertake any action himself, he assumes, almost involuntarily, that he must not, cannot, dare not exclude whites, because he cannot succeed without them. He has been so conditioned that he cannot separate personal and individual associations with individual whites in the everyday business of striving and existing, from that interior business that is the specific concern of his group's existence. Every other ethnic group in America, a "nation of nations," has accepted the fact of its separateness and used it to its own social advantage.[5]

Fundamental to his critique of Jones for being a Black radical but not a Black separatist is Cruse's claim that African Americans in general and the intelligentsia in particular have been brainwashed ("conditioned" is Cruse's term) into "individual associations with . . . whites."

Cruse's Comparison of Blacks and White Ethnics

Cruse reinforced his tendency toward psychologism when explaining interracialism among Black intellectuals with a cultural-separatist characterization of white ethnic groups. According to Cruse, unlike African Americans as an American ethnic community, the major non-WASP white ethnic groups like the Irish, Italians, Poles, and Jews had forged themselves into viably modernizing ethnic communities without systemic-incorporation linkages or interactions with the WASP-hegemonic American mainstream system. As Cruse put it above, unlike African Americans, "Every other ethnic group in America, a 'nation of nations,' has accepted the fact of its separateness and used it to its own advantage."

Here Cruse, rather inadvertently I think, offers an important insight relating to the ethnic character of African Americans relative to white ethnics. He is suggesting that African Americans are both a racial group (shaped by white supremacist oppressive patterns) and an ethnic group (shaped by generic cultural patterns). In this seemingly unintentional formulation about Black American ethnicity, Cruse shares a similar perspective to one put forward by W. E. B. Du Bois in his essays in *Dusk of Dawn* (1940).

Cruse, however, is mistaken in his observation that white ethnic groups possessed during their twentieth-century evolution some special variant of ethnic cultural separateness in American society that enabled them to gain modern capabilities without linkages to the WASP-hegemonic mainstream American system. The observation was not as such historically valid, lacking a basis in the actual historical development of these non-WASP white ethnic groups.

When compared to the trajectory that African Americans followed, these non-WASP whites did indeed rely heavily upon linkages and interactions with the dominant WASP patterns, even while having to challenge the enormous levels of bigotry and nativism practiced by WASPs. For one thing, the vast majority of the white-ethnic working class gained viable employment not in businesses owned by other white ethnics, but in WASP-owned businesses and factories. Furthermore, the business sector among white ethnic groups relied heavily on WASP-owned banks and financial institutions, and they depended upon close alliances with WASP political elites and power brokers within both the Democratic and Republican Parties. And when, from the late 1930s onward, a second- and third-generation middle and professional class emerged among white ethnic groups like the Irish, growing numbers of upwardly mobile Irish males—defying religious resistance by the Catholic Church—sought wives among elite WASP women, as did men from the third-generation Italian and Jewish professional class beginning in the 1960s.

Thus, the successful creation of a viable modern socioeconomic mobility among white ethnic groups from the late nineteenth into the early twentieth century occurred through multilayered linkages and alliances between groups like the Irish, Italians, and Jews on the one hand and the dominant WASP ethnic cluster on the other. Cruse appears quite ignorant of the real social-system interactions between white groups in twentieth-century American development. This ignorance, however, was convenient for his Black Nationalist–oriented critique of the integrationist development trajectory followed by the mainline African American intelligentsia and professional class.

Accordingly, I question one of Cruse's core claims in *The Crisis of the Negro Intellectual*: that the weak modern development of twentieth-century African American society, as compared with that of white ethnic groups, was primarily a result of the Black intelligentsia's failure to come to grips with the Black Nationalist perspective. According to Cruse's analytical schema, mainline Black leadership neglected to learn from the special uses by white ethnic groups of their so-called cultural separateness in their pursuit of viable modern development without linkages with the WASP-dominated mainstream American system. As I argued earlier, however, Cruse's historical understanding of the twentieth-century modern development of white ethnic groups was totally wrong.

I also question Cruse's second explanation of the weak modern development of twentieth-century African American society. He believed the mainline African American intelligentsia were "conditioned" into "individual associations with . . . whites," or what I call brainwashed. Employing a crude kind of psychologism, Cruse said that the mainline Black intelligentsia suffered "from a psychology that is rooted in the Negro's symbiotic 'blood-ties' between slave and master, bound together in the purgatory of plantations. The American Negro has never yet been able to break entirely free of the ministrations of his white masters."[6]

Here, Cruse indulges a crude form of cultural reductionism, one that resulted in a one-dimensional explanation of the weak modern development of African Americans from the late nineteenth through the twentieth century as compared to that of white ethnic groups. Furthermore, from this foundational explanatory vantage point, Cruse constructed the core sections of *The Crisis of the Negro Intellectual* that treat the ideological and political leadership manifestations of the twentieth-century development of African American society.

Cruse's Interface with Black Leadership Dynamics, 1905–1940s

Cruse's portrait of the Black American leadership dynamics as they evolved during the early twentieth century is informed by a strong affinity for Booker T. Washington's accommodationist leadership paradigm on the one hand and a strong antipathy toward W. E. B. Du Bois's civil rights activism leadership paradigm on the other. In Cruse's analytical schema, the indifference of the Washingtonian leadership mode to advancing African Americans' human and citizenship rights— its indifference to challenging American society's white supremacist edifice—was its unique strength. Why? Because it freed up or allowed Black leadership resources to concentrate upon what might be called Black-communitarian advancement or, in Cruse's words, the "rise of black economic nationalism."[7]

By contrast, the civil rights activism leadership paradigm, of which Du Bois was the period's representative spokesperson, is viewed by Cruse as intrinsically incapable of producing viable forms of modernization for African American society. According to Cruse, Du Bois's methods resulted in a dysfunctional dissipation of the Black leadership resources required to challenge America's white supremacist hegemony and gain equal citizenship rights within the broader American social contract, at parity with white Americans.

Unfortunately, Cruse's historiographic acumen is rather poor, because nowhere in his narrative on the practice of Bookerite accommodationism in early twentieth-century Harlem does he show appreciation of the fact that Washington's conservative white elite patrons never provided Black elite proponents of accommodationism (believers in Cruse's "economic black nationalism") adequate capital resources. This meant that the claim of Bookerite accommodationism as a viable modernizing paradigm for Black people in American society was an overblown pretense, phony and absurd.

Interestingly enough, a similar failure to appreciate the Bookerite accommodationist leadership paradigm in racist American society resurfaced four decades later, in the twenty-first century, in Michael Rudolph West's 2008 book *The Education of Booker T. Washington: American Democracy and the Idea of Race Relations*.[8] Unlike Cruse, however, who articulates his affinity for the Bookerite accommodationism candidly, the Black scholar West embraces the philosophy in a circuitous manner and a florid narrative style, claiming that the underlying ideas represented a higher vision of American civilization. From this extravagantly pro-Washington position, West intimates that the Du Boisian NAACP strand of civil rights activism was mistaken and that it should have followed the accommodationist trajectory. West offers his rather bizarre claim and argument as follows:

> The . . . appeal of [Washington's] race relations construction . . . lies in its allowing democracy and racist proscription to stand by each other (indeed overlapping) seemingly without the latter affecting the former. It is here we find Washington's real wizardry and the real genius of race relations as an idea in providing a magic formula to create two worlds out of one world of difficult . . . conflict, and, prospectively, offering up "the Negro" as tabula rasa: a clean slate upon which a better future could be charted. . . . This was the idealist rendering of the Negro problem.[9]

Fortunately for the progressive side of the African American intelligentsia legacy, an evaluative counterbalance to West's apologia for Washington's leadership had been bequeathed to progressive Black leaders in the early twentieth century by the Reverend Francis Grimké, pastor of the Fifteenth Street Presbyterian Church in Washington, DC, who reflected in a scathing manner on Washington's leadership legacy in 1915. As Grimké put it, "His death will be a loss to Tuskegee, but will not be to the race. The race will not in any way suffer from his death. It will not suffer in its higher aspirations, nor in its efforts on behalf of its rights, as it did in the death of Frederick Douglass. In neither of these respects did Mr. Washington make himself felt."[10]

It should also be pointed out that in 2006, the Yale University African American studies scholar Hazel Carby had suggested caution apropos phenomena like the Bookerite accommodationist "race relations" management schema that enchanted West in the early twenty-first century. In short, Washington's accommodationism bespoke autocracy, not democracy. As Carby, whose work cited here predated West's by two years, put it, "As we know from the history of the Tuskegee Machine . . . Booker T. Washington sought to hold in his hands to approve appointments [in African American institutions], to control and dominate access to the [African American] media . . . and mainstream sources of support. One hundred years later, dominant institutions and foundations, for example, are still too eager to assign to one or two black celebrity figures the right to grant a seal of approval to black intellectual and cultural work."[11]

Be that as it may, Cruse lays the groundwork for his intellectual affinity for the Washingtonian accommodationist strand of the evolving twentieth-century Black leadership or elite in chapter 2 of *The Crisis of the Negro Intellectual*, "Harlem Background." Here, Cruse presents a celebratory narrative history of the role of Black capitalist entrepreneurship in the rise of "Black Manhattan" (James Weldon Johnson's term) in the early 1900s to the 1930s. For Cruse, the preference among early Harlem businessmen for Washington's leadership paradigm was crucial. T. Thomas Fortune, the owner-editor of Black America's leading weekly newspaper of the era, the *New York Age,* was one of the more prominent proponents of Washingtonian accommodationism. Another leading pro-Washington business figure was the real estate developer Philip A. Payton.

According to Cruse, a unique form of Black economic development prevailed in early twentieth-century Black Manhattan because there was a surplus of good middle-class housing and apartments—built initially by white real estate speculators—that white Americans in New York City virtually ignored. This provided an opportunity for Black middle-class property acquisition in Harlem "in mass proportions around 1905," he observed. Cruse saw this as the foundation of an environment that favored Black Nationalism in early twentieth-century Harlem, stating, "The origins of Harlem's black community are to be found in the rise of black economic nationalism."

The entrepreneur Philip Payton was the central figure in this regard, along with his Afro-American Realty Company. Cruse waxes euphorically on the Bookerite accommodationist strand among Harlem's emergent twentieth-century Black elite:

> The spirit behind this [Harlem development] was [Black] economic nationalism. The economic organization behind this nationalism was the Afro-American Realty Company, a group of Negro leaders, businessmen, and politicians of whom the leading voices were Philip A. Payton, a real estate man, and Charles V. Anderson, a Republican Party stalwart who, in 1905, was appointed Collector of Internal Revenue in New York by Theodore Roosevelt. Behind these men stood T. Thomas Fortune of the *New York Age*, the oldest and most influential Negro newspaper in New York. But behind them all stood the guiding mind of Booker T. Washington and his National Negro Business League founded in 1900. All of the personalities in or around

the Afro-American Realty Company were proteges of Washington and members of his business league. They were, thus, representatives of Washington's Tuskegee Machine, a power in Negro affairs, and the bane of civil rights radicals led by W. E. B. Du Bois and his Niagara Movement of 1905.[12]

To Cruse's mind, the experience of the Afro-American Realty Company in Harlem paved the way for the high point of Black Americans' modernization in future years. The preparatory conditions for such Black economic nationalism owed a great debt to Washington, Cruse believed, so much so, in fact, that Cruse reports on the fourteenth annual gathering of Washington's Tuskegee Negro Conference, originally founded in 1891. There, his hero waxed rosily about the Afro-American Realty Company, advising his Black audience to "Get some property. . . . Get a home of your own." Above all, at the conference, Washington articulated one of his favorite uplift-the-Black-race mantras: "When [our] Race gets Bank Book, its Troubles will cease."[13]

In this astonishingly pro-Washington moment, Cruse seems devoid of solid analytical capability. After all, any cogent member of the civil rights leadership sector among African Americans in the early twentieth century (Du Bois, Grimké, Monroe Trotter, Ida Wells-Barnett) could have told Washington's audience at his fourteenth annual Tuskegee Negro Conference that without government-protected human and citizenship rights within a non-racist democratic American society, this was one of myriad Bookerite mantras that was supremely naive—and to quote it in 1967 was even more so! Furthermore, there's something approaching intellectual dishonesty on Cruse's part in this discussion, because he does not inform his readers that the civil rights activists among the early twentieth-century Black leadership represented by Du Bois fully understood the importance of Black-communitarian advancement. Du Bois explicitly articulated the importance of this perspective throughout his 1903 masterwork *The Souls of Black Folk* and in numerous subsequent writings, as expounded upon by Elliott Rudwick in *W. E. B. Du Bois: A Study in Minority Group Leadership* (1960) and by Henry Lee Moon in *The Emerging Thought of W. E. B. Du Bois* (1972).[14]

Be that as it may, Cruse lets his readers in on just how thrilled he himself is to have discovered the historical record of the Afro-American Realty Company's business successes in the period of modern Harlem.

"The Afro-American Realty Company lasted about five years," Cruse informs us, "[initiating] a wave of real estate buying among Harlem's new [middle-class] Negro arrivals."[15] What is more, he says, Payton and his company used capitalist modalities for Black modernization without causing anxiety among white Americans—which is to say, Payton's strategies sat well with white Americans; there was no fear among white residents or business owners of Black people "getting out of their place" or "uppity" thanks to the accommodationist-oriented business sector of the evolving twentieth-century Black elite.

Indeed, in Cruse's research on the early development of Black Harlem, he was satisfied to discover that conservative white people easily adjusted to the Black capitalist successes represented by Payton's Afro-American Realty Company, which in turn was influenced especially by accommodationism. As Cruse puts it, "Despite much bitter feeling [between Blacks and whites] during a fifteen year struggle of Negroes to gain a foothold, Harlem was won [by the accommodationist sector of Black leaders] without serious violence." This amounted to a major African American breakthrough, in Cruse's eyes, which he celebrated with the observation that the accommodationist brand of "nationalism had become aggressive and assertive in economics, but conservative in civil rights politics."[16]

Put another way, in Cruse's analytical scheme of things, the accommodationist-oriented Black entrepreneurs and politicians in early Harlem were the genuine Black leadership or elite sector. But what about the Black leadership sector oriented toward civil rights activism that launched the Niagara Movement in 1905 and, four years later, in alliance with upper-class white liberals, the National Association for the Advancement of Colored People?

Problematics of Cruse's Pro-Black Nationalism

Harold Cruse, I think, was rather adroit at producing a historical narrative that elevated the Black capitalist activity in Harlem of Philip Payton and his circle who subscribed to Booker T. Washington's accommodationist Black leadership methodology. Cruse also made clever use of his narrative to delegitimize the Black leadership sector oriented toward civil rights activism. In fact, at one point, Cruse is furious at Black scholars who sympathized with civil rights activism, noting that "Even writers such as John Hope Franklin and E. Franklin Frazier fail to mention either Payton, his realty company or even the men around him. . . . This omission of the role of [Black economic] nationalism leaves much of the analysis common to Negro historiography open to question."[17]

Indeed, for Cruse, the fact that leading Black intellectuals neglected economic and financial successes among the accommodationist-oriented leadership in Black Harlem's nascent years was unforgivable, nearly traitorous behavior. James Weldon Johnson's writings on the early period of Harlem's development placed him at the top of Cruse's hit list. As executive director of the NAACP during the 1920s, Johnson was the period's preeminent Black civil rights leader, and as such, his views about figures like Payton, who represented Washington's accommodationist version of what Cruse called Black economic nationalism, carried enormous weight. In *Black Manhattan* (1930), Johnson's portrait of early twentieth-century Harlem, he offered a fair-minded appraisal of Payton and his leadership circle: "The matter of better and still better housing for colored people in New York became the dominating idea of . . . [Payton's] life," observed Johnson, "and he worked on it as long as he lived. When Negro New Yorkers evaluate their benefactors in their own race, they must find that not many have done more than Phil Payton; for much of what has made Harlem the intellectual and artistic capital of the Negro world is in good part due to [him]."[18]

Yet Johnson also understood the larger systemic American dynamics within which the Black business advances of Payton and his circle occurred: within the white supremacist edifice that broadly subordinated African American citizens in general and hemmed in sectors among the Black elite as well. For Johnson, then, no serious forward-looking appraisal of the advances made by Payton and his cohort in early Harlem could be achieved without placing those advances in the broader context of a racist American society, one that tenaciously restricted the human and citizenship rights of Black people. This analytical strategy on Johnson's part was a matter of much annoyance to Cruse.

It happened that during the World War I era, Payton's Afro–American Realty Company went bankrupt. As Johnson appraised the company's failure, it was not merely a technical matter of the breakdown of a single Black capitalist's enterprise. Rather, for Johnson, the bankruptcy of Payton's business was connected with systemic racist patterns in the United States. He put it astutely in *Black Manhattan*: "It is idle to expect the Negro in Harlem or anywhere else to build business in general upon a strictly racial foundation or to develop it to any considerable proportions strictly within the limits of the patronage, credit, and financial resources of the [Negro] race."[19]

In other words, Johnson was saying that Black people required fully realized American citizenship rights so that those who were business inclined, like Payton, could have access to the full range of American capitalist opportunities, just as white entrepreneurs among ethnic groups like the Irish were achieving in the post–World War I era. Furthermore, for Johnson and other proponents of the activism leadership paradigm, challenging American racism in general meant opening the broader social-mobility doors of American society as a whole, not maintaining or creating separate avenues of modern social existence for Black people. In his 1935 essay "Negro Americans, What Now?," Johnson wrote,

> We should by all means make our schools and institutions as excellent as we can possibly make them; and by that very act we reduce the certainty that they will forever remain schools and institutions for "Negroes only." . . . We should gather all the strength and experience we can from imposed segregation. But any good we are able to derive from the system we should consider as a means, not an end. The strength and experience we gain from it should be applied to the objective of *entering into*, not *staying out of*, the [American] body politic.[20]

Now, what especially perturbed Cruse about Johnson's linkage of the Afro-American Realty Company's glass-ceiling experience in 1915 to the racial-caste marginalization of Black people in American society generally was the reinforcement this perspective gave the civil rights activism and integrationist sectors among the Black elite. Thus, in responding to Johnson's commentary on the company's demise, Cruse asserted his most strident pro–Black Nationalist thinking: "This was, of course, an old NAACP 'integration' type of argument, and became the interracial rationalization for evading the issue of [Black] nationalism and its economic imperatives for the Negro community. The logic of this argument has been retarding and detrimental to the Negroes' ghetto welfare."[21]

Cruse went on to reject in full Johnson's integrationist-leaning commentary on the experience of the Afro-American Realty Company. For Cruse, the correct leadership methodology for African American modern development in the early twentieth century was some variant of Black Nationalism, and Washington's accommodationist variant was, Cruse believed, tested and workable. Labeling Johnson, Du Bois, Trotter, and other proponents of civil rights activism mouthpieces for "an old NAACP 'integration' type of argument," Cruse observed that "The real reason Negro businessmen have not been able to gain 'patronage [and] credit' outside the 'financial resources of the [Negro] race' is because they failed precisely to 'build business upon a strictly racial foundation.' In other words, Negroes in Harlem have never achieved economic control inside Harlem or inside any other major black community."[22]

More assertively than in any other place in *The Crisis of the Negro Intellectual*, Cruse presents a deep preference for the Black Nationalist developmental approach here. This notwithstanding, it must be noted in this regard that Cruse also exhibits a great deal of conceptual confusion, because early in his discussion of "economic black nationalism," he supports this approach by way of analogy with what he views as the modern developmental experience of white ethnic groups, holding in high regard those groups' ability and savvy in using their ethnocentric patterns, their "separateness," their skill at maintaining separatist ethnic enclaves. While this formulation rings sympathetically in the ears of Cruse and many other Black Nationalist intellectuals, we know it to be historically erroneous.

Although the extensive historical literature on the development of white ethnic groups shows that they undertook ethnic-separatist mechanisms equivalent to what African American intellectuals like Cruse have in mind when propagating Black Nationalist mechanisms, in terms of business and industry, none of the white ethnic-separatist mechanisms would have been capable of producing viable modernization development for even 10 percent of their population on their own without connections to WASP-owned and -run institutions.

Thus, in light of the real historical experience of white ethnic groups in the evolving twentieth century, the social system of African Americans at the time was no more capable of fashioning ethnic-separatist modernization development than white ethnic groups were. Indeed, it is rather strange that Cruse allowed his fervent commitment to Black Nationalism to prevent him from recognizing that the American racist edifice imposed crippling constraints on the ability of African American citizens to establish viable, Black-run modernization development mechanisms.

This, of course, is precisely what Johnson so clearly grasped about the bankruptcy of Payton's Afro-American Realty Company during the World War I era. In years prior and years to come, it was precisely those white supremacist processes that had to be challenged and vanquished before the entrepreneurial talents of Black people like Payton could begin to gain adequate access to national-level banking, investment, and technical resources. It wouldn't be until the second half of the twentieth century, under the mass-based pressure of the African American civil rights movement, that this occurred. And I believe it is a certainty that this never would have occurred had Washington's accommodationist leadership paradigm trumped the civil rights activism leadership paradigm among the Black elite.

Writing some forty years since the publication of *The Crisis of the Negro Intellectual*, I find it strange just how badly Cruse misconstrued the pertinaciously oppressive impact of American racism on African Americans' quest for viable modernization development. Furthermore, in a curious way, this aspect of Cruse's discourse was a kind of prelude to that of the first-generation cohort of conservative Black intellectuals who emerged in the late 1970s, who share both Cruse's preference for Bookerite accommodationism and his misperceptions.

Cruse's Critique of Civil Rights Activism and Interracialism

At the core of *The Crisis of the Negro Intellectual*, Harold Cruse devotes most of his discourse to the experiences of civil rights activism networks and organizations, and of academics, novelists, and playwrights, artistic performers, and journalists or media personalities of that bent. His arguments are skewed toward Black Nationalism, and two fundamental propositions inform Cruse's thinking in this area: one, that civil rights activism and interracialism among the evolving Black intelligentsia was governed by "psychological umbilical ties to [white] paternalism"; and two, that the mediating process between the Black intelligentsia and "white paternalism" owed much to "the Jewish [leftist] involvement in this interracial process over the last fifty-odd years. The American Jew as political media-tor between Negro and Anglo-Saxon [WASPs] must be terminated by Negroes themselves."[23]

Sources of Interracialism Among Black Intellectuals

The issue of Jewish leftist intellectuals' involvement as interracial media-tors for Black intellectuals obsessed Harold Cruse. In chapter 6 of *The Cri-sis of the Negro Intellectual*, "Jews and Negroes in the Communist Party," Cruse strains for an explanation of their role as "mediator between Negro and Anglo-Saxon":

> In Negro-Jewish relations in the Communist left, there has been an intense undercurrent of jealousy, enmity, and competition over the prizes of group political power and intellectual prestige. In this strug-gle, the Jewish intellectuals—because of superior organization, drive, intellectual discipline, money and the motive power of their cultural compulsions—have been able to win out. In the name of Negro-White unity (the party's main interracial slogan), the Jewish Communists acted out the role of political surrogates for the "white" working class, and thereby gained the political whip of intellectual and theoretical domination of the Negro question.[24]

One might ask, Why was Cruse obsessed with the relationship between Jewish leftists and African American intellectuals? I think this issue offered Cruse at least a partial explanation for what he considered a baffling phe-nomenon among the evolving Black intelligentsia: the failure of civil rights activists and members of the radical Black intelligentsia to fashion a broad-based Black-ethnic infrastructure, a group-wide Black Nationalist agency, if you will; or, alternatively, the failure of mainline Black activists and intel-ligentsia during this time to at least fashion limited alliances with Marcus Garvey's UNIA, which, after all, had secured a broad appeal among urban working-class African Americans, and some middle-class ones too.

Alas, in Cruse's analytical schema, white "umbilical paternalism" pre-vented the rise of serious Black Nationalism among the evolving African American intelligentsia. In keeping with other white ethnics, he saw

Jewish intellectuals as executing the umbilical paternalist role, partly by spawning intra-Black cleavages within the mainline African American intelligentsia, especially the Black American–West Indian cleavage. Cruse traces this cleavage as follows: "as far back as 1919 one of the problems of the first Negroes to enter the newly emerging Communist leftwing was the ideological split between American and West Indian Negroes." From the late 1920s onward, says Cruse, "the split was exacerbated by the rise of Garvey [Black] Nationalism."[25]

Cruse's Staunch Anti-leftist Mind-Set

Important as the Black American–West Indian intellectual cleavage was in Cruse's discourse, the decisive factor that undercut a prominent place for Black Nationalism among the period's African American intelligentsia was the ideology and practice of interracialism. Listen to his formation of the reasons for his staunch antipathy to interracialism and its white leftist purveyors:

> During the Communist Party's "Anglo-Saxon" period of Dunne, Minor, William and Earl Browder, etc., there was more open inquiry into the precise nature of the Negro question than there was to be later on. . . . There was a certain flexibility and a willingness to survey and debate. But this open-mindedness and freshness went out of the Communist Party very rapidly. By 1929, when the West Indian–American Negro era of debate began, an unyielding, narrow-minded rigidity permeated the Party's thought on all questions. . . . [It was] a period of cheap militancy, imitative posturing, and blind evasion of Negro realities. The West Indian–American Negro braintrust could not utter a single theoretical idea about themselves unless they first invoked the precedent of the Moscow "line." . . .
>
> This situation led inexorably to the period of Jewish dominance in the Communist Party. It culminated in the emergence of Herbert Aptheker and other assimilated Jewish Communists, who assumed the mantle of spokesmanship on Negro affairs, thus burying the Negro radical potential deeper and deeper in the slough of white intellectual paternalism.[26]

There might be something to say for Cruse's bitter skepticism toward the relationship of interracialism and African American intellectuals in the American Marxist movement from the 1920s and into the 1950s. But Cruse carries his bitterness toward white leftist (in particular Jewish) purveyors of interracialism much too far, ruling out the possibility that progressive white intellectuals might possess that combination of radical intellectual acumen and a Black-friendly humanism required to produce strategies serviceable to the needs of working-class African Americans. It seems that a paranoid Black Nationalist view of leftist white intellectuals was rather axiomatic in Cruse's thinking.

Indeed, he could be contemptuous and catty in the manner in which he dismissed leftist white intellectuals as contributors to progressive strategies serviceable to Black people. "The white Left," says Cruse, "does not possess a single idea, tactic or strategy in its theoretical arsenal that can make the Negro protest movement [of the 1960s] a revolutionary one. All it can achieve is to intervene and foster such tactics as will get some persevering Negro activist leader jailed, framed, or exiled for utterly romantic reasons." Cruse goes on with this putdown of white leftists, and thus of interracialism:

> Association with white Marxists warps the social perception of left-wing Negro intellectuals to the extent that they also fail to see the factors of their own dynamic. Over the past forty-five years many of the best Negro minds have passed on, through, and out of the Marxist Left [some of whose experiences Cruse criticizes in his book—Richard Wright, Claude McKay, Ruby Dee, Ossie Davis, Julian Mayfield, etc.]. Their creative and social perceptions have been considerably dulled in the process, and their collective, cumulative failures over the decades have contributed to the contemporary poverty and insolvency of Negro intellectuals as a class.[27]

Despite Cruse's rather fierce antipathy to the role of white leftist intellectuals, Jewish and otherwise, as mediators of a variety of interracialist ideological patterns among the evolving twentieth-century Black intelligentsia, he reserved a special place in his discourse for assaulting the role of foreign-born Black intellectuals as purveyors of interracialism. His targets were from the Caribbean, and throughout his discussion of the place of West

Indian intellectuals within the African American intelligentsia, one detects a certain neurotic edge, an emotive rigidity.

Cruse's Antipathy to West Indian Intellectuals

Although Cruse viewed white intellectuals as primarily responsible for spreading what he saw as an interracialist virus among the evolving twentieth-century African American intelligentsia, thereby weakening its ability to develop a Black Nationalist developmental trajectory, he also believed that the leftist strand among immigrant West Indian intellectuals contributed to furthering this contagion among the African American intelligentsia. Indeed, Cruse believed that immigrant West Indian intellectuals possessed something akin to a generic need to traffic in interracialism. For Cruse, during the era between the two world wars there prevailed among Caribbean immigrant intellectuals "a psychology of . . . accommodation to American white bourgeois values . . . [more than with the] essentials of the American Negro struggle."[28] This, in turn, resulted in multilayered disputes and conflicts within the ranks of progressive African American intellectuals as to political relationships with leftist white intellectuals, and thus also with white Americans in general.

It should be pointed out that a major historical scholar has disputed the veracity of Cruse's claim that Caribbean immigrant intellectuals maneuvered interracialism in a way that produced corrosive fissures within the ranks of progressive Black intellectuals. The Columbia University historian Winston James has demonstrated—quite conclusively, I think—in his seminal work *Holding Aloft the Banner of Ethiopia: Caribbean Radicalism in Early Twentieth-Century America* (1998) that West Indian intellectuals were no more prone to that "psychology of . . . accommodation to American white bourgeois values" than were progressive elements among the African American intelligentsia. James reveals numerous historiographical and evidentiary errors in Cruse's treatment of the historical record regarding the relationship between Caribbean immigrant intellectuals and domestic-born Black intellectuals.[29]

Cruse develops his portrait of the cleavage-making role of West Indian intellectuals within the African American intelligentsia through a probe of the activities of the African Blood Brotherhood, a radical Black organization founded after World War I by a group of Caribbean-born intellectuals that included Cyril Briggs, Richard Moore, W. A. Domingo, and Grace Campbell. According to Cruse, the African Blood Brotherhood "represented two or three simultaneous aspects of Harlem radical developments in the 1920s" and operated at the crossroads of "a conflict between American and West Indian Negroes over radical policies, inasmuch as [A. Philip] Randolph and his co-editor [of *The Messenger*, Chandler] Owen considered themselves the leaders of 'the New Negro' trend, a strictly African-American development."[30] However, in his deeply researched critique of Cruse's portrayal of the Black American–Caribbean cleavage among the Black elite, James squarely challenges Cruse's story line: "Contrary to Cruse's repeated notion of a West Indian versus American Negro split at the *Messenger* . . ., the fact is that in 1923 Domingo was the only Caribbean person who severed connections with the magazine. Caribbeans such as Frank Crosswaith continued to write for it; so did Eric Walrond and, most prodigiously, J. A. Rogers, from Jamaica, who continued to make his distinguished contribution."[31]

It would appear that Cruse was not as precise as he should have been in his treatment of the relationship between immigrant and domestic Black intellectuals. For example, at another point in Cruse's exploration of this relationship, he chastises African Blood Brotherhood intellectuals like Briggs and Moore for what he called their turncoat behavior toward the Garvey movement, in whose networks the two men gave shape to the brotherhood. Between 1919 and the early 1920s, however, Cruse claims that they opportunistically deserted the Garvey movement for greater resources derived from ties with interracialist white leftists. James's research, however, disputes this interpretation of the leftist political trajectory among Caribbean intellectuals during the 1920s.

Be this as it may, it is important to recognize that Cruse's take on the history of Caribbean leftist intellectuals' relationship with their Black American counterparts was informed by his strongly held belief that Caribbean intellectuals advanced interracial patterns among African Americans. Furthermore, Cruse reserved a special antipathy for what he considered a veritable form of political treachery among Caribbean intellectuals when it came to their relationship with Black Nationalist–oriented groups. As Cruse put it in his discussion of these issues in *The Crisis of the Negro Intellectual*, he viewed West Indian leftists' "onslaught against Marcus Garvey [and the UNIA] . . . [as] one of vituperation, rancor and bitter accusations of deceit, dishonesty, fraud, lunacy, racial disloyalty, charlatanism and ignorance."[32]

His contempt toward Caribbean leftist intellectuals exploded when he delved into the interactions between these intellectuals and white leftists—within the Communist Party—during the 1924 convention of Garvey's UNIA in Harlem:

> It was very apparent that these infiltrators used by the Communists were none other than the West Indian members of the African Blood Brotherhood. In this regard it is ironic that in the legend built up around the personality of Garvey, the notion has come down that his worst enemies and detractors were all American Negroes [e.g., Du Bois, Randolph, Owen, etc.] who did not appreciate the man's nationalist genius. However, the truth of the matter was that while Garvey's most inspired followers were West Indians, so were his most vitriolic and effective enemies—both in the United States . . . and in the West Indies. . . .
>
> West Indians are never so "revolutionary" as when they are away from the Islands.[33]

Finally, it should be noted in Cruse's discussion of the role of Caribbean intellectuals that his overall conclusion is that there was nothing genuinely radical or militant about these intellectuals. Why? Because they structured their variant of civil rights activism against American racism along the lines of the same kind of interracialism and political relationships employed by mainline African American intellectuals like W. E. B. Du Bois and James Weldon Johnson. For Cruse, shedding interracialist patterns, not advancing them, was the true route to Black modernization development.

Pseudo-Militancy in Cruse's Discourse

Cruse believed that the only genuinely radical or militant political patterns available to twentieth-century African Americans were those associated with Black Nationalist modes of modernization development. Furthermore, he viewed Booker T. Washington's accommodationist leadership approach as a variant of the Black Nationalist mode, owing to the accommodationist preference for not utilizing African Americans' resources to conduct civil rights activism against America's white supremacist edifice.

The preference of the mainline Black leadership represented by Du Bois, Johnson, and the NAACP for challenging American racism through civil rights activism rendered them a bête noire in Cruse's analytical schema.

Indeed, throughout *The Crisis of the Negro Intellectual* there is a basic argumentative and narrative strategy whereby Cruse—by manipulating the term "interracialism" to delegitimize the civil rights activism or NAACP sector of the mainline African American intelligentsia—attempts to disabuse African Americans (the author's target readership) of the popular notion that the term "militant" should apply to the NAACP leadership sector. He thereby proceeds to appropriate the term for Black-owned entrepreneurial business patterns among the evolving twentieth-century African American elite, a narrative maneuver Cruse commences in chapter 2 of *The Crisis of the Negro Intellectual*, where he relates the rise of Harlem in the early 1900s.

Cruse often uses the expression "economic black nationalism" when discussing Black-owned business endeavors, and simultaneously introduces the names of Booker T. Washington and the National Negro Business League in that context. Moreover, when Cruse writes of the civil rights activism of the period, he draws attention to its integrationist and interracial patterns, characterizing these patterns as reflective of a pathological psychic dependence on white people. Nowhere in these accounts, however, does Cruse mention that the practitioners of "economic black nationalism" were also involved in interracial patterns, such as loans from white-owned banks, or that Washington's nationwide power base among African Americans in business and the professions was sustained by financial grants from white capitalist patrons.

Thus, with the analysis that he embroiders with militant rhetoric, Cruse turns on its head the normal understanding of so-called militant leadership. The fact of the matter was that the kind of Bookerite accommodationist economic relationship between the evolving twentieth-century Black elite and the established white business class was totally conservative—indeed, reactionary—because it was a Black-white relationship that permitted very little if any challenge of America's white supremacist edifice by the Black elite.

But never mind. In Cruse's eyes, and thus in his analytical schema, his Black-communitarian understanding of Washington's leadership methodology—an outlook that connected Bookerite accommodationism with the "economic black nationalism" element in the Black elite—produced a composite legitimate African American leadership sector. Let's call it a composite Black-communitarian elite, for want of a better term.

Thus, with such narrative maneuvers—deception, really—Harold Cruse turns upside down the usual understanding of the last century's Black leadership among his African American readership. For his target audience, he introduced a new understanding of the comparative attributes of Black Americans' civil rights activism or of the NAACP leadership sector on the one hand and the composite Black-communitarian leadership sector on the other. In this way, Cruse's narrative strategies in *The Crisis of the Negro Intellectual* gave the Black Nationalist–type leadership, noted for its inclusion of Black-communitarian features, a certain militant aura when contrasted with the civil rights activism notion of leadership.

Personal Reflections on Cruse's Pseudo-Militant Analysis

It was, of course, in the late 1960s, during the Black-consciousness phase of the civil rights movement, when Cruse put forth what I view as his pseudo-militant analysis in *The Crisis of the Negro Intellectual*. When Cruse was producing a facile Black-militant patina for his narrative style, both the integrationist element and the Black-communitarian element coexisted within the larger civil rights movement. Cruse, I think, was aware that important constituencies within the broader movement would be especially attentive to the gloss he applied to his narrative and text.

Leftist and progressive African American intellectuals and professionals like myself were surprised—stunned even—at Cruse's success at employing a shallow argument to shape such a critical narrative about and against the mainline civil rights activism sector of the African American intelligentsia and leadership. I recall vividly how caught off guard I was to discover firsthand this aspect of the appeal of Cruse's book among the expanding population of activist-oriented African American students on white college campuses starting in the late 1960s. I had numerous discussions about Cruse's book with Black students at Harvard in this period, which overlapped with the rise of what we then called Afro-American studies and Black studies programs on white campuses, an experience I documented in the chapter "From the Birth to a Mature Afro-American

Studies at Harvard, 1969–2000," in Lewis Gordon and Jane Anna Gordon's *A Companion to African American Studies* (2006).[34]

Harvard's dean of students, Archie Epps, one of the university's first Black administrators, had brought Malcolm X to speak at Harvard in 1963. He used this coup, one might call it, as a means of luring Cruse to come as well. Ten years later, Epps and I mounted a panel on Cruse's book, in conjunction with the staff of the *Harvard Advocate*, during the Alain Locke Forum. Held in the fall of 1973 in Harvard's Boylston Hall, the forum brought a host of speakers, including Cruse himself; Ralph Ellison; Albert Murray; Ewart Guinier, professor and chair of Afro-American studies at Harvard; and Nathan Huggins, then a history professor at Columbia University who would succeed Guinier as chair at Harvard in 1979–1980. Virtually all of the African American students who participated in this discussion accepted Cruse's analysis as a valid critique of the mainline civil rights activist sector of the African American intelligentsia and its leadership. Through the 1970s and into the 1980s, *The Crisis of the Negro Intellectual* secured a broad readership and even an iconic status among African American students on white campuses around the country, and at Black colleges in the South as well. It was Cruse's shrewd manipulation of narrative style that allowed him to achieve this ideological success.

Cruse Misconstrues the Liberal Impact of Civil Rights Activism

As I suggested in the early part of this chapter, *The Crisis of the Negro Intellectual* contains numerous conceptual, interpretive, analytical, and historiographical weaknesses. Perhaps the most important of these was Cruse's inability to grasp that the liberal and progressive use of interracialism—as a political orientation and modus operandi—by the civil rights activist sector of the evolving twentieth-century African American intelligentsia and leadership was a phenomenon of enormous political significance. It was, I think, Cruse's fierce, rather one-dimensional Black Nationalist mind-set that derailed his analytical and historiographical acumen in this matter.

In regard to challenging the American white supremacist oppression and pariahization of African American citizens from the late nineteenth century through most of the twentieth, the liberal-progressive use of interracialism by the civil rights activist sector of Black leadership eventually sparked what might be called progressive political spin-offs—namely, the feminist movement among white women. Similarly, the disability rights movement, in existence throughout the century, experienced a rebirth around this time, primarily among white Americans during its first wave. Still another progressive political spin-off of the 1970s was the gay liberation movement.

In short, *The Crisis of the Negro Intellectual* reveals unmistakably that Cruse was intellectually unable to grasp the idea that African American civil rights activism spawned progressive political movements among white Americans. It was perhaps a historical mission of this leadership mode—the mode associated with Du Bois, Johnson, and the NAACP—to fashion a challenge to American racism that, in turn, spawned viable liberal systemic outcomes for American society in general.

A Concluding Note: An Evaluative Balance Sheet

What kind of evaluative intellectual ranking can one apply to Harold Cruse's *The Crisis of the Negro Intellectual*? In evaluating Cruse's book alongside works by African American authors that warrant the designation "classic," because they set forth an enduring understanding of core dynamics that shaped modern African American existence, *The Crisis of the Negro Intellectual* does not, as far as I am concerned, warrant such a designation. I have in mind works such as *The Negro Wage Earner* by Lorenzo Green and Carter G. Woodson (1930); *Black Reconstruction in America* by Du Bois (1935); *Negro Education in Alabama* by Horace Mann Bond (1939); *The Negro Family in the United States* by E. Franklin Frazier (1939); *Deep South* by Allison Davis (1940); *Growing Up in the Black Belt* by Charles S. Johnson (1940); and *Black Metropolis* by St. Clair Drake and Horace B. Cayton (1945).

Let's put it another way: Is Cruse's book worthy of the intellectual ranking associated with the term "monumental"? Monumental works on core historical issues can have what might be called a mixed history in that they can be gauged over time by either their argumentative quality or by what I call their symbolic-ideological emissions. I'm inclined to measure the monumental dimension of Cruse's book less by its argumentative quality and more by these symbolic-ideological emissions, which have been an especially important feature of Cruse's book because of the particular era in which it appeared, and therefore, because of the contemporary needs that readers—above all, African American readers—brought to it, a matter of "the eyes of the beholder (reader)," as it were.

The beholders' eyes that I have in mind particularly were those of the Black-consciousness sector during the phase of the civil rights movement occurring from the 1960s to the early 1970s. A crucial component of the movement was located among an exploding population of Black students on white campuses, as well as students at traditional Negro colleges. Many who espoused Black consciousness had experienced dissatisfaction with the mainline civil rights activism among African American leadership. This dissatisfaction, in turn, produced a political leadership vacuum at the national level of African American society.

A variety of Black Nationalist–type organizations, such as the Nation of Islam, had resurfaced by the early 1960s, attempting to fill this vacuum in political leadership. The riotous upheavals among working-class African Americans in numerous urban areas, North and South, from 1964 onward can also be viewed as responses to this vacuum. Thus, one way to understand the impact of the symbolic-ideological emissions of *The Crisis of the Negro Intellectual* is to view its publication in this context. Cruse produced a work that was designed as a response to a perceived void in political leadership at the core of African American society, and there were thousands upon thousands awaiting its message. And its Black Nationalist–skewed ideological and political message—generating the book's powerful cathartic-racialist emissions—was skillfully rendered.

In regard to the operational processes governing American politics during the 1960s and 1970s, however, Cruse's ideological and political message was misguided. I suggest that it was rather bizarre of Cruse to advise African Americans in the late 1960s—thereby laying out an agenda for the 1970s—that the historical civil rights activism of the national Black leadership from the emancipation era into the twentieth century, spanning Frederick Douglass, W. E. B. Du Bois, Ida Wells-Barnett, James Weldon Johnson, A. Philip Randolph, and Walter White to Martin Luther King Jr., Ella Baker, Rosa Parks, Fannie Lou Hamer, was an error; that instead, Black Americans from the early twentieth century would have been better served politically and systemically had Booker T. Washington's accommodationist sector of the Black elite dominated national Black leadership. Listen to Cruse's formulation of this leadership issue in the context of twentieth-century African American developmental dynamics:

Failing this [civil rights leaders' refusal to bow to Washington's accommodationist doctrine], the black bourgeoisie has been condemned to remain forever marginal in relation to its own innate potential within American capitalism. It has also remained politically subservient, intellectually unfulfilled, and provincial. Thus, the black bourgeoisie was unprepared and unconditioned to play any leading sponsorship role in the Harlem Renaissance; this class was and still is culturally imitative and unimaginative.[35]

Here, Cruse lets his ideological and visceral antipathy to the civil rights activism strand of the evolving twentieth-century Black elite run amok, allowing it to obstruct good thinking and fair-minded historiography. First, I've already shown that the accommodationist-oriented sector of the emergent Black elite in the early 1900s could not have effected a Black-separatist or Black-communitarian mode of viable modernization any more than the elite of white ethnic groups were able to do for themselves in the same period. Thus, Johnson and the NACCP believed—correctly, I think—that until the racist marginalization and pariahization of Black people were legally obliterated, Philip Payton's Afro-American Realty Company and other Black business enterprises would continue to suffer gross inequalities in the political-economic sphere.

Second, it was a flagrant distortion by Cruse to argue that the political weakness of African Americans and their leadership during the twentieth century came about as a result of the civil rights leaders' rejection of Washington's accommodationist leadership approach. In Cruse's words, this rejection doomed that sector to a "politically subservient" status. Contrary to Cruse's interpretation, any honest reading of the historical record of American racism tells a very different story—namely, that the mainline Black elite as represented by the NAACP and other activist organizations remained in a "politically subservient" status because of the vicious and oppressive functioning of America's white supremacist edifice.

Although nowhere in *The Crisis of the Negro Intellectual* does Cruse demonstrate enough intellectual honesty to recognize it, nothing about Washington's accommodationist leadership methodology—including its alliance with what Cruse called "black economic nationalism"—would have enabled African American leadership to lay a political foundation that might allow them to overcome the politically subservient status imposed by American white supremacism. Only the civil rights activism sector of the

Black elite—the sector that Du Bois helped to fashion—eventually produced, from the 1950s onward, a mass-based political mobilization among African Americans that vanquished the legal structures of America's white supremacist edifice. It is, I think, one of the intellectually pathetic features of Cruse's book that its author could not textually grant this indisputable fact!

Note, finally, that Cruse formulates his overall evaluative reflections putting down the Black elite oriented toward civil rights activism by borrowing from E. Franklin Frazier's caricature in his book *Black Bourgeoisie* (1957). In Cruse's version of Frazier's argument, this Black elite played no role in the rise of the New Negro movement or Harlem Renaissance of the 1920s through the 1930s. As Cruse put it, the mainline Black elite during that time "remained . . . intellectually unfulfilled, and provincial. . . . The black bourgeoisie was unprepared and unconditioned to play any leading sponsorship role in the Harlem Renaissance."

Now, anyone familiar with the extensive literature on the New Negro movement or Harlem Renaissance does not have to dig very far into it to dispute Cruse's observation. The Black bourgeoisie or the elite elements associated with civil rights activism facilitated the period's artistic, literary, and overall intellectual output. Just read the pages of the Urban League's journal *Opportunity: Journal of Negro Life*, edited by the sociologist Charles S. Johnson, and the pages of the NAACP's journal *The Crisis*, edited by Du Bois, where can be found numerous examples of aesthetically rigorous art, literature, and philosophical discourse promulgated by African Americans.

Or just read the pages of weekly Negro newspapers around the country whose bourgeois owners and editors opened their publications to African American contributors to the New Negro and Harlem Renaissance movements—newspapers like the *Philadelphia Tribune*, the *Chicago Defender*, and the *Pittsburgh Courier*, to mention just a few. Furthermore, middle- and upper-middle-class African Americans influenced many Black churches to contribute to the New Negro and Harlem Renaissance movements, and many Black professional associations, women's associations, and colleges did likewise. In short, Cruse's dismissive observation on the mainline Black elite illustrates that he simply didn't know what he was talking about.[36]

It might also be mentioned that Cruse's overall evaluative putdowns of the civil rights activism sector of the Black elite condemned it not only as "intellectually unfulfilled and provincial" but also as "culturally imitative and unimaginative." Although here again Cruse is piggybacking on Frazier's arguments in *Black Bourgeoisie*, it happens that Cruse is just as wrong in this observation as Frazier was. Of course, this observation essentially levels a charge of intellectual charlatanism against the civil rights activism sector of the evolving twentieth-century Black elite. No doubt there were charlatans in the ranks of this Black elite, but no more so than in the bourgeois or elite ranks of its evolving white ethnic and WASP counterparts too.

Unfortunately, throughout perhaps two-thirds of the text of *The Crisis of the Negro Intellectual*, Cruse employs his crude polemical formulation charging charlatanism to dismiss the creative works of first-rate African American intellectuals of the twentieth century, including Claude McKay, Paul Robeson, Lorraine Hansberry, John Killens, Ruby Dee, Ossie Davis, Julian Mayfield, and LeRoi Jones. It should be stated plainly, however, that Cruse had neither academic training nor hands-on professional experience in art, creative writing, or theater that would lend much authority to his discourse on the creative facet of these Black intellectuals' productions. As a result, his polemical account of their careers was a jumbled mixture of dilettantish cultural criticism and ideological hubris.

Be that as it may, looking back from the vantage point of forty years at *The Crisis of the Negro Intellectual*, it deserves to be ranked as a monumental work. The book's audacious conceptual range in terms of topics treated, combined with its bold interpretive quest, make it so.

CHAPTER V

E. Franklin Frazier and
Black Bourgeoisie Reconsidered

As of this writing, it has been nearly fifty years since E. Franklin Frazier published his book *Black Bourgeoisie.* Frazier ranked at the top of a brilliant group of first-generation African American social scientists trained in the 1920s and 1930s, including Horace Mann Bond, Ralph J. Bunche, Allison Davis, John Aubrey Davis, St. Clair Drake, and Charles Spurgeon Johnson. By the time of Frazier's death in 1962, the economic and political groundwork were in place for the growth of the African American middle-class and professional sectors (Frazier's *la bourgeoisie noire*). Thus, the size of the Black bourgeoisie today surpasses anything Frazier could have imagined; it is several times what it was when Frazier wrote his book. And the dual status that the Black bourgeoisie holds within the Black and American settings is today infinitely more complex than it was two generations ago.

What was Frazier's initial focus in his study of what he called the "Black bourgeoisie"? In general, his probe of the African American middle- and upper-middle-class strata focused less on these strata's power-structure dimensions than on their societal dimensions. He took this analytical vantage point because the racial-caste marginalization of African Americans' status in American society prevented Blacks from winning any serious access to roles in the power structure.

Thus, inasmuch as racial-caste practices rigidly marginalized Black Americans and truncated their modern development, this in turn translated into a systematically distorted and dysfunctional African American subsystem within the overall modernizing American system. To describe the distortions that characterized this subsystem, Frazier and other social observers of African American life used the term "social pathology." Of course, many of these social pathologies were concentrated among the weak working-class and poor-majority sectors of Black Americans in the form of high crime rates, intragroup or fratricidal violence, weak family patterns, and so on. But in Frazier's analytical approach, the Black middle- and upper-middle-class strata—the bourgeoisie—also exhibited signs of social pathology.

In a review of Gunnar Myrdal's *An American Dilemma* that appeared in *The Crisis* in 1944, Frazier formulates his conception of a social pathology as follows: "Myrdal recognized the Negro community for what it was—a pathological phenomenon in American life. . . . He recognized that segregation [of the racial-caste variety] kept the Negro in poverty and ignorance. . . . It is not surprising then that he did not indulge in over-rating the achievements of the Negroes and the ability and character of their leaders." Of course, from this formulation, it is just one small step to Frazier's rather slashing critical formulations on the character of the Black bourgeoisie offered in his book of the same name. As he observes in the American edition,

The exclusion of middle-class Negroes from [equal] participation in the general life of the American community has affected their entire outlook on life. It has meant that whites did not regard the activities of Negroes as of any real consequence in American life. It has tended to encourage a spirit of irresponsibility or an attitude of "play" or make-believe among them. Consequently Negroes have "played" at conducting their schools, at running their businesses, and at practicing their professions. The spirit of play or make-believe has tended to distort or vitiate the ends of their most serious activities. Since the black bourgeoisie live largely in a world of make-believe, the masks which they wear to play their sorry roles conceal the feelings of inferiority . . . that haunt their inner lives. . . . Their escape into a world of make-believe with its sham "society" [conspicuous status seeking] leaves them with a feeling of emptiness and futility.[1]

Thus, looking back on the development of the African American bourgeoisie through the first fifty years of the twentieth century, Frazier focused on what I call its societal dimensions. For Frazier, these societal dimensions exhibited mainly dysfunctional tendencies as described above. Now, while there is undoubtedly an element of systemic truth in Frazier's pathological perspective on the Black bourgeoisie's first five decades, I would also argue that he exaggerated the application of his perspective. His discussion of consumeristic frivolity among the Black middle and upper-middle classes are exaggerated, for instance, especially in the context of similar obsession with conspicuous consumption among the bourgeoisie sector in white groups including WASPs, Irish Americans, and Jewish Americans. The same could be said for his thoughts on professional frivolity among Black and white groups. Evidence for the social pathologies among white ethnic groups can be found in Andrew Greeley's studies on Irish Americans, in *That Most Distressful Nation: The Taking of the American Irish* (1972), and in studies on the white-ethnic political class, such as Harold Foote Gosnell's *Machine Politics: Chicago Model* (1935), and Harold Zink's *City Bosses in the United States: A Study of Twenty Municipal Bosses* (1930).

Furthermore, for Frazier's discussion on this topic to be taken seriously, he was, I think, obligated to produce direct evidence for specific Black professionals and/or professional institutions that fell into his pathological category. Moreover, it seems to have never occurred to him that during this time there were countervailing patterns that involved high-level professional behavior among the African American middle- and upper-middle-class strata, represented broadly within the Black bourgeoisie among lawyers, doctors, teachers, businesspersons, dentists, engineers, scholars like himself, and so on. Following Frazier's death in 1962, a number of studies of high-performing professionals among middle-class African Americans during this period were published.[2]

In this connection, it should also be mentioned that Frazier exaggerated the role of middle-class Black women as purveyors of materialistic consumerism. Frazier failed to recognize that they performed constructively as contributors to the aggregate incomes of middle-class Black households. And as of the 1920s, they were employed outside their homes at two or three times the rate of middle-class white women.

An Overview

Within a decade of Frazier's death in 1962, the African American middle-class and professional sectors experienced significant advances in social mobility, sparked especially by public policies extracted from the federal government by the civil rights movement. In the first instance, between the 1960s and 1980s, there was a simultaneous growth of white-collar occupations among African Americans and a marked occupational differentiation. During the first five years of the 1960s, in fact, some 380,000 nonwhites (mainly African Americans) acquired white-collar employment, increasing the number of nonwhites in the middle class to some 4 million. And by 1980, about 40 percent of working African Americans had obtained white-collar jobs, this compared with 52 percent of white Americans and 32.4 percent of Latinos. There was also educational advancement for African Americans, with the number of Blacks graduating high school increasing from 42 to 75 percent between 1960 and 1980.[3]

A panoramic perspective on the position of African Americans in white-collar jobs is shown in table 5.1—covering the era from the end of the Great Depression in 1940 to 1980—from the National Academy of Sciences' major survey of the overall status of African Americans organized by Gerald David Jaynes and Robin M. Williams in the late 1980s. Numbering about 200,000 Black white-collar jobholders in 1940, this category had increased to 474,000 by 1960, and by 1980 the Black white-collar category had more than doubled, standing at 1,564,914.

An equally important feature of the expansion of white-collar employment among African Americans during the post-Frazier years was that both males and females shared in this transformation. Both at the lower and upper ranks of white-collar jobs, Black women strengthened their position relative to their white counterparts, more so, in fact, than did Black men. For example, by 1980, some 14 percent of Black women held professional/technical jobs compared to 17 percent of white women, whereas 8 percent of Black males held such jobs compared to 16 percent of employed white males.

Viewed in terms of specific professional/technical occupations by the early 1980s, the female/male percentage of these occupations among African Americans had advanced significantly. Within their categories (jobs held by all women/jobs held by all men),

- Black females held 7.4 percent and Black males 3.6 percent of accounting positions
- Black females held 9.4 percent and Black males 4.1 percent of computer specialist positions

TABLE 5.1
Selected white-collar occupations filled by Blacks, 1940–1980

	Number (Percent)									
Occupation	1940		1950		1960		1970		1980	
Managerial	62,220	(33.2)	112,020	(37.5)	121,762	(25.7)	170,035	(21.8)	487,432	(31.1)
Self-employed	49,760	(26.5)	73,560	(24.6)	63,357	(13.4)	34,893	(4.5)	21,781	(1.4)
Private salary	10,940	(5.8)	32,580	(10.9)	44,318	(9.3)	87,765	(11.2)	282,488	(18.1)
Government	1,240	(0.7)	5,250	(1.8)	12,282	(2.6)	46,388	(5.9)	181,847	(11.6)
Professional and technical	125,330	(66.8)	186,930	(62.5)	352,298	(74.3)	611,334	(78.2)	1,077,482	(68.9)
Clergy	17,920	(9.6)	19,110	(6.4)	14,530	(3.1)	12,850	(1.6)	16,195	(1.0)
Engineers	300	(0.2)	2,730	(0.9)	12,049	(2.5)	13,679	(1.8)	36,019	(2.3)
Lawyers and judges	1,000	(0.5)	1,530	(0.5)	2,970	(0.6)	3,728	(0.5)	15,277	(1.0)
Physicians	4,160	(2.2)	4,500	(1.5)	9,983	(2.1)	6,106	(0.8)	13,509	(0.9)
Social workers	2,720	(1.5)	6,750	(2.3)	15,345	(3.2)	40,791	(5.2)	88,512	(5.6)
Teachers	67,660	(36.0)	90,180	(30.2)	150,743	(31.8)	240,073	(30.7)	424,755	(27.1)
	187,520	(100.0)	298,950	(100.0)	474,060	(100.0)	781,369	(100.0)	1,564,914	(100.0)

Source: Gerald David Jaynes and Robin M. Williams Jr., *A Common Destiny: Blacks and American Society* (Washington, DC: National Academy Press, 1989), 170.

- Black females held 10.8 percent and Black males 7.9 percent of personnel and labor specialist positions
- Black females held 0.5 percent and Black males 2.1 percent of medical and dental practitioner positions
- Black females held 9.2 percent and Black males 8.4 percent of health technician positions
- Black females held 5.3 percent and Black males 3.3 percent of college teaching positions
- Black females held 10.2 percent and Black males 5.5 percent of school teaching positions
- Black females held 12.2 percent and Black males 2.6 percent of school administrative positions
- Black females held 4.6 percent and Black males 2.6 percent of banking and financial official positions
- Black females held 6.7 percent and Black males 5.6 percent of engineering and science technician positions
- Black females held 7.1 percent and Black males 3.1 percent of lawyer and judge positions[4]

Moreover, the impact of affirmative action policies and practices persisted into the 1990s, resulting in a steady advance of middle-class and professional-level occupations among African Americans. Selected aspects of this advance are shown in table 5.2.

New Mainstreaming Patterns

Middle-class and professional-sector employment patterns among African Americans in the post-Frazier era have shifted from a Black "ghetto" market to nationwide job markets, including bank chains, insurance companies, rental firms, airline companies, white college campuses, chemical firms, computer businesses, a broad range of government jobs, and scientific research firms. New occupations provided by government agencies have played a role in this process of job-market mainstreaming; government agencies now employ some 30 percent of white-collar Black families, compared to 16 percent of white-collar white families.

Sociologically, the new occupational dispersion—which was inconceivable among the middle class studied by Frazier in the middle of the twentieth century—affects a broad range of social relationships among the Black bourgeoisie, thereby altering the historical patterns. New kinds of workplace milieus for middle-class and professional Blacks afforded them new social networks and cultural orientations. When those changes were reinforced, in turn, by the growing shift from residing in compact Black urban communities to residing in more racially dispersed suburban communities, we have in place the preconditions for a new kind of systemic mainstreaming of the Black bourgeoisie—a phenomenon that was not on the agenda when Frazier wrote about the potential for mobility among that community.

We have no better source for documenting the new occupational and sociocultural dispersion of the African American upper stratum than *Black Enterprise*, the first Black multimillion-dollar entrepreneurial magazine, owned and edited by Earl Graves. For example, in September 1975, *Black*

TABLE 5.2
Selected middle-class occupations held by Black people, 1990 (numbers in the thousands)

Occupations	U.S. total	Percent Black
Managers (marketing, management, public relations)	630	2.1
Managers (properties, real estate)	302	6.3
Computer systems analysts	987	5.8
Engineers	1,919	3.6
Registered nurses	2,494	7.1
Therapists (occupational and physical)	479	7.2
Computer programmers	882	6.7
University teachers	846	4.8
Special education teachers	467	9.5
Health technologists	2,595	12.9
Biological scientists	83	2.0
Chemists	96	5.2
Engineering technicians and technologists	1,640	7.2
Accountants and auditors	1,325	7.6
Educational and vocational counselors	192	15.5

Source: Adapted from "What You're Worth," *Black Enterprise*, February 1993, 67.

Enterprise evaluated the degree of Black penetration of the executive ranks of major American foundations. Among them were the Kettering Foundation, the Borden Foundation, the Avon Foundation, the Lilly Endowment, the John Hay Whitney Foundation, the TRW Foundation, the Josiah Macy Jr. Foundation, the Twentieth Century Fund, the Borg-Warner Foundation, the Charles Stewart Mott Foundation, the Phelps Stokes Fund, the Rockefeller Brothers Fund, the Rockefeller Foundation, the Ford Foundation, the Cleveland Foundation, and the Chicago Foundation.

Equally noteworthy has been the Black penetration of mid-level technical and managerial ranks of medium-size and large corporations. For more than twenty-five years, monthly issues of *Black Enterprise* carried the column "Making It," comprising a job profile of persons exemplifying the occupational dispersion of the Black bourgeoisie into mainstream corporations. In the September and October 1979 issues, the column listed the following instances of occupational breakthrough by the Black elite:

Hallie Anderson—promoted to supervisor of the group claims department at the Phoenix Life Insurance Company (Hartford); Bill Baker—appointed manager of communications for Blue Cross/Blue Shield (Colorado); Jack Bell—elected president of the Texas Restaurant Association and the first Black person to head his 5,500-member group; Columbus Coleman—promoted to executive vice president and general manager of Wells Fargo Securities Clearance Corporation (New York); Tom Finch—formerly director of matrix operations for Meadowlands and Giants Stadium (New Jersey) was appointed director of promotions at Arlington Park Race Track Corporation (Arlington Heights, Illinois); Jay Francis—elected vice president of Westinghouse Broadcasting Company; Edward T. Gilliam II—appointed internal audit manager at Toro Company (Minneapolis); Cressworth Lander—appointed managing director of Civil Aeronautics Board; James Lockhart—formerly vice president of legal affairs at Budget Rent-a-Car Corporation was appointed vice president for public affairs for TransAmerica Corporation; George Brown—appointed to executive vice president at Grumman Energy Systems, Inc. (Bethpage, New York); Stephen Daniels— appointed manager for Reservationist Trans World Airlines (New

York region); and Alfred Fornay—appointed creative director at Revlon Corporation.

The importance of these social-class transformations in the job market among middle-class and professional African Americans cannot be over-emphasized. Such transformations freed the new Black bourgeoisie from the traditionally segregated job market that had socially rigidified and politically emasculated the old Black bourgeoisie, spawning the social pathologies described by Frazier. These job-market transformations among middle-class and professional Black people represent an unprec-edented randomization of white-collar occupations and white-collar job-market regional locations for African Americans. This has meant above all that members of the new Black bourgeoisie have access to a variety of technical and cultural networks that ultimately facilitate a new kind of systemic mainstreaming of middle-class and professional African Americans.

In general, the systemic mainstreaming of the Black bourgeoisie in the post-Frazier era has occurred along a protracted and uneven developmen-tal trajectory, not a straight line. This is not only because of the tenacity of racist sociocultural patterns among white Americans but also because of the sway of sociocultural friendship and network patterns among African Americans. Thus, in the first instance, the new opportunities available to middle-class and professional African Americans catalyzed a new range of Black social networks. Among the new associational infrastructure that evolved within the post-Frazier Black bourgeoisie, the following have been representative: the National Association of Black Accountants (founded in 1970); the National Association of Black Manufacturers (1971); the National Black Contractors Association (1972); the National Black Media Coalition (1973); the National Black Network (1973); the Council of Concerned Black Executives (ca. 1975); and the Organization of Black Airline Pilots (1976). Furthermore, an institutionalized African American political class of elected and appointed officeholders has evolved along with other professions in the new Black bourgeoisie (with eight thousand elected and perhaps thirty thousand appointed officials), and this sector has also fashioned a network of nationwide associations. These include the National Black Caucus of State Legislators, the National Association of Black County Officials, and the National Black Council of School Board

Members. Moreover, the nationwide associations are reinforced at the local level (city especially) by a plethora of similar Black organizations, ranging from the Dallas Alliance for Enterprise and the Durham Business and Professional Chain to New York City's influential One Hundred Black Men.

Though all Black in composition like the professional associations of the pre-1960s era, the new post-Frazier-era associations have a fundamentally different relationship to mainstream American bourgeois patterns. Keep in mind that pre-1960s Black professional organizations like the National Negro Business League (founded by Booker T. Washington in 1900) functioned protectively. They shielded middle-class African American business and professional activities from the pressures of white supremacy and shored up Black ghetto markets, while the post-Frazier associations function integratively. They opened broad job-market and professional and business opportunities for middle-class and professional African Americans throughout the American political, economic, and social systems. Put another way, even while the new Black professional associations among lawyers, engineers, administrators, architects, and accountants in the post-Frazier era continued as primarily African American in membership, they began to operate broadly within the mainstream American economy, becoming "deghettoized," meaning that operationally the members of these Black professional associations would interact frequently with white professionals beside whom they worked in mainstream white-owned law firms, accounting firms, computer businesses, and so on. Thus, over time, we can expect a growing proportion of middle-class and professional African Americans to acquire social and political attitudes that will also become deghettoized, influenced less by racial realities confronting the working-class and poor sectors of the African American populace. A similar shift occurred in the social and political attitudes among the middle-class sector of white ethnic groups when, from the 1940s through the 1960s, large numbers of these groups migrated to middle-class suburbs, leaving behind their working-class and poor neighborhoods. Among the post–World War II white-ethnic middle-class elements, a less combative attitude toward the status-dominant WASP group emerged, and this, in turn, was reflected in more conservative, Republican-leaning voting habits. So far in the post-Frazier era, however, a significant shift in voting patterns among middle-class and professional African American elements away from the Democratic Party has not occurred.

New Systemic Dynamics Among the Black Bourgeoisie

In Frazier's critique of the Black bourgeoisie as it was in the 1950s, in addition to identifying distortions in their performance of modern middle-class and professional functions or tasks, he also identified distortions in what might be called the leadership thrust or leadership aura of this social stratum. The Black bourgeoisie's leadership thrust was, in Frazier's view, rendered flaccid and directionless by too many members' indulgence in what he variously called "make-believe" or "high society" behavior, which is to say, they acted out the frivolous aspects of genuine bourgeois elite behavior, expending their limited wealth in conspicuous consumerism and a leisure style of expensive gaiety. In Frazier's view, this was the opposite of what a truly viable Black bourgeoisie required as its guiding motif—namely, what might be called a power-seeking leadership aura.

Now, while there was much truth in this aspect of the Frazierian critique of middle-class and professional African Americans in the early 1950s, it is clear from our vantage point today that the revolution in civil rights laws and practices that uprooted a century of white supremacist marginalization of African Americans was a necessary precondition for correcting the leadership distortions that Frazier identified among the Black bourgeoisie. Above all, it was the revolution in civil rights laws and practices that—as I have demonstrated—transformed the opportunities available to middle-class and professional Blacks from a so-called ghetto job market to a nationwide job market.

Indeed, concurrent with this new access, African Americans fashioned new professional networks among accountants, engineers, lawyers, computer technologists, media entrepreneurs, and so on. This new Black organizational process was the beginning of a significant shift in the leadership aura of the Black bourgeoisie away from the high-society pattern that Frazier so sharply critiqued and toward what I call a power-mustering or power-promoting bourgeois outlook. The individuals who headed up the new professional organizations viewed them overwhelmingly as power-mustering agencies in terms of technocratic, educational, and professional standing for their new job-market members.

This new style of leadership also evolved through other modalities, especially through new African American journals. Beginning in the 1970s, the most prominent of these Black journals appeared monthly and attained a nationwide Black readership. *Black Enterprise* led the way, reaching 250,000 readers by the mid-1980s and increasing its influence enormously, with subscribers in the millions. Another such journal directed mainly toward new African American women of the middle-class and professional sectors was *Essence*, which by the mid-1980s had around 600,000 readers and whose current circulation tops a million. While *Essence* readers are offered content on fashionable clothing or the interior design of upper-middle-class homes, they are also informed about the professional and business careers of successful African American women.

Perhaps the biggest surprise among the genre of Black magazines that emphasize these power-mustering orientations were the changes in the contents of *Ebony*, the premiere Black magazine of its genre. Founded in 1945, *Ebony* has always fed its Black readers a steady diet of what Frazier called high-society orientations, articles that emphasized the consumerist lifestyles of Black entertainers mainly but also of Black professionals and businesspersons. Beginning in the 1970s, however, *Ebony* increasingly focused on the new professional and business careers among African Americans as opposed to their spending habits, with articles tracing the methods and processes that made these careers possible. A final entry among this group of power-mustering Black journals is *Black Collegian*, with its vast array of articles on topics related to how Black college graduates can prepare themselves to enter the mainstream job market.

The overriding goal of these Black journals has been to galvanize the systemic mainstreaming of the Black bourgeoisie. And the cumulative impact of these developments is transforming the customary character of American race relations in a manner that Frazier, writing in the early 1950s, could not have imagined. Above all, there is emerging what might be called a status-deracialization process among the post-Frazier Black bourgeoisie. To speak of status deracialization is another way of identifying those alterations in the historical dynamics of racism in American life that William Julius Wilson has characterized as the "declining significance of race." But unlike Wilson's, my conception of status deracialization does not imply that racism as such has ceased to exist. Far from it. The term "status deracialization" denotes that racism now has less capacity than it did two generations ago and beyond to dictate the systemic patterning of an expanding segment of mobile African Americans, the bourgeois sector especially. Today this sector among African Americans constitutes a kind of upper stratum made up of middle-class and professional households that amount to some 35 percent of Black households. Another 25 percent of Black households fall into the stable blue-collar or stable working-class sector, making up a middle-stratum Black sector. The remaining 40 percent, the lower-stratum Black sector, comprises weak or struggling working-class and poor Black households.

In general, the new systemic incorporating process that I call status deracialization is likely to proceed in an erratic manner at best, characterized by breakthroughs on one front and setbacks on another. Owing to residual racist practices among white Americans, the setbacks slow down the replacement of race- and class-linked attitudes among the post-Frazier Black bourgeoisie, thereby restricting the ideological range of class differentiation among African Americans. Put another way, as status deracialization proceeds in the post-Frazier era, class perceptions and identity among the Black bourgeoisie will display numerous inconsistencies. On some issues, upper-stratum Blacks will converge with upper-stratum whites. On others, however, upper-stratum Blacks will converge with middle- and lower-stratum Blacks and the broader African American community. Why are there such inconsistencies in the status-deracialization process?

The erratic manner by which upper-stratum African Americans are co-opted into the American mainstream in our post-Frazier era leaves them, as it were, both insiders and outsiders. While processing full-fledged elite capabilities in a way that Frazier could not have foreseen more than a half century ago, today's Black bourgeoisie is still vulnerable to powerful patterns of residual racism in American life. Furthermore, the insider/outsider condition facing today's Black bourgeoisie (a bourgeoisie that is without, or rather has fewer of, the pathologies identified by Frazier) comes from blue-collar or upper-working-class and lower-middle-class African American families, with only a small segment of today's Black bourgeoisie having second-generation bourgeois origin. Thus, most of the new Black bourgeoisie continue to have overlapping class and cultural ties deep in the everyday realities of Black ethnicity. They experience a kind of sociocultural asymmetry, a pattern also found in the upward-mobility trajectories of such white ethnic groups as Irish Americans, Italian Americans, and Jewish Americans.

Be that as it may, owing to both residual racism among white Americans and sociocultural asymmetries among African Americans, the insider/outsider aspect of status deracialization among the post-Frazier Black bourgeoisie indicates that status deracialization is quite problematic. It is not always easy to function as a member of the post-Frazier Black bourgeoisie today, for it is a mercurial ethnic class. However, given African Americans' origins in slavery and their travails under a century of white supremacist patterns down to the 1960s, the current "split-personality" pressures facing some members of today's Black bourgeoisie are, I suggest, a significant though comparatively minor burden to bear.

In addition to status deracialization as a systemic feature or dynamic associated with the post-Frazier Black middle-class and professional sectors, the post-Frazier Black bourgeois stratum has produced a wholly new kind of class stratification among African American society. Owing to the qualitatively new level of nationwide job markets, nationwide recourse to higher education, and access to competitive income and overall compensation, the post-Frazier Black bourgeoisie has fashioned a systemically stronger position for itself within African American society. This stronger position has, in turn, been curiously reinforced by the mobility ceiling that residual neoracist patterns in American society have imposed on the lower stratum that makes up nearly 40 percent of African American households. The African American sociologist Andrew Billingsley has organized data that illustrate well the job-market and income basis of this new kind of class-stratification dynamic among African American society. These data are shown in table 5.3.

A corollary set of data organized by Billingsley is shown in table 5.4. These data suggest a growing differential within the African American social system in terms of what might be called societal efficacy among class or status ranks. For example, of all Black families, the 9 percent in the upper class include 96 percent two-spouse families; the 27 percent middle-class Black families include 83 percent two-spouse families; and the 34 percent working-class nonpoor families include 60 percent two-spouse families. But poor working-class households are 67 percent single-parent families, and among underclass households, 75 percent are single-parent families.

Ultimately, the new politicization capability of the post-Frazier Black bourgeoisie will enable it to influence both the public policy and private power sectors in American society to upgrade the status of the weak

TABLE 5.3

Social-class structure of African American families, 1969–1986

	1969		1983		1986	
	Families	%	Families	%	Families	%
Upper class	143,000	3	267,000	4	624,000	9
Middle class	1,100,000	25	1,500,000	25	1,910,000	27
Working class (nonpoor)	2,100,000	44	2,400,000	36	2,420,000	34
Working class (poor)	688,000	14	963,000	14		
Underclass (nonworking poor)	716,000	14	1,500,000	23	2,142,000	30

Source: Andrew Billingsley, "Understanding African American Family Diversity," in *The State of Black America 1990*, ed. Janet Dewart (New York: National Urban League, 1990).

TABLE 5.4

African American social class and family structure

	Family structure		
Class	Married Couple	Single Parent	Working Wife
Upper class	04%	96%	50%
Middle class	83%	17%	78%
Working class (nonpoor)	60%	40%	45%
Working class (poor)	33%	67%	33%
Underclass (nonworking poor)	25%	75%	25%

Source: Andrew Billingsley, "Understanding African American Family Diversity," in *The State of Black America 1990*, ed. Janet Dewart (New York: National Urban League, 1990).

working-class and poor sector among African Americans. This politicization was one of the important transformations in the systemic character of the post-Frazier Black elite.

Concluding Note: Politicization of the Post-Frazier Black Bourgeoisie

As I have already suggested, the critical thrust of E. Franklin Frazier's keen analysis of upper-stratum African Americans (the middle class and professional sectors) focused on this stratum's societal dimensions, which exhibited the pathologies that Frazier pinpointed for a very good reason—namely, because during the several decades in the development of the Black bourgeoisie, this leadership sector of African American society was prevented by American racist patterns from creating for itself a parallel political dimension. Thus, while the systemic strengthening of the socio-structural attributes of the Black bourgeoisie or upper stratum was a crucial aspect of developments during the post-Frazier era from the late 1960s to the present, an equally important aspect of the post-Frazier era has been the full-fledged politicization of the Black bourgeoisie. This was a development that Frazier, writing in the early 1950s, could not possibly have foreseen. Indeed, Frazier wrote *Black Bourgeoisie* under the assumption that the viable political incorporation of African American citizens in the American mainstream was not likely to occur during the twentieth century.

It is important to recognize that a significant structural difference between the African American middle class and professional elements on the one hand and the white-ethnic bourgeoisie on the other during the long period between World War I and the 1970s was that the latter had three generations of lead time in reinforcing their socio-structural development with access to political power at both the local and national levels of American politics. While white groups during these decades were pursuing viable electoral empowerment and advancing to the next stage of political development, which I call power-consolidation politics, the African American community—some twelve million strong by 1930, twenty million by the 1950s—was largely confined to protest politics. During that period, the NAACP, the National Urban League, Black professional associations, activist religious bodies, activist civic associations, and some activist trade unions like A. Philip Randolph's Brotherhood of Sleeping Car Porters were the African American population's conveyer belts of protest politics, what after World War II was dubbed civil rights movement politics.

The task of Black protest politics was to smash the rigidity and systemic viciousness of America's racist patterns, epitomized from the 1890s to the 1950s by nearly four thousand recorded lynchings. Even so, ending systemic racism ultimately required massive federal judicial and legislative intervention (e.g., the Civil Rights Act of 1964, the Voting Rights Act of 1965) before the African American bourgeoisie could viably enter the realm of electoral empowerment, with a cutting-edge role played by newly elected Black mayors from 1968 onward, and move toward power-consolidation politics. By the early 1960s, there were fewer than three hundred Black officials in the United States (for a Black population of about twenty million), six of whom were in Congress—five in the House of Representatives and one, Edward Brooke of Massachusetts, in the Senate. But seven years after the Voting Rights Act of 1965, there were about four thousand Black elected officials; as of the 1990s, there were over eight thousand— some 2 percent of all elected officials nationwide. When perhaps thirty thousand or so appointed and civil service officials are added, the aggregate African American political class at the time of this writing totals nearly forty thousand.

Thus, new developments in terms of electoral empowerment and power-consolidation politics from the 1970s through the 1990s produced a kind of generically liberal tilt to the political orientation of the African American middle-class and professional sectors. The electoral empowerment that commenced in the late 1960s was linked to the liberal wing of the Democratic Party during the Kennedy and Johnson administrations, and this linkage between the Black elite and liberals was reinforced first during the Carter administration and then even more strongly during the two terms of the Clinton administration. Under Clinton, the African American professional class hit its peak in national political power thus far: four cabinet positions during the first Clinton administration (agriculture, commerce, energy, veterans' affairs), as well as important second-level executive positions, which included assistant secretary of defense, assistant secretary of state for African affairs, Federal Communications Commission director, director of the Office of Management and Budget, and director of the Department of Justice's Civil Rights Division.

These developments in the consolidation of political power during the post-Frazier era have, I suggest, ensured at least for the short run an orientation toward generic liberalism within the majority wing of the Black bourgeoisie. Today none of the nonwhite ethnic bourgeoisie in American society registers as strong and as consistent a liberal orientation, measured by the degree of support for liberal Democratic Party policies, as does the post-Frazier Black bourgeoisie.[5] The strong Democratic liberalism of the Black bourgeoisie today has trickled down, as it were, through middle- and lower-strata African American households. Today, no serious expectations of presidential electoral victory by a Democratic Party candidate are conceivable without the full backing of African American voters. I like to think that had he lived, E. Franklin Frazier would have been pleased.

CHAPTER VI

Adelaide M. Cromwell's Intellectual Odyssey

Black Elite Modernity in America and Africa

MARION KILSON

Adelaide M. Cromwell belongs to the third generation of twentieth-century African American intellectuals. Born into a distinguished professional family in Washington, DC, in 1919, Cromwell attended Dunbar High School before entering Smith College in 1936, where her beloved aunt Otelia Cromwell had been a trailblazer at the turn of the century. Unlike most of her generational cohort of professional African Americans, Cromwell has always been affiliated with white institutions—as an undergraduate, graduate student, and faculty member.[1] Nevertheless, her sociological scholarship consistently focused on Black elites in the United States and Africa and their interconnections.

Three themes inform Adelaide Cromwell's sociological perspective in her major publications: race, class, and women's roles. Her 1952 Harvard University doctoral dissertation, which remained unpublished until 1994, focused on a comparative sociological analysis of Black and white elite women in mid-twentieth-century Boston and on the development of the Black Boston elite over three hundred years. For her second major study of race and class, Cromwell produced a sociological portrait of an elite African woman in *An African Victorian Feminist: The Life and Times of Adelaide Smith Casely Hayford, 1868–1960*, published in 1986. In 2007, Cromwell published a historical study of her own elite African American family based primarily on family documents, *Unveiled Voices, Unvarnished Memories: The*

Cromwell Family in Slavery and Segregation, 1692–1972.[2] Finally, in 2010, Cromwell composed a portrait in letters of her relationship with her aunt, in *My Mothering Aunt: Otelia Cromwell.*[3] In exploring Cromwell's work, I will start with the last of her publications, as it details a person whose impact on her formative years was immeasurable.

My Mothering Aunt: Otelia Cromwell

Otelia Cromwell, the first African American to attend and graduate from Smith College, had graduated in 1900; her only niece followed in her footsteps, graduating in 1940. Cromwell's tribute to her aunt Otelia is divided into two sections. Part 1, "Aunt Tee," is based on eighty weekly letters that her aunt sent to Adelaide during three of her years at Smith College. Aunt Tee's letters reveal her concern for her niece's well-being and success at the college. She clearly sees that Adelaide's college years were a preparation for the future. "Studying is the main business of college life, surely, for those who are preparing to earn a living and scholarship is in no sense a cause or an achievement to be scoffed at except by short-sighted, light-hearted, or thoughtless people."[4]

Aunt Tee's advice about academic work includes the importance of getting advice on study problems from faculty and administrators, emphasizing the importance of mastering German, focusing more on the humanities at Smith than on the social sciences in which Adelaide would pursue graduate study, and options for graduate study. She also encourages Adelaide to write to her other aunts and her father and to save money from her monthly allowance. She inquires about Adelaide's college activities, reports on Adelaide's father's unsuccessful case for reinstatement in Dunbar High School's Mathematics Department, and her own interest in the theater and in creating Adelaide's wardrobe. In this first section, only occasionally does Aunt Tee mention discrimination issues, including the problems that the singers Roland Hayes and Marian Anderson encountered in getting hotel accommodations in Northampton, the town in which Smith is located, and the racially discriminatory membership policy of the Smith College Club of Washington, DC.

In part 2, however, titled "Miss Cromwell," Aunt Tee probes the subject of discrimination more deeply. In it she focuses on a 1913 racial discrimination case at Smith College in which an African American student was denied campus housing until influential members of the board of trustees intervened. Otelia Cromwell was among the first to protest the discriminatory situation to the college's then president. The 1913 case was the occasion for the Smith College dean to survey the housing policy regarding students at the Seven Sisters;[5] according to Adelaide Cromwell, only Wellesley College had a nondiscrimination policy at the time. Part 2 concludes with Adelaide Cromwell's discussion of integrated residential policies during her years at Smith.

The Cromwell Family in Slavery and Segregation, 1692–1972

If *My Mothering Aunt* pertains to a limited period in a long and affectionate familial relationship, *Unveiled Voices, Unvarnished Memories* encompasses almost three hundred years of Cromwell family history with particular emphasis on Adelaide's notable grandfather and his children, among whom Adelaide Cromwell spent her formative years in Washington, DC. John Wesley Cromwell Sr. was born enslaved in Virginia, spent his boyhood in Philadelphia, and as a young man moved to Washington, DC, where he became a lawyer, civil servant, and educator, as well as a productive scholarly member of the emancipation-era African American intelligentsia.

In 1875 Cromwell founded the Virginia Educational and Historical Association, serving as its president until 1883; in 1886, he started a newspaper, the *People's Advocate*. In 1877 he and the Episcopalian minister Alexander Crummell, particularly notable as the first Black graduate of Cambridge University, founded the short-lived Negro American Society, which was supplanted by the American Negro Academy in 1897, which he also cofounded. In 1915, the same year that Cromwell helped establish the Negro Book Collectors Exchange, the American Negro Academy he was instrumental in developing published his book *The Negro in American History*. He was interested not only in African American society and its evolution but in the development of African societies as well.

J. W. Cromwell Sr.'s wide-ranging network of relationships was often sustained through correspondence. The letters he saved constitute the "archive" on which his granddaughter's book is largely based. Letters from family members underlie the chapters chronicling the Cromwell family's evolution from enslavement to freedom before the Civil War; from working-class to elite professional status in the emancipation era; and between father and college-going daughter and son (Otelia at Smith and John at Dartmouth). In addition to family letters are two chapters devoted to letters from friends and colleagues—one to the letters from the journalist John Edward Bruce and the other from the historian Theophilus Gould Steward. Adelaide Cromwell edited and extensively annotated this collection of letters. Had the rich content of the footnotes informed the analytical structure of the book, it would have been even more comprehensive than it is. Be that as it may, *Unveiled Voices, Unvarnished Memories* presents a remarkable multigenerational chronicle of one African American family extending from the late seventeenth century into the late twentieth century.

Boston's Black Upper Class, 1750–1950

Adelaide Cromwell's first major foray into the social and historical study of African American elites, especially elite women, was her doctoral dissertation. This study, which Cromwell began to research in the late 1940s and ultimately led to her Harvard doctorate in 1952, was not published until more than forty years had passed.[6] In her valuable afterword, which traces the evolution of community-class studies since her Boston research, she notes that more attention has been paid to underclass Blacks than to elites in the intervening years and that the study of elite Blacks in suburbia remains a virtually unexplored area of study.[7]

In *The Other Brahmins*, Cromwell traces the growth of the African American community in Boston from its earliest days in the seventeenth century into the mid-twentieth century. She outlines four major stages of development: the historical period, with its phases of enslavement and freedom, and which ended in 1831; the period of integration of the antebellum and war years, with its initial stage of abolitionist and social protest; the post–Civil War period, which saw the florescence of the upper class; and the period of decline in the early twentieth century that ultimately ushered in the "contemporary" period beginning with Roosevelt's New Deal in 1933. At the time of her research, Boston was perceived as an atypically liberal, Black-friendly northern city, but by the time her study was published, the city had developed the reputation of being racist and unfriendly to African Americans.

The focus of Cromwell's sociological study is a comparative exploration of elite Boston women, both white and Black. Basing her analysis primarily on responses to questionnaires by white women randomly selected from the Boston *Social Register* and by members of six elite Black women's clubs, as well as on interviews and participant observation, Cromwell identifies similarities and differences in elite Bostonian women at the mid-twentieth century. Both sets of elite women were engaged primarily in domestic responsibilities and secondarily in charitable and cultural activities, though Black elite women emphasized charitable pursuits over cultural activities and white elite women cultural over charitable. Both sets emphasized family heritage, political conservatism, and education.

Few elite white women, however, were college educated themselves, whereas almost two-thirds of Black elite women had at least some college education. Cromwell argues that limited occupational opportunities for Black Bostonians had constrained the community's economic development and probably influenced the prevalence of small family size among Black elites in contrast to white elite women, who valued large families. Fissures within the Black community related not only to class factors but to ethnic cleavages primarily between Caribbean and northern-born community members.

Cromwell's discussion of the evolution and continuing importance of social clubs within the Black Boston community is particularly insightful. In post–Civil War Boston, "the social clubs of the Negro elite . . . emerged as a key to the Black society's inner structure. These trends were the increasing diversification of class lines within the Negro structure and the concomitant tendencies toward greater separation between the two racial groups in social affairs and uplift work. . . . With the exception of two literary societies and clubs based on place of birth, they were class-limited, sex-limited, and race-limited—thus establishing a social pattern that prevailed well into the twentieth century."[8] Cromwell identifies five types of elite Black women's clubs in the mid-twentieth century: local chapters of national organizations such as the Links; charitable clubs like the League of Women for Community Service; Greek-letter organizations; auxiliaries associated with men's professional associations; and special interest groups like literary clubs.

Cromwell's African Studies Sojourn

Like her grandfather John Wesley Cromwell Sr., Adelaide Cromwell always was drawn to the study of Africa and its peoples as well as the interconnections between Africans and African Americans. This interest led to three very different books: *Apropos of Africa*, *Dynamics of African/African American Connection*, and *An African Victorian Feminist*. The first is an anthology of major texts by African Americans on their views of Africa and their roles on the African continent; the second a series of papers emanating from a conference on African and African American scholars planned in Boston and held in Monrovia; and the third a biography of a notable Sierra Leonean woman.

African American and African Ties

Cromwell initially probes the topic of the ties between African Americans (the contemporary term, which she uses, was "Afro-Americans") and Africans in her 1969 book *Apropos of Africa: Sentiments of Negro American Leaders on Africa from the 1800s to the 1950s*. Her own analytical commentary, along with coeditor Martin Kilson's,[9] accompanies texts she selected, ranging from Paul Cuffe's log of his first trip to Sierra Leone in 1811 to Congressman Charles C. Diggs Jr.'s writings on the role of American Negroes in American and African relations in 1959. Arrayed under four topical headings—(1) "Let's Go Home to Africa"; (2) "How Negro Americans Can Help as Individuals and as Organizations"; (3) "When I Was in Africa"; and (4) "Negro Self-Identity and Pan-Africanism"—each topic is introduced with a summary of major themes, and each selection begins with a biographical sketch of its author.

One of the distinctive merits of the anthology is its illumination of varying views on the same subject, such as African American emigration to Africa, which was opposed by Frederick Douglass but supported by the Reverend Henry McNeal Turner and later Marcus Garvey. The contribution of African Americans to the establishment of Christian institutions, education, and economic development in Africa is a persistent theme from the writings of Paul Cuffe and Lott Cary in the early nineteenth century to those of Garvey and the Reverend James H. Robinson in the twentieth. Perhaps the most valuable account of the multiple ties between people of African descent in the New World and in Africa is W. E. B. Du Bois's 1955 review of the various Pan-African Congresses, ending with his optimistic conclusion that "When once the blacks of the United States, the West Indies, and Africa work and think together, the future of the black man in the modern world is safe."[10]

In regard to African American and African ties, Cromwell further develops this topic in *Dynamics of the African/Afro-American Connection: From Dependency to Self-Reliance* (1987).[11] This volume reflects Cromwell's masterly organizational skills. For the project she garnered Ford Foundation funding to support a preliminary 1981 planning workshop in Boston and a 1983 seminar at the University of Liberia that addressed the issue of enhancing communication between Africans and diaspora Blacks; she enlisted the support of the two oldest sub-Saharan universities—the University of Sierra Leone and the University of Liberia—as well as her home institution, Boston University; and she assembled a notable group of diaspora and African scholars to address various aspects of the relations between Blacks on both sides of the Atlantic within the current global system. Cromwell's own writing in the volume is restricted to a brief preface noting the enhanced communication between Africans and African Americans during the twentieth century and introducing the content of the volume.

The Life and Times of an African Victorian Feminist

Cromwell's biography of Adelaide Smith Casely Hayford constitutes her major sociological contribution to the exploration of the relations between Africans and African Americans.[12] This remarkable professional African woman captured Cromwell's interest as representative of Sierra Leonean Creoles "who were at home in the world of the West and who could look both ways—to roots in Africa or to historical and kinship ties with Europe and Great Britain, in particular."[13] Cromwell met Casely Hayford only briefly on a 1959 visit to Freetown, but through interviews, review of correspondence, archival research, and access to her unpublished memoirs, Cromwell uncovered the other Adelaide's story. As in her later Cromwell family books, she relied heavily on Casely Hayford's own words. In fact, Cromwell asserts, "This book . . . is truly a joint venture; her words in the *Memoirs* and elsewhere, are used whenever possible and the organization of the book is naturally determined by her experiences and the sequence in which they occurred."[14]

Cromwell traces Casely Hayford's life from its beginnings in Freetown to her family life and education in England and Germany to her initial work as a teacher in Africa, followed by her marriage to the barrister Joseph Ephraim Casely Hayford and their three years together in the Gold Coast before her return to the place of her birth. In Freetown she resumed her career as an educator and began to discuss her plan for a technical and industrial school for girls. To facilitate the realization of this goal, Casely Hayford spent more than two years in the United States learning about education for African American girls and raising funds to launch her own school, which she did in the mid-1920s. After closing the school for a year, Casely Hayford reopened it in 1926 with the help of her daughter Gladys and served as its principal from 1927 until 1940.

Noting that African historians rarely discuss the personal lives and families of notable Africans, Cromwell devotes considerable attention to Casely Hayford's family of origin, which represented "every major thread from the which the fabric of Creole society was woven," as well as to her unsuccessful marriage to J. E. Casely Hayford and her difficult but loving relationship with her daughter Gladys, whose son she raised after Gladys's death.[15] Throughout Casely Hayford's long life, insufficient financial resources were a persistent problem, first in supporting her own education and later in obtaining support for her daughter's medical care, for financing her school for girls, and for maintaining her own lifestyle. Cromwell concludes her biography with this statement: "In her life on three continents over nine decades, Mrs. Casely Hayford managed to symbolize the problems of modern women—and of modern Black women. Identity (cultural and racial), marriage, motherhood, career goals, community responsibility are all reflected in the life of this remarkable woman."[16]

Cromwell's scholarly interest in Black women's lives and achievements on both sides of the Atlantic is also reflected in the contributions that she made to two books authored by women. The first was an afterword to the 1982 edition of Dorothy West's first novel, *The Living Is Easy*. The second was the introduction to *Jellemoh*, Mary Antoinette Brown Sherman's biography of her mother.[17]

Cromwell's afterword to *The Living Is Easy* begins with a musing on why pre-1960s African American women writers have long been neglected in the literary canon. West wrote her first novel from her home on Martha's Vineyard. Cromwell details her life there, where West not only penned weekly columns for the *Vineyard Gazette* but supplemented her income by working as a restaurant cashier during the bleak, non-touristy winter months. She goes on to delineate West's Boston beginnings and subsequent participation as a junior member of the Harlem Renaissance. Cromwell notes that West's novel both informs and disguises the fragile Black Boston community that West knew growing up. The afterword concludes with a discussion of the expansion of economic opportunities for Black Bostonian professional and organizational people since the period West captured in *The Living Is Easy*. Cromwell considers that the novel provides "an understanding of another dimension of the black experience. . . . From her island retreat Dorothy West has expanded our knowledge of black America."

Cromwell's introduction to Mary Antoinette Brown Sherman's *Jellemoh: The Life and Times of Victoria Elizabeth Jellemoh Grimes, a Liberian Wife and Mother* opens with a brief survey of African literature from the eighteenth century through the twentieth, pointing out the rarity not only of Liberian authors but of biographies of African women more broadly. Cromwell notes that her own study of the Sierra Leonean Adelaide Casely Hayford, published in 1986, was only the third-ever contemporary biography of an African woman. She praises Sherman for writing her mother's biography, maintaining that Africans have an "obligation . . . to tell the rest of the world . . . what it is really like to grow up and live in a particular African setting." Victoria Elizabeth Jellemoh Grimes's life (1898–1970) reveals the interconnections between up-country and settler peoples as well as the strong ties within "extended families" comprised of foster children and natural-born children in the Liberian setting. Cromwell concludes her introduction with highlights of Grimes's life as presented by her distinguished daughter.

Cromwell's Essays

Over the years, Cromwell published many essays. Noteworthy among them are "What Is Africa to Us?" (1968); "Black Education in the Seventies: A

Lesson from the Past" (1970); and "The Black Presence in the West End of Boston, 1800–1864" (1993).[18] Each essay developed out of one of her major scholarly interests. Initially delivered at the Newark National Conference on Black Power in 1967, "What Is Africa to Us?" explores African American identity over time in relation to Africa. Cromwell asserts that not until Marcus Garvey articulated a positive Black identity in the first decades of the twentieth century did Africa become more than a "fragile source" of African American identity. With the civil rights movement and the fruition of independence movements in Africa, however, African Americans' "separate identity . . . has been strengthened by having its most basic ingredients, Africa and our blackness, viewed positively. . . . The identity itself is old; its roots are spreading and strengthening."[19] Some of Cromwell's African American intellectual peers, among them W. E. B. Du Bois, Rayford Logan, and E. Franklin Frazier, elaborated on this proposition in the 1958 volume *Africa Seen by American Negroes*, published in Paris by *Présence africaine*.

If "What Is Africa to Us?" presents a positive view of the efforts toward social equity for the institutional integration of Black Americans during the fifties and sixties, "Black Education in the Seventies" reveals some ambiguous consequences of these efforts through a case study of Cromwell's alma mater, Dunbar High School, in Washington, DC. From its founding in 1870 until 1954, Dunbar was an all-Black institution in which "respect for learning and an expectation of superiority based on knowledge and pride emanating from [Black] teachers and instilled into [Black] students made Dunbar a special educational environment."[20] Dunbar graduates were high achievers who went on to integrated northern colleges and universities and often distinguished careers in later life. Following the Supreme Court decision to integrate schools throughout the country, Black students in Washington, DC, attended schools throughout the city and Dunbar students were drawn from the local neighborhood, and Cromwell concludes that "The irony of Dunbar . . . is that at the time when opportunities were opening, the school was unable to provide an adequate educational environment."[21]

While "Black Education in the Seventies" develops from Cromwell's experiences as an adolescent in a major Black institution, "The Black Presence in the West End of Boston, 1800–1864" describes the antebellum Black community in the city in which Cromwell spent most of her professional life. In this important historical essay, Cromwell describes the geographical contours of this community, the principal occupations its members pursued, and its leadership patterns, as well as presenting vignettes about some of the major figures within the community, such as the physician John V. De Grasse, the journalist William Cooper Nell, the entrepreneur John P. Coburn, and the hairdresser Madame Christiana Carteaux Bannister.

Cromwell also includes a demographic map showing the residences of significant community personalities as well as the location of churches and schools. Appendices list Black women heads of households, prominent Black men living in the West End, and a partial list of Black voters in the 1864 election. Over the years, Cromwell was instrumental in placing historic markers and placards on West End houses identifying the prominent Black community members who once lived in them.

Conclusion

In this essay I have explored the sociological topics that concerned Adelaide Cromwell in her major publications. From her 1952 dissertation through her 2010 book about her aunt Otelia, Cromwell focused on African American families and the roles and challenges of elite Black women. Often these foci are presented in their historical and community contexts as well as in comparative perspective—Black and white elite Boston women in *The Other Brahmins*; African and African American elites in *An African Victorian Feminist* and in *Unveiled Voices, Unvarnished Memories*. More often than not, Cromwell relies on her subjects' own words to develop her theme, most notably in *An African Victorian Feminist*, *My Mothering Aunt*, and, of course, in the anthology *Apropos of Africa*. In initiating sociological consideration of African American and African elite families as well as African American and African elite women's experiences, Adelaide M. Cromwell made an invaluable contribution to the scholarship of the third generation of African American intellectuals.

CHAPTER VII

Ishmael Reed and Cornel West

Anatomy of Black Public Intellectuals

Introduction: Why Public Intellectuals?

To paraphrase the adage about the status of the poor in modern society, public intellectuals will always be with us. The context out of which the public intellectual phenomenon evolves has been the problem-solving ethos at the core of the identity of modern nation-states, especially those that are democratically governed. Unlike feudal and other modes of premodern society, the modern nation-state was viewed by its formulating elites as distinct from its antecedents precisely because it permitted citizens to place their expectations and claims before a so-called public marketplace of ideas, thereby creating a perpetual need for persons who fashioned moral/ethical/policy criteria and options for discourse on the character of the society.

Our awareness today of the public intellectual phenomenon is especially keen because we have witnessed during the half century since the end of World War II a broad diversification in the ranks of persons performing these tasks, especially among women, Latino Americans, Asian Americans, and African Americans. In this chapter I probe the unique features of the developmental dynamics relating to the place of African Americans in the public intellectual phenomenon during the twentieth century.

Illustrative case-study examinations of the discourse of two contemporary African American public intellectuals will be undertaken as well: those

[215]

of Ishmael Reed and Cornel West. I will also explore a major shift in the archaeology of Black intellectuals in general from the late 1970s onward, when the long-standing dominance of liberal and civil rights activist patterns within the African American intelligentsia confronted for the first time a viable stratum of conservative Black intellectuals. Prominent personalities among the initial cadre of conservative Black intellectuals are the economists Glenn Loury and Thomas Sowell; the literary studies scholar Shelby Steele; the sociologist Anne Wortham; the economist Walter Williams; and the political scientist Alan Keyes.[1]

One of the first theoretical discussions of what today we call the public intellectual phenomenon I ever read can be found in the late C. Wright Mills's classic work *White Collar: The American Middle Classes* (1951). In the chapter "Brains, Inc.," Mills used the term "political intellectuals" to characterize an intellectual function very much like what today we have in mind when employing the term "public intellectual": "Political intellectuals are special dealers in . . . symbols and states of political consciousness; they create, facilitate, and criticize the beliefs and ideas that support or attach ruling classes, institutions and policies; or they divert attention from these structures of power and from those who command and benefit from them as going concerns."[2]

In addition to its generic problem-solving ethos, there are several core dilemmas in the functioning of the democratic nation-state that spawned what has become the public intellectual process. If we conceive of the modern nation-state—in contrast with the ancient or traditional state (e.g., chieftain, feudal, aristocratic, monarchic, etc.)—as an opportunity-driven rather than a privilege-driven system, then it is in regard to the inevitable discrepancy between the modern state's opportunity-enhancing ideal and its real-world toleration of privilege and greed that the public intellectual process evolves. Thus, in terms of function, public intellectuals in their most generic capacity generate reflections and perspectives relating to the opportunity-privilege gap at the heart of the democratic nation-state.

Public intellectuals in American society might be said to have commenced this function as early as the 1830s. What the social historian Arthur Schlesinger Jr. dubbed "the Age of Jackson" witnessed the appearance of intellectuals who queried the opportunity-privilege gap in the American system of that era. They pinpointed shortcomings in opportunities in education, in landownership, and above all in citizenship and political rights. Keep in mind, too, that the scope of issues relating to the opportunity-privilege gap in the democratic state has always been multi-layered, ranging across numerous segments of the class and status systems, along lines of wealth, ethnicity, race, gender, age, and so forth. Moreover, what I call the opportunity-privilege gap has interfaced with another generic fault line at the heart of democratic nation-states: namely, the sacred-modernist or sacred-profane gap, by which I mean the inevitable tension and fissure between modern society's ideal of infinite value choice juxtaposed with the perennial tenacity of sacred or traditionalist values.

Thus, since the mid-nineteenth century, the typical democratic nation-state required arbiters for its two-tier systemic fissures: the opportunity-privilege gap on one tier and the sacred-profane gap on the other. While a variety of segments among the intelligentsia had performed the function of arbiters for these systemic fissures, those individuals we call public intellectuals have been especially prominent in this regard. Alexis de Tocqueville, the shrewd French observer of the fledgling American republic during the Jackson era, had already identified a stratum among the professional classes that looked rather like today's public intellectuals. That stratum was composed of writers, among whom de Tocqueville noted two generic types: those he called "authors" and those he called "journalists." De Tocqueville posited that in the genuine democratic nation (as contrasted with an aristocratically skewed nation—say, nineteenth-century Britain, as opposed to the United States), there was an intrinsic need for literary discourse and reflection. As he put it in *Democracy in America* (1835), "Democracy . . . infuses a taste for letters among the trading classes [i.e., the bourgeoisie]."

De Tocqueville went on to observe that only his first category of "authors" performed something like what we now recognize as the public intellectual function—namely, "they . . . act upon the manners of the people." De Tocqueville's second category of writers, "journalists"—who he thought were dominant among American writers and whom he described as "not great writers"—were considered a tawdry version of public intellectuals, for "they amuse the mind." This Tocquevillian dilemma among writers who "act upon the manners of the people" as compared with writers who "amuse [read: entertain] the mind," is in some respects replicated in our own era.

This leads us to an operational definition of public intellectuals and their function. What public intellectuals do, historically and presently, is to fashion moral, ethical, and policy criteria or options for mediating among the opportunity-privilege issue and the sacred-profane issue spheres. From about the early nineteenth century onward, public intellectuals have focused mainly on the opportunity-privilege issue sphere. Why is this so? Because problems relating to the opportunity-privilege sphere were prominent in such national crises as agrarian issues, monopoly capitalism issues, cheap- or tight-money issues, and the slavery issue. Then, in the twentieth century, additional national crises arose, including but not limited to workers' compensation issues, women's voting rights, agrarian subsidies, labor union rights, and the citizenship rights of African Americans.

Debut of African American Public Intellectuals

In the late 1980s, when a spate of magazine articles appeared focusing on a highly visible set of Black public intellectuals and written by freelance writers like Robert Boynton, two misinformed arguments about the American public intellectual phenomenon surfaced. One argument proclaimed that the public intellectual process was of no real significance in American public life before the appearance of a cadre known as the New York intellectuals, primarily consisting of liberal and leftist Jewish Americans, during the era between the 1930s and the immediate post–World War II years. A second argument was that an African American presence in the American public intellectual arena was not felt until the militant phase of the civil rights movement and thereafter. As I will discuss momentarily, both of these arguments reflect a shallow historical grasp of the generic sources and character of the public intellectual phenomenon in the development of the American democratic republic.

The entry of Black intellectuals into the public intellectual process was related to the fact that problems stemming from that opportunity-privilege issue sphere have historically played a major role in shaping the boundaries of American society's public intellectual phenomenon. Thus, the initial appearance of Black intellectuals on the public intellectual scene extends back to the period before the Civil War, when a very small cohort of largely self-educated African Americans—many of whom were born in slavery and escaped to freedom—emerged as members of the antislavery abolitionist movement. Most prominent among this pioneering group was Frederick Douglass. Others were James W. C. Pennington, John Sella Martin, and

William Howard Day, to mention only a few. This prewar development of an embryonic Black public intellectual process has been brilliantly studied by R. J. M. Blackett in *Beating Against the Barrier: The Lives of Six Nineteenth-Century Afro-Americans* (1986).[3] African Americans' special subordinate status continued as a major defining theme in the character of the opportunity-privilege issue sphere in American public life in the post–Civil War era, following upon the refusal of the federal government to use its armed and legal powers to protect the extension of democratic rights to Blacks living in the South, where 95 percent of African Americans resided by 1900.

Accordingly, African American status at the dawn of the twentieth century was defined by fierce and unrelenting racial-caste marginalization. This was essentially an authoritarian-imposed status, for that same number of Black Americans—95 percent—were denied representative rights in the American political process. This authoritarian-imposed status was juridically sanctioned by white-controlled legislatures and courts and reinforced everywhere in America—South and North—by police power and white terrorist violence in the form of lynchings and riots against African American communities. In a review of Richard Wright's novelized autobiography *Black Boy* from 1945, the literary scholar Lionel Trilling, a charter member of the New York intellectuals, provided an unflinching characterization of the white supremacist racial-caste delineation of the status of African Americans in the twentieth century. Calling the book "a precise and no doubt largely typical account of Negro life in Mississippi," Trilling remarked,

> That it is the account of a tragic situation goes without saying. Here is the Negro poverty in all its sordidness: here is the calculated spiritual imprisonment of one racial group by another; here, above all, is the personal humiliation of Negro by white, the complex cruelty of the dominant race practiced as a kind of personal, spiritual necessity, sometimes direct and brutal, sometimes sophisticated with a sensual, guilty, horrible kindness. . . ."Black Boy" is an angry book, as it ought to be. . . . It is also in proportion to the author's desire to live a reasonable and effective life. For what a Negro suffers in the South—what, indeed, he might suffer in the North—calls for illimitable anger.[4]

Trilling's vivid identification of what can only be called the antihumanitarian rawness of twentieth-century American white supremacist processes might seem to ignore some modicum of democratic space available to African Americans, but he nonetheless put his finger on its most central, cruel, authoritarian ethos. Or, to borrow a phrase from Toni Morrison's Nobel Prize acceptance address, Trilling's vision "arcs toward the place where meaning may lie."[5]

In fashioning a public response to the white supremacist victimization of Black realities in recent American life, the first- and second-generation cohort of twentieth-century African American intellectuals (overwhelmingly trained at Negro colleges) utilized a variety of Western-derived modes of thought and action. Social activist Christianity—rooted in the social gospel mode of Christian discourse—loomed large in this regard, partly because of its salience in forging the abolitionist movement during the nineteenth century. Typically open to egalitarian orientations, African American intellectuals fashioned social activist Christianity into platforms of Black civil rights activism, and they did not hesitate to co-opt secular modes of radicalism as well. Primary among these were the radical egalitarian ideas associated with socialist thought generally and Marxism in particular, along with ideas rooted in the social activism of ethnic or national communities within democratic nations. This first, fledgling cohort of African American public intellectuals were often Negro college–based personalities but also other members of the evolving Black professional class. Among this group was W. E. B. Du Bois, trained as a sociologist at Atlanta University; Booker T. Washington, the president of the Tuskegee Institute; Horace Mann Bond, a Dillard University sociologist and later Lincoln University president; Anna Julia Cooper, only the fourth African American woman to earn a PhD, obtained at the University of Paris; John Wesley Cromwell, editor of the *People's Advocate* newspaper and founding member of the American Negro Academy; St. Clair Drake, also a Dillard University sociologist, later at Roosevelt University; the Reverend Francis Grimké and his brother, the lawyer Archibald Grimké; John Hope, the president of Atlanta University; Charles S. Johnson, magazine editor and future Fisk University president; Monroe Trotter, a newspaper editor; Ida Wells-Barnett, the journalist and antilynching activist; and Carter G. Woodson, the founder of *Journal of Negro History* and director of the Association of Negro Life and History.

While some of the foregoing personalities participated in early twentieth-century African American organizations like the National Negro Business League, the American Negro Academy, the NAACP, and the National Urban League, others, like William Hastie, Charles Houston, James Nabrit, and John Aubrey Davis, started their careers as public intellectuals by founding the New Negro Alliance in 1933 as a direct-action organization concerned with job discrimination in the nation's capital. And in the late 1930s Bunche, along with E. Franklin Frazier, the Howard University educator Doxey Wilkerson, the Harvard-trained lawyer Benjamin Davis, the founder of the Brotherhood of Sleeping Car Porters, A. Philip Randolph, and others formed a nationwide radical organization, the National Negro Congress, which joined the NAACP and National Urban League as forums for fashioning moral/ethical/policy responses for public discourse on the racial-caste status of Black people in the American system.

Furthermore, though it is often assumed that what might be called the NAACP sector among African American intellectuals during the proto–public intellectual era between World War I and the end of World War II was tantamount to this experience generally, this is not accurate. There was, in fact, a two-sector proto–public intellectual process among African American intellectuals during that time. There is no doubt that what I call the NAACP sector—those intellectuals influenced by Du Bois and associated with organizations like the NAACP, the National Urban League, the New Negro Alliance, and the National Negro Congress—contained the main cluster of publicly assertive Black intellectuals in this period. A second cluster, though, might be called the UNIA sector, which comprised those intellectuals who favored a Black-separatist orientation toward white American society and in general revolved around Marcus Garvey and his Universal Negro Improvement Association.

In general, both the UNIA sector and the NAACP sector shared the fact that what might be called their public market consisted primarily of African American citizens. Both sectors functioned operationally through African American social relationships and organizational agencies as their legitimating milieu. At the same time, however, within their mainly African American public market, the intellectuals in the UNIA sector consciously restricted their appeal to African Americans, whereas those in the NAACP sector attempted to make their public market as interracial as possible. Leading NAACP-sector civil rights activists and intellectuals during the interwar era like Du Bois, James Weldon Johnson, Charles S. Johnson, Frazier, Bunche, Randolph, Trotter, and Wells-Barnett combined an activist anti–white supremacist orientation with an interracialist or integrationist civil rights one. During their first several decades, both the NAACP and the National Urban League had significant representation by liberal white professionals on their executive boards, and among this white representation were important financial contributors to these civil rights activist organizations, such as the brothers Joel and Arthur Spingarn in the NAACP and Julius Rosenwald in the National Urban League. The UNIA-sector intellectuals, however, functioned out of a militant cultural-separatist Black identity pattern.

We should also note in these contextual observations that in overall numerical terms, for the first decade of the twentieth century there were about 5,000 college-educated African Americans among a total population of about 9 million, which meant that many persons functioning as professionals among African Americans were trained through apprenticeship arrangements. By 1930, the total Black population increased to nearly 12 million, and the first major study of the college-educated category among African Americans, conducted in the late 1920s by Charles S. Johnson—*The Negro College Graduate*—placed the college-trained population at 18,918.[6] Thus, during the proto–public intellectual phase among African Americans, the range of Black citizens available to perform the intellectual function was not very large, and African Americans did not gain a sizable college-educated category until the mature public intellectual phase, beginning in the era of massive civil rights mobilization in the 1960s.

Typology of Black Public Intellectuals

From the 1960s onward, the formative or proto–public intellectual phase among Black intellectuals began to give way to a full-fledged or mature public intellectual phase. Several things contributed to this metamorphosis. As I have already noted, the proto–public intellectual phase was defined by—and restricted by—a rigid ethnic- or racial-boundary demarcation of the public arena available to the early twentieth-century cohort of African American intellectuals. With few exceptions, those who could function as public intellectuals during the era between the two world wars had mainly the African American population and a minuscule sliver of white Americans as a public arena, or a public marketplace, on which to project a Black intellectual's outlook on moral, ethical, and political options for guiding American society. Thus, what was new in operational terms in regard to the maturation phase of the Black public intellectual process was the expansion of the white public market.

This expansion of the white public market, moreover, had two important constituent features. On one side of the political spectrum, there was a liberal dynamic owing to the 1960s civil rights movement's appeal to a small sector of liberal and progressive white Americans, mainly within the Democratic Party. On the other side, the white public market took on conservative, even reactionary atavistic features with regard to mounting a broad and undeniably terrorist resistance (via the KKK and the White Citizens' Councils) to the civil rights movement's challenge against American racism and to the movement's broader goal of egalitarianizing the American system in general.

Ironically and interestingly enough, both of these transformations in the character of the post–World War II white public market involved more white American citizens paying attention to the activity of Black public intellectuals. There were also similar ironic shifts in the character of the Black public market during the 1960s. Above all, what began as the Garvey movement's cultural-separatist orientation in the pre–World War II era among African Americans reemerged in the postwar era, simultaneously with the integrationist civil rights movement, as an even more militantly anti-white political thrust in the form of the Nation of Islam or Black Muslim movement, and later in the form of the Afrocentric movement.

From the vantage point of these post–World War II transformations in the white and Black public markets, it is possible to conceptually identify a variety of styles that have evolved since the 1960s among Black public intellectuals. I suggest we can hypothesize at least four core styles that have developed among Black public intellectuals.

Type 1: I call this category reform-leftist or pragmatic-activist Black public intellectuals. For my analytical purpose, this label connotes a sector of Black public intellectuals who combine a preference for the liberal-leftist or progressive spectrum of American society with a firm but pragmatic intellectual obligation to Black-ethnic patterns. Since the 1950s, the mainline African American intelligentsia has been identified with some variant of the type 1 category.

Type 2: I call this category ethno-activist Black public intellectuals. This label connotes a sector of Black public intellectuals who insist on a totalist ethnocentric nexus with Black-ethnic patterns in modern society, reinforced by a beleaguered or Black-fortress perspective as well. Whereas the reform-leftist outlook can view American white supremacist patterns as variable (capable, that is, of some ebbing and attenuation), the ethno-activist outlook views American racism as rigid or relatively totalist in character. Since the 1950s, a crucial minority sector of the African American intelligentsia have identified with some variant of the type 2 category.

Type 3: I call this category conservative Black public intellectuals. It designates a sector of Black intellectuals who take their defining cues from dominant American sociopower realities. An intellectual so defined functions in terms of perspectives governed by what the dominant socio-power orientations are toward African American patterns. Since the mid-1970s, there has emerged for the first time in the life cycle of the African American intelligentsia a cadre of conservative Black public intellectuals.

Type 4: I call this category establishmentarian Black public intellectuals. The term designates a sector of Black intellectuals who take their defining cues mainly from dominant American socio-power realities but simultaneously articulate a degree of Black-ethnic fidelity. The Black intellectual in this category is a hybrid Black intellectual, exhibiting a kind of generic opportunism characterized on the one hand by ideological genuflection toward dominant American socio-power patterns, while on the other hand expressing Black-fidelity mannerisms.

Dynamics of the Types of Black Intellectuals: Ideological Issues

Inevitably, as one's analysis progresses from the definitional to the operational, it must be recognized that the boundaries between one's definitional or typological categories are not necessarily rigid. Thus, a given establishmentarian Black public intellectual might increasingly emphasize the Black-ethnic-fidelity facet of his or her type 4 persona as, say, Professor Stephen Carter of Yale Law School began to do in 1996 when he shifted his ground regarding affirmative action practices from opposition to support. Though any such issue-specific shift from the establishmentarian side of the policy spectrum to the liberal side may not in itself amount to a fulsome typology-category or ideological-identity metamorphosis on the part of an establishmentarian or conservative Black intellectual, we can hypothesize that a steady pyramiding of such issue-specific shifts would indeed be tantamount to a fulsome shift on Carter's part.

The interplay of the definitional and operational aspects of analysis can be seen in regard to type 1 Black public intellectuals as well. For one thing, there is an important activist ideological range among reform-leftist Black intellectuals. This range can proceed from, say, Professors Adolph Reed and Manning Marable on the progressive left to, say, Marian Wright Edelman and Julian Bond on the liberal left. Progressive-left Black intellectuals like Reed and Marable can entertain a distinctly socialist perspective on ameliorating the racial-opportunity gap and the overall class and power divisions within American society today, whereas liberal-left intellectuals usually seek such amelioration through incremental activist approaches that do not take an explicit socialist packaging.

We can make further sub-analytical permutations among the above-mentioned typology of Black public intellectuals. For example, there can be migration between full-fledged types among Black public intellectuals, from reform-leftist to establishmentarian, from establishmentarian to conservative, and so on. Something like this seems to have occurred in the case of the economist Professor Glenn Loury. A close reading of Loury's writings over the past several years—sparked by the publication of Richard Herenstein and Charles Murray's *The Bell Curve* (1994) and Dinesh D'Souza's *The End of Racism* (1995)—shows that Loury has publicly condemned the American Enterprise Institute's role in the publication of these books. Loury resigned from his role as researcher at the institute, aggressively denounced it and American conservatives in general for lacking a proactive approach toward the crisis of African American poverty, critiqued the corporate wealth gap, and endorsed affirmative action policies. As such, it might be said that Loury has shifted from a type 3 (conservative) to a type 4 (establishmentarian) ideological identity for himself, which means that while he still genuflects toward America's established socio-power patterns, he combines this with the articulation of a clear Black-ethnic fidelity.[7] This kind of transition from one full-fledged typology to another has occurred as well among type 1 Black public intellectuals, as when the leftist LeRoi Jones shifted from type 1 (reform-leftist) to type 2 (ethno-activist) during the 1970s—changing his name to Amiri Baraka in the process—a metamorphosis portrayed in a monumental study by Jerry Gafio Watts, *Amiri Baraka: The Politics and Art of a Black Intellectual* (2001).[8]

An important analytical proposition for advancing one's comparative understanding of the several types of Black public intellectuals relates to what might be called their legitimizing milieu. The leadership persona of the several categories of Black public intellectuals varies as to the mode of gaining their particular pattern of support, appeal, and respect, which is to say that the leadership persona among the types of Black public intellectuals derives from their legitimation differently. For example, what distinguishes the type 2 (ethno-activist) category from all the other types of Black public intellectuals is that type 2 intellectuals operate almost exclusively through Black-ethnic blocs (milieu) for legitimating their leadership persona, generally ignoring white American legitimating milieu. Ethno-activist Black intellectuals function mainly through media connected with African Americans (magazines, newspapers, television stations, radio stations); they mount speaker platforms mainly related to African American audiences; they recruit only African Americans as members or fellow travelers; and they forge political networks mainly through African American groups.

All of the other three types of Black public intellectuals—reform-leftist, conservative, establishmentarian—share a common tendency to seek some facet of legitimation for their leadership persona among white American patterns. As such, they reject the cultural-separatist paradigm typical of ethno-activist Black public intellectuals. In other words, types 1, 3, and 4 share with African Americans generally the interracialist goal of penetrating the broader cultural-societal institutional processes of American life.

Of course, among Black public intellectuals, types 1, 3, and 4 differ from each other as to how they achieve the penetration or integration of mainstream American patterns. In general, reform-leftist Black public intellectuals—ever since the formative phase represented by leading personalities like Du Bois and James Weldon Johnson—have historically insisted on an assertive challenging of white supremacist patterns, combined with a proactive governmental role (on the part of the federal government especially) in redressing the mobility gap that American racism has engendered between Black and white Americans.

By contrast, the establishmentarian Black public intellectuals have favored only a moderately challenging demeanor toward America's white supremacist patterns. They prefer caution to overly rocking the boat of dominant American patterns, and therefore prefer also what the establishmentarian Black historian Jonathan Holloway characterizes as an individualistic Black identity mode (as contrasted with the Du Boisian Black-ethnic commitment mode) of mobility inclusion into mainstream American patterns.[9]

Also by contrast, the conservative Black public intellectuals exhibit a virtually non-challenging demeanor toward America's white supremacist patterns, or more precisely toward the post–civil rights era's neo-racist variants of historical American racist practices. Instead, conservative Black public intellectuals reify laissez-faire capitalist processes, preferring market-driven and private modalities for correcting the consequences for African Americans of a century of cruel authoritarian and mobility-restrictive American racist processes. It was a Black intellectual trained at Harvard in the 1950s who surfaced on the American public intellectual scene in the early as the initial articulator of a Black conservative ideology paradigm: Thomas Sowell, long affiliated with Stanford University's Hoover Institution. Beginning in the 1970s, Sowell was joined by a cadre of conservative Black public intellectuals, among them Shelby Steele, Anne Wortham, Walter Williams, Glenn Loury, Alan Keyes, Stanley Crouch, and Orlando Patterson.

Dynamics of the Types of Black Intellectuals: Group Leadership Issues

If we functionally classify African American leadership patterns in terms of power-institutional leadership (the task of interlocking African Americans with mainstream American processes) and cultural-cathartic leadership (the Black-ethnic and celebratory task), throughout the twentieth century, the Black American population has exhibited an interesting process of distributing these two generic leadership functions among the several types of Black public intellectuals.

For one thing, what I call the cultural-cathartic leadership task has always been the most contentious, owing to the fact that it involved a sociocultural assertion over and against the mainstream American sociocultural system. Also, the high-level political contentiousness of the cultural-cathartic leadership task operated not simply between the dominant white

American cultural system and the African American subsystem, but within the African American subsystem itself. In general, the Black American population during the twentieth century allocated an important part of the cultural-cathartic leadership task to type 2 (ethno-activist) Black public intellectuals. This practice has extended back in time to the Garvey movement of the 1920s and 1930s, and today a cadre of ethno-activist Black public intellectuals, known popularly as Afrocentrists, are key articulators of cultural-cathartic patterns among African Americans. There was no period in the twentieth century, however, when type 2 (ethno-activist) Black intellectuals—whether the Garveyites after World War I or the Afrocentrists of today—were given the required degree of popular support among African Americans to perform power-institutional leadership roles. In general, power-institutional leadership roles have gone to reform-leftist or pragmatic-activist Black intellectuals. This is the same category of Black intellectuals whom I characterized above as the NAACP sector of the evolving twentieth-century African American intelligentsia, represented most prominently by W. E. B. Du Bois. And when the holding of elected office became available to African Americans, the required popular support among African Americans for election to city council offices, state legislatures, and congressional office went to intelligentsia personalities associated with the NAACP sector, such as Black congressmen elected from Chicago like Oscar DePriest (1928), Arthur Mitchell (1932), and William O. Dawson (1942), or the Black congressman elected from New York City, Adam Clayton Powell Jr. (1944).

We can strengthen our understanding of the interaction between the cultural-cathartic leadership and power-institutional leadership modes among the evolving twentieth-century African American intelligentsia if we recognize that the white ethnic groups of the same period also experienced a variant of this cleavage between the cultural-cathartic and power-institutional leadership modes. From the late nineteenth century through the first half of the twentieth, during which white ethnic groups (Irish, Italian, Jewish, and so on) faced strong patterns of bigotry emanating from the dominant status of WASPs in American society, the major white ethnic groups had cultural-cathartic leadership patterns that took the form of ethnic-defense organizations. Among Irish Americans there were organizations like the Knights of Columbus (conceived with the goal of unity across all Catholic American communities); among Jewish Americans, organizations like the Anti-Defamation League; and among Italian Americans, organizations like the Sons of Italy.

In comparative terms, of course, Black Americans have endured both more vicious and more systemically rigid bigotry and pariahization in American life than did members of white ethnic groups, and thus the cultural-cathartic leadership mode has been more pervasive and enduring among African Americans than among white ethnic communities. Usually when a white ethnic group develops a sizable professional class or bourgeoisie (say about 35 percent of the group's households), the cultural-cathartic leadership mode recedes significantly and gives way to an unquestioned prominence of the power-institutional leadership mode. However, as African Americans developed a sizable professional class or bourgeoisie during the post–civil rights era, there was no major decline in the cultural-cathartic leadership or intellectual mode among African Americans. What, we might ask, has sustained an important position for the cultural-cathartic leadership or intellectual mode among African Americans?

The answer is that an asymmetrical class pattern—a lot of Blacks moving up socially but many moving down too—existed among African Americans during the post–civil rights era. In this asymmetrical class pattern, even though some 60 percent of Black households during this time have entered what I call the mobile stratum (middle-class and professional ranks), during the same post–civil rights era, some 40 percent remained caught in the weak working-class and poverty ranks—a Black static stratum. Thus, in terms of the everyday political and cultural dynamics of African Americans, enough feelings of alienation and disenchantment prevailed among static-stratum Black households (and even among some upwardly mobile Black households) that there remains a lot of room among African Americans for performance of the cultural-cathartic leadership of intellectual tasks.

It is, then, under these circumstances among African Americans during the post–civil rights era that important personalities associated with the type 2 (ethno-activist) sector among Black public intellectuals have evolved. Indeed, type 2 intellectual personalities have kept the cultural-cathartic leadership task quite vibrant since the 1960s. The largest representation of type 2 intellectuals function as schoolteachers and university scholars in the Black studies field, the most prominent among these scholars being the

Temple University historian Professor Molefi Asante. A few ethno-activist intellectual personalities have functioned as self-made intellectual figures, one of the best known being the minister Louis Farrakhan of the Nation of Islam. His prominence was illustrated by Farrakhan's ability to pull together the Million Man March in the fall of 1995. An unprecedented eight hundred thousand or so participants gathered in Washington, DC, to march in an event focused on the status of the African American family. Farrakhan was the event's public face, but at the community organizational level, it was pragmatic-activist-oriented persons among middle-class and professional African Americans who performed most of the tasks to get out the marchers. Black professionals like my nephew Thomas Kilson Queenan joined a cadre of other middle-class Black civic-oriented persons to mobilize a delegation of sixty thousand Philadelphia-area African Americans to the Million Man March, the largest single deputation from a given region. My nephew, the deputy treasurer of the City of Philadelphia in the summer of 1995, and his professional colleagues and peers recognized the importance of mobilizing around family issues facing African Americans, and the ethno-activist origin of the idea for the Million Man March was for my nephew and his colleagues no reason not to participate in it.

Now, while the exhibitionist militant style among ethno-activist Black public intellectuals like Farrakhan and Asante has given them a kind of media-hyped high visibility, the ethno-activist intellectuals have only minimal impact in terms of the everyday functioning of mainline institutions in African American society (e.g., churches, Black trade union branches, Black professional associations, and women's organizations like sororities, branches of the National Council of Negro Women, etc.). Instead, type 1 (reform-leftist or pragmatic-activist) Black public intellectuals have predominated in the institutional leadership sector among African Americans throughout the post–civil rights era. Moreover, the type 1 intellectual sector among African American leadership—from the early 1900s down to our era—has remained ideologically on the liberal side of the American political/ideological spectrum. Above all, the type 1 intellectual sector among African Americans has persistently combined a leftist tilt with its generally liberal political/ideological orientation, and has operated through a pragmatic assertive challenging of America's white supremacist interface with African Americans.

Thus, when one thinks of the most influential leadership and intelligentsia personalities among African Americans from 1900 to our day, one inevitably thinks of personalities who ideologically fall on the liberal and leftist side of the political spectrum—Du Bois (as always), Mary McLeod Bethune, and Jesse Jackson, to mention a scant few. Martin Luther King Jr. must be included on this list as well. Since the public policy and social mobility successes of the civil rights movement in the late 1950s through the 1960s, the reform-leftist thrust in the composition of Black public intellectuals has continued throughout the post–civil rights era down to our day.

This era (from the 1970s on), characterized as it is by a prominent position of the liberal and leftist sector among the mainline African American intelligentsia, has not been subject to a straight-line development, though. In particular, the establishmentarian and conservative forces in the mainline WASP-dominated American power and institutional processes have, during the post–civil rights era, opened their leadership ranks to African American intellectuals. When the WASP-dominant conservative political and intellectual networks opened their ranks to Catholic and Jewish intelligentsia starting around the 1950s to the early 1960s, numerous of these newcomers rushed in where angels had feared to tread. In the late 1970s, some African American intellectuals, sensing a historic opening, similarly began to clamor at the conservative WASP gates. And why shouldn't some Blacks quest to join WASP-conservative patterns, one might muse?

It happens that in the long struggle for non-WASP white ethnic groups and African Americans (also Latino Americans) to escape the bigotry and pariahization practices of WASPs (with Black Americans, of course, facing the cruelest bigotry and pariahization at the hands of WASPs and other white ethnic groups alike), there has always been a powerful "hope we can join WASP conservative networks" consciousness among non-WASP American groups, regardless of ethnicity and color. Of course, in the more than century and a half since the end of the Civil War, African Americans have been more realistic than white ethnic groups like the Irish, Jews, and Italians in assessing their chances of acceptance. This was partly because of the special viciousness and rigidity of anti-Black bigotry in American society and also because of the powerful role of Christian humanist consciousness (social gospel consciousness, that is) in the making of the ideological mind-set of the founders of the post–Civil War and early twentieth-century African American intelligentsia.

Thus, owing to the factors of the nastiness of anti–Black bigotry in American life and the Christian humanitarian ideological sway among early generations of African American intellectuals, there has been throughout the previous century a weak influence among the African American intelligentsia of the upward-mobility fantasy to participate as ideological confreres (or, more plainly, as ideological errand boys) of the WASP-dominant networks. Simultaneously, though, there has been since the early twentieth century a strong influence of the WASP-deferential upward-mobility fantasy among Irish Americans, Jewish Americans, Italian Americans, and other white-ethnic intelligentsia.

It was, of course, the goal of the accommodationist leadership paradigm among African Americans, fashioned by Booker T. Washington between the 1880s and World War I, to advance among Black leadership circles the upward-mobility fantasy of joining America's conservative networks. But the civil rights activist leadership paradigm fashioned by Du Bois and others associated with the Niagara Movement and later the NAACP competed effectively with Washington for the broader support of both the Black professional class and African American citizens in general. As a result, it was not until the post–civil rights era that anything like a viable cadre of Black intellectuals could realize the upward-mobility fantasy of becoming ideological confreres of or joining forces with the conservative networks that control the power gates of the American system. I will discuss this momentarily.

The remainder of this chapter will probe instances of the continuation of the reform–leftist thrust among the African American intelligentsia during the post–civil rights era through case studies of Ishmael Reed and Cornel West. I will also discuss efforts to displace the long-standing reform-leftist trend, efforts mounted by new establishmentarian and conservative Black intellectuals.

Public Intellectual as Populist: Ishmael Reed

During his decades-long professional career, Ishmael Reed has been one of the most prolific Black creative writers associated with the reform–leftist category among African American intellectuals. Reed's fine creative output includes dozens of poems, plays, essays and criticisms, and novels.[10] Among the latter is his brilliant novel of satire and pathos, *Japanese by Spring*. Reed's style as a Black public intellectual is Tocquevillian, for he endeavors through his writings seriously to "act on the manners of people," as de Tocqueville put it. Reed is equally Tocquevillian in his penchant for critiquing that category of "authors" for whom de Tocqueville had little regard: "journalists." For Reed, this means especially journalists whose particular area of discourse earned them the label "Black-pathology writers." Reed has targeted his keen left-critical vision on three Black-pathology writers for New York City organs—namely, Joe Klein of *New York* magazine, Pete Hamill of the *New York Post*, and Jim Sleeper of *New York Newsday*.

For Reed, the neoconservative era from the early 1970s onward has witnessed a mushrooming of veritable Negrophobic discourse on the multilayered crises facing the 30 percent of African Americans who have been poverty-ridden, and especially that discourse focused on societal dimensions of Black poverty, such as teenage pregnancies, unwed births, high crime, and rates of violence. There have been two dimensions of Black-bashing and Black-denigrating discourse among white journalists and pundits that have perturbed Reed.

First, Reed informs us that this Black-denigrating discourse is saturated with falsehood in the form of failure by Negrophobic-leaning commentators who compare patterns of societal breakdown among Blacks with those of whites and other groups. In the case of drug use, for example, this is particularly pernicious. Nationwide data have revealed for some time that illegal drug use is greater among white Americans than among Black Americans, but, owing to racist practices in the logistical allocation of police and their arrest methods, African American citizens are disproportionately arrested and imprisoned for illegal drug use.

Second, the Black-denigrating discourse among conservative white pundits has also been saturated with what might be called evaluative distortions. For Reed, this means especially the cynical causal connections drawn by conservative white pundits between systemic malaise in American society generally on the one hand and the multilayered features of poverty and urban crises among African Americans on the other. Here, Reed has in mind the argument about a presumptive cultural/moral decline in American life as propagated by conservative white evangelist clergy figures like the Reverend Jerry Falwell. This pattern of evaluative distortion of Black urban crises has also been propagated, to the detriment of the African American poor, by conservative white intellectuals like James Q. Wilson, Richard Herrnstein, Charles Murray, and John Dilulio, as well as the Indian

American Dinesh D'Souza, and others associated with research institutions like the Heritage Foundation and the American Enterprise Institute.[11]

A basic component of Reed's persona as a public intellectual has been fashioned by this Negrophobic-skewed, Black-denigrating discourse, which was broadcast by conservative white intellectuals and pundits from the 1970s through the 1990s. If we borrow a moment from the notion of the "Water Dowser"—the person who aids communities facing water crises—then we might think of Reed's demeanor in assisting Black communities facing bashing from Negrophobic white pundits as that of a "Truth Dowser," speaking truth to Black-denigrating distortions and falsehood.

In several essays collected in *Airing Dirty Laundry* (1993),[12] Reed has performed his "Truth Dowser" function by zeroing in on a particularly specious and odious version of Black-denigrating discourse, a 1988 article by Pete Hamill titled "Breaking the Silence," about which Reed observed that Hamill claims that "the Black underclass is a greater threat to our national security than the Russians."[13] Declaring the Irish American Hamill's charge a "preposterous," naked falsehood, Reed goes on to underscore the irony of white-ethnic intellectuals positioning themselves at the forefront of the era of Black-denigrating conservative discourse on urban crises: "It is ironic that the same claim [as Hamill's against African American poor] was made by Irish-pathology writers [WASP writers] only two generations ago." Reed continues:

> Hamill's criticisms of the Black underclass have been made [in the late nineteenth and early twentieth centuries] about Irish Americans, the group to which Hamill, William Buckley, and Moynihan belong. . . . As for illegitimacy, Bob Callahan, author of the *Big Book of the American Irish*, points to the stereotype that the typical Irish American was a person with thirty-five children that he couldn't support, all of whom were headed for the poor house. As for crime, Callahan remembers growing up in a New England city in 1930s where the newspapers separated information about "American Crime" from "Hibernian Crime."[14]

Moreover, in numerous essays and newspaper columns, Reed continued his populist-intellectual defense of the honor of Black folks, uncovering and lambasting the evaluative distortions and falsehoods associated with what he calls Black-pathology-oriented white conservative intellectuals and pundits. Taking up the issue of drug use, for example, Reed observes that "while the media bombard the public with images of black women as irresponsible cocaine mothers," less attention is given to related data that "indicated that the white suburban rate for cocaine pregnancies is about the same as that in the inner city." Reed continues this particular populist-intellectual defense of Black folks' honor as follows:

> According to a *New York Times* survey, the typical crack addict is a forty-year-old white male professional, married, and suburban. . . . Even though studies show that white teenagers are more prone to drug abuse than black teenagers, the image of drugs as a black problem prevails, not only in the media and political circles where the war on drugs means a war against black neighborhoods, but the country's leading intellectual publications.[15]

By the 1990s, Reed could have easily drawn in his sails as a populist intellectual defending Black honor after a two-decades-long enterprise of critiquing Black-denigrating discourse in the media among conservative white intellectuals and commentators, satisfied with his achievement in the public intellectual arena. But Reed's populist soul did not permit him this satisfaction. Quite the contrary. He has instead gone a step further with his populist public intellectual demeanor, harnessing organizational resources to create a biracial alliance charged with boycotting television networks found to be peddling a grossly negligent Negrophobic discourse on African American urban issues. One of the instances that ignited the spark for Reed's boycott movement was a television news essay by the commentator Roger Rosenblatt. As Reed tells it,

> After I began to collect and examine [media] material [for a boycott movement] I began to notice that . . . even places like National Public Radio had accepted the corporate think tankers' "underclass" theory . . . that a majority of America's social problems were related to the personal behavior of Black people. . . . One particularly shocking to me was a commentary by Roger Rosenblatt of the McNeil/Lehrer News Hour, during which the Black youth involved in the Central Park rape of a young stockbroker was used to smear all Black youth, whose activities were equated with "Satanism." . . . The Roger Rosenblatt tape, for me, was the last straw.[16]

Reed's media-boycott movement was forged through a network of writers he had encountered in the writers' association PEN International, some of whom functioned as local organizers for the boycott in cities across the country. The start-up year was 1989, and the first formal event—a boycott week—was launched in 1991. Two additional boycott weeks would follow. Evaluating the impact of his boycott activity in the pages of *Airing Dirty Laundry*, Reed offers the following observation:

> For our first boycott [in 1991] we were able to assemble a coalition unheard of in these days of division and polarization. Buddhists in Boulder, Colorado; blacks and whites in Berkeley; Latinos in Houston, Texas and New York; gays and lesbians, integrationists in Berkeley, and nationalists in Atlanta, Georgia. Writers in Boston, Brooklyn, New Orleans, Washington, D.C., and Detroit. During some of the events, writers addressed the stereotypes of African Americans, Latinos and Asian Americans that pour into the nation's living rooms each night.[17]

Thus, as a leading figure among Black public intellectuals over the past several decades, Reed has carved out a special niche for himself in his populist-defense posture on behalf of the honor of Black folks in general and the African American poor in particular. The incredible sway that conservative white pundits' Negrophobic bashing of the African American weak working class and poor sector gained in America's media was shameful, and it took a brilliant and courageous Black public intellectual like Ishmael Reed to challenge and checkmate it. In doing so, he set an example that has sparked numerous other African American intellectuals to take up where he left off. Like Du Bois, Wells-Barnett, and others among the formative cohort of civil rights activist African American intellectuals, Reed and his protégés know well that the struggle to secure respect for Black folks' honor in America's media remains ongoing.

Public Intellectual as Radical Humanist: Cornel West

Although Ishmael Reed and Cornel West, as Black public intellectuals, overlap in regard to their progressive orientation, they also diverge in some basic ways. For one thing, Reed is a creative writer and literary studies scholar whereas West is a philosophy of religion and culture scholar. More fundamentally, if Reed can be characterized as a populist-challenger intellectual personality, West might be labeled a "let me commiserate with you" personality.

At West's core lies a solid radical-humanist strain. Jervis Anderson, the African American essayist and pacifist intellectual, offers an apt characterization of West's public intellectual persona in describing West as "a religious and intellectual freedom fighter." And Anderson fleshes out quite deftly this image of West: "He regards philosophy as a weapon that should be used in the arena of social action—to clarify issues and to help build progressive alliances across racial lines."[18] West himself expanded on Anderson's portrayal of his radical-humanist persona during an interview in 1990 on the PBS television series *World of Ideas with Bill Moyers*: "I understand the vocation of the intellectual as trying to turn easy answers into critical questions, and ask these critical questions to those with power. . . . The quest for truth, the quest for good, the quest for the beautiful, for me, presupposes allowing suffering to speak, allowing victims to be put on the agenda of those with power."

What stands out in West's self-characterization during his Moyers interview is his deft intertwining of both the philosophical and Black-ethnic sources (stemming especially from the traditions of the Black church) of his humanist persona. The interplay of formal philosophy (particularly pragmatism and what West views as ethical Marxism) and Black religious forms contribute acutely to his humanism, for they enable him to harness ethically both the ideal-world and problem-solving-world realities within his radical-humanist identity. In regard to pragmatism's contribution to what might be called West's dualistic philosophical fusion, West observes in his astute work *The American Evasion of Philosophy* (1989) that "the distinctive appeal of American pragmatism in our postmodern moment is its unashamedly moral emphasis and its unequivocally ameliorative [problem-solving] impulses." And as regards Black religious patterns, West draws attention especially to the way in which a Black religious ethos differs from a Marxist one. As he put it in his book *The Ethical Dimensions of Marxist Thought*: "As a [Black] Christian, I recognize certain irreconcilable differences between Marxists of whatever sort and Christians of whatever sort. . . . My Christian perspective mediated by the rich traditions of the Black Church that produced and sustains me—embraces depths of despair, layers of dread . . . and ungrounded leaps of faith alien to the Marxist tradition[, which] . . . is silent about the existential meaning of death, suffering, love, and friendship."[19]

There is a seemingly contradictory dimension about the constituent philosophical elements in West's radical-humanist persona (the pragmatist, Marxist, and Christian elements), causing one to ask how West resolves this. For the ethical Marxist element in West's humanist position, it is important to focus on the "man makes his own history" facet of Marxist thought—its emphasis on human agency, that is—not on the naked power-tactical facet of Marxist thought, or the Leninist and Maoist facet, so that when Marxism's focus on human agency is synergistically entwined with what West calls in *The American Evasion of Philosophy* the "ameliorative impulse" of pragmatism on the one hand and interlaced with the folk-pragmatism of Black Christianity on the other, then an internally consistent humanistic outlook emerges. As already noted, West offered a cogent characterization of how he threads the several philosophical strands—pragmatist, Marxist, and Christian—into a modern-day progressive humanist position during his 1990 interview with Moyers. West informed his audience that what he called "The quest for the good . . . presupposes allowing suffering to speak, allowing the victims to be visible, and allowing social misery to be put on the agenda of those with power."

Thus, at the core of West's radical-humanist persona is a kind of dual mandate, one concerned with expanding human knowledge regarding the sources of human suffering, especially in the context of the modern state, which West fulfills as an academic philosopher, and the second concerned with fashioning real-world strategies for egalitarianizing the modern human condition, which West fulfills as a public intellectual. It has been the second face of West's humanistic dual mandate that has made him a household name among most African Americans, and he endeavors to become a household name among a much broader range of Americans. To this end, West has fashioned what might be called a civic-culture contextualization of public discourse among American citizens—white/Black, Jew/gentile—in relation to our society's most fundamental moral and democratic failure as a leading nation-state—namely, its cruel and tenacious racist heritage.

Numerous public appearances in civic milieus are key to West's civic-culture mobilization of public discourse on the human wreckage wrought by America's racist heritage. West's mobilization has also been aided by the publication of his essays in *Race Matters* (1993), which enjoyed best-seller status for a half year in combined hardcover and paperback formats. With *Race Matters*, West was able to regularize his quest to fashion a moral tormenting of Black souls associated with American racism, a confrontation that continues to elude the vast majority of white Americans.

The Reverend Martin Luther King Jr. had hoped that the civil rights movement's nonviolent quest would provide the moral spark for white Americans to end their long-standing denial of the human ravages wrought by American racism, but the rise of Black-bashing neoconservatism under the Republican administrations of Richard Nixon, Ronald Reagan, and George H. W. Bush stymied this development. When contemplating the moral thrust of West's journey as a public intellectual, it is helpful to compare it to a similar uphill quest by Günter Grass and other postwar German humanist intellectuals to compel Germans to confront the legacy of Nazism. The disaster of Nazism caused Grass to cry out in anguish at his first visit to the death camps, "What manner of human evil did we Germans bequeath to mankind?" In a similar vein, I suggest that West is telling his white American compatriots in his public talks and in *Race Matters* that an American version of Grass's redemptive cry must be forthcoming in response to the wreckage wrought upon Black lives by the heritage of American slavery and racism.

West also reveals in *Race Matters* an astute understanding that the problematic associated with contemporary society's quest to vanquish America's neurotic racist mystique cuts across white victimizers and Black victims alike. In other words, the ultimate goal of vanquishing America's racist heritage and cosmopolitanizing all Americans' cultural identity requires a simultaneous assault on both white American progenitors of the country's racist mystique and on the defensive xenophobic-chauvinist copycat inventions of both African Americans and other nonwhite Americans, such as the Black separatism of Garveyism and the Nation of Islam.

For guidance on this awesome goal, West and other reform-leftist African American intellectuals have often turned to Ralph Ellison's insights on the defining role of racism in the American experiment. For Ellison, history has saddled Black folks with the special burden of weaning American civilization off of its racist denial of its generally pluralist cultural heritage. This high-humanist calling, as it were, demands that African Americans look beyond the oppressive heritage of American racism and affirm what Blacks have in common with whites—namely, a common peoplehood. In a variety of essays and short stories and his major novel, *Invisible Man* (1952),

Ellison posits that Blacks and whites share a common cross-racial Americanness, a common American identity notwithstanding perpetual efforts by white supremacist boosters (the KKK, White Citizens' Councils) and to a lesser degree xenophobic Black chauvinist elements (the Garveyites, the Nation of Islam movement) to fracture this cross-racial Americanness into warring cultural enclaves. In Ellison's conceptual schema on a common cross-racial Americanness, there are few defining white cultural realities that are simultaneously not Black, and similarly there are few defining Black cultural realities that are simultaneously not white. Thus, for Ellison, affirming this common generic cross-racial Americanness is the preeminent American moral imperative.

In general, West's interface with the Ellisonian perspective is best understood if we first dissect the political dimension of Ellison's searching insights on America's generic cross-racialness into two constituent parts. In one part, the political dimension of Ellison's cross-racial Americanness suggests that African Americans can concur with Ellison's formulation while at the same time mounting an activist movement to unseat America's white supremacist edifice. West's discourse in his addresses and writings suggests that this progressive reading of Ellison is his political take on the Ellisonian perspective. Another part of the political dimension of Ellison's cross-racial Americanness tilts in an establishmentarian direction.

As suggested by the essayist and critic Michele Wallace, the establishmentarian element implied in Ellison's formulation of cross-racial Americanness relates to his insistence that Blacks' invisibility has few socio-power dimensions—that is, related to systemic constraints associated with America's racist patterns and heritage—but rather is a function merely of white people's visual failure. Thus, from this vantage point on Ellison's cross-racial Americanness, African Americans are obliged politically not to rock the American systemic boat; rather, they should patiently allow white Americans' visual failure to mature, which means minimizing challenges to the vestiges of hegemonic racist patterns.

So seen in its establishmentarian dimension, then, Ellison's vision of Americanness dictates that Black intellectual discourse should put a premium on Americanness, persistent vestiges of white supremacist patterns and their tormenting of Black people's lives notwithstanding. Ellison's advice is that Blacks should trust in white Americans' intrinsic goodness, a presumptive tilt toward an egalitarian American society—advice that a generation and a half later, from the late 1970s onward, would be adopted by the first cadre of conservative Black intellectuals, as I'll discuss momentarily. Inasmuch as Ellison had, by the end of the 1940s, shed his progressive and leftist networks and was politically inert or noncommittal during the radicalization phase of the civil rights movement from the mid-1950s onward (making him a rare figure among African American creative writers in this period, along with Lorraine Hansberry and James Baldwin, among others), the establishmentarian view of Ellison's cross-racial Americanness was indeed Ellison's own intrinsic position.

Now, as West endeavored to calibrate his quest to challenge white Americans' indifference to America's legacy of the racist tormenting of African American lives on the one hand with an equal challenge of tenacious xenophobic Black chauvinist elements on the other, he responded unhesitatingly to the need to stand down the Black chauvinist elements. By the time of the publication of *Race Matters* in 1993, the most prominent variant of xenophobic Black chauvinism was represented by Minister Louis Farrakhan and his Nation of Islam organization. Farrakhan's Black-racialist group, it should be noted, has always had a media visibility far beyond its objective organizational strength. Its membership is said to have peaked at around one hundred thousand in the mid-1990s, with estimates today falling somewhere between ten thousand and fifty thousand—this compared with a combined membership of perhaps four million for reform-leftist civil rights organizations like the Southern Christian Leadership Conference, the National Council of Negro Women, the National Urban League, the Rainbow Coalition, and the NAACP, not to mention the multimillion-person membership of other African American civic associations, professional organizations, mainline African American religious denominations, and sororities and fraternities.

Be that as it may, by the time of the publication of *Race Matters* in 1993, West recognized that there is no hope ever in realizing genuine racial healing in American society without a two-front strategy, one challenging white Americans' long-standing denial of America's racist legacy of tormenting Black lives, and one challenging persistent xenophobic Black chauvinist elements. Remarking on his recognition of the need for such a two-front strategy, West informs his readers in *Race Matters* that xenophobic Afrocentrism "is misguided." What's more, he says, xenophobic Afrocentrism operates "out of fear of cultural hybridization and through . . .

retrograde views on black women, gay men, and lesbians, and a reluctance to link races to the common good [for all Americans]—it reinforces the narrow discussions about race."[20]

West is aware, of course, that challenging xenophobic Afrocentrist elements is a multidimensional undertaking. He does not shy away from recognizing the need for him and other reform-leftist Black intellectuals to engage some outreach to Afrocentrists, for example, to be willing to dialogue with them and even engage short-run coalitional activity too. West did this, as did numerous other reform-leftist Black intellectuals, including myself, in regard to the Farrakhan-initiated Million Man March in Washington, DC, in the fall of 1995.[21]

While it is not yet known whether West's mode of pragmatic but skeptical engagement with the xenophobic sector of Afrocentrists can produce his hoped-for transformation in their extremist ways, my own feeling is that West is quite correct in this engagement posture. His overall radical-humanist persona as a Black public intellectual would be deficient without this orientation. Deficient, too, would be West's long-standing quest to assist a creative and progressive version of an Ellisonian coalescence of Black and white identities in the everyday life stream of his American compatriots.

The New Archaeology of Black Intellectuals

Owing significantly to affirmative action practices that the civil rights movement inspired, the past thirty-plus years have witnessed the African American intelligentsia's penetration beyond the old occupational and institutional boundaries of the Black American social system. The process associated with this development has amounted to a new archaeology of the African American intelligentsia. Basic to this new archaeology is a simple yet multifaceted fact: that non-Black agencies now have an important degree of socialization influence over the formation of the Black intelligentsia.

Our view of this transformation can be highlighted if we contrast it with the 1930s era. When the British Marxist intellectual Nancy Cunard organized her brilliant compilation of essays and creative works by Black intellectuals in 1934, titled *Negro Anthology*, the vast majority of African American intellectuals had gained their modern formation through Black ethnic-bloc agencies and relationships.[22] From the late nineteenth century through the first sixty years of the twentieth—some five generations—the modern formation of the African American intelligentsia was realized overwhelmingly through Black colleges, Black churches, Black civil rights associations, Black professional associations, and the like.

It was, of course, the ideological and institutional rigidity of white supremacist American patterns that restricted the socialization role of non-Black agencies to the Black intelligentsia socialization process. Where there was some measure of deviation in this regard, it was found among an infinitesimal number of white colleges and professional schools that admitted a small number of African American students and among marginal sectors of white intellectual circles that opened their networks to participation by African Americans, such as those of bohemian WASP intellectuals; a few liberal WASP intellectuals; radical Quaker pacifists; a few liberal Jewish American intellectuals, especially those groups that supported the formation of the National Urban League and the NAACP; and leftist Jewish American intellectuals.

Thus, for the most part, mainline professional organizations and networks among whites in law, medicine, teaching, business, academia, technology and science, and entertainment were off-limits to participation by persons of African ancestry, whether of domestic Black or immigrant Black backgrounds. Professor Kenneth Manning's biography of the brilliant twentieth-century African American biologist Dr. Ernest Just demonstrates graphically how professionally frustrating and restricting Just's career was, even when he was granted a degree of associational membership in a white scientific research organization during the 1930s and 1940s.[23]

In our contemporary post–civil rights era, however, something new has evolved in regard to the long-standing exclusion of African American intellectuals from white-controlled intelligentsia agencies in American society. Since the late 1960s and early 1970s, numerous mainstream agencies associated with intelligentsia formations in American society have shed enough of their white supremacist ways to accommodate growing numbers of African Americans. Above all, the degree of attenuation of naked racist posturing by white intellectual and professional processes has been enough to induce blatantly conservative white forces to participate in the socialization of African American intellectuals.

The shift in the behavior of conservative quarters toward African American intelligentsia was preceded by a rather broad base of new conservatism among Jewish American intellectuals, starting in the mid-1960s. By the mid-1970s, this development had translated into a situation whereby these conservative intellectuals were functioning as a conveyor belt between mainstream American conservatism and an emergent cadre of conservative Black intellectuals. Journals and magazines associated with Jewish intellectuals, such as *Commentary*, the *New Republic*, and *Public Interest*, played an important role in fostering conservative Black intellectuals, as did other conservative journals, such as the *National Review* and *Policy Review*. Furthermore, conservative Jewish American intellectuals, functioning within well-financed WASP-run conservative research organizations like the Heritage Foundation, the Bradley Foundation, the American Enterprise Institute, and the Hoover Institution, also played an important role since the mid-1970s in institutionalizing the status of the first-generation cohort of conservative Black intellectuals on the American scene.[24]

It should be noted here that the new cadre of conservative Black intellectuals represents what might be called a fabricated Black conservatism. Were this conservatism organic, it would emanate from intrinsic African American status- and class-conflict patterns. But it is not. Their fabricated Black conservatism is phony, a pseudo-conservatism that is induced and fostered by forces extrinsic to African American society. As such, in the first instance anyway, the new Black conservatism is calibrated as a satellite of established American conservative forces. As a satellite intellectual phenomenon, conservative Black intellectuals function mainly as strategic performers, so to speak. They perform strategic tasks in political, social, and cultural spheres in the service of establishmentarian and conservative power patterns in American society. To this end, talented figures among conservative Black intellectuals like Sowell, Steele, Wortham, and Stanley Crouch are granted special access to media, to the editorial pages of leading newspapers like the *New York Times* and the *Washington Post*, and to leading magazines such as *The Atlantic*, *Harper's*, the *New Republic, and Commentary*.

In discourse terms, since the mid-1980s, new conservative Black intellectuals have fashioned what I call a "trasher demeanor" toward African American realities. As practiced by this group, the trasher demeanor operates in opposition to the mainline liberal and progressive definitions of African American sociopolitical processes, as these processes gained articulation by the mainline African American intelligentsia during most of the twenti-eth century.

In functional terms, two strands have evolved since the mid-1980s within the ranks of conservative Black intellectuals. Among the original trailblaz-ers or first-generation cohort of Black intellectuals we find a conservative strand of true believers—a hard sector, the aforementioned scholars among them. By the late 1980s and early 1990s, a second-generation cohort sur-faced among conservative Black intellectuals, constituting a kind of soft-core conservative sector who function in a more sporadic manner than the trailblazer true-believer strand. The soft-core sector functions rather like a guerrilla sniper corps, which is to say they produce writings shaped by neo-accommodationist expectations (harking back to Booker T. Washing-ton's conservatism mode) and a demeaning tone toward the honor of Black folks. Yet their writings can return to a semblance of Black-respecting ori-entations that might be just for a period of time, only to surface once more in an establishmentarian or conservative mode.

Put another way, proponents of the trasher demeanor toward mainline African American patterns who fall into the soft-core sector aren't exactly card-carrying members of the conservative party. In this respect, they're rather like the left-leaning American intellectuals during the 1930s and 1940s who remained fellow travelers just outside of the official Communist Party ranks. The chief thinkers of this trasher demeanor have not formally joined with their natural hard-core Black conservative allies; rather, they have hedged their bets, chameleon-style, and remained with the soft-core sector of Black conservatives instead hedge their bets. The establishmentar-ian classification applies rather aptly to this set of conservative Black intel-lectuals, among whom I would identify intellectuals such as the law scholar Randall Kennedy, the literary critic Hilton Als, the literary studies scholar Henry Louis Gates Jr., the philosophy of culture scholar K. A. Appiah, the Afro-American studies scholar Gerald Early, and the sociologist Orlando Patterson. Several recent newcomers to the ranks of soft-core Black conser-vatives include the historian Daryl Michael Scott, the Afro-American stud-ies scholar Paul Gilroy, the literary studies scholar Philip Richards, and the linguistic studies scholar John McWhorter.

The progressive sector among Black intellectuals today has, I believe, a special obligation to scrutinize the new ranks among conservative and establishmentarian Black public intellectuals. It is a task we owe our forefathers and foremothers of the twentieth-century African American intelligentsia who laid the foundations on which we function—founding forerunners like Alexander Crummell, Reverdy Ransom, John Wesley Cromwell, W. E. B. Du Bois, Monroe Trotter, Ida Wells-Barnett, Anna Julia Cooper, Francis Grimké, James Weldon Johnson, and Carter G. Woodson, among so many others. The goal of such scrutiny is to challenge the strategic satellite political function that conservative Black intellectuals perform for conservative forces in American society in general. After all, the strategic satellite political role played by conservative Black intellectuals endeavors to weaken the fulfillment of a maximal impact by African Americans on behalf of liberal and progressive patterns in the American system.

Notes

Prologue

1. Raymond Wolters, *The New Negro on Campus: Black College Rebellions in the 1920s* (Princeton, NJ: Princeton University Press, 1975).
2. Seymour Martin Lipset, "American Intellectuals: Their Politics and Status," *Daedalus: Journal of the American Academy of Arts and Sciences* 88, no. 3 (Summer 1959): 460.
3. R. J. M. Blackett, *Beating Against the Barriers: The Lives of Six Nineteenth-Century Afro-Americans* (Ithaca, NY: Cornell University Press, 1986).
4. W. E. B. Du Bois, *The Souls of Black Folk* (Chicago: A. C. McClurg & Co., 1903), 164.
5. David Levering Lewis, *W. E. B. Du Bois: Biography of a Race* (New York: Henry Holt, 1993), 170.
6. Michelle Valerie Ronnick, *The First Three African American Members of the American Philological Association* (Philadelphia: American Philological Association, 2001).
7. William M. Banks, *Black Intellectuals: Race and Responsibility in American Life* (New York: William Morrow, 1996), 56.
8. Text of the American Negro Academy manifesto can be found in Alfred Moss, *The American Negro Academy* (Baton Rouge: Louisiana State University, 1981), 291.
9. Roger Lane, *William Dorsey's Philadelphia and Ours: On the Past and Future of the Black City in America* (New York: Oxford University Press, 1991).

10. See Vincent P. Franklin, *The Education of the Philadelphia Negro: The Social and Educational History of a Minority Community, 1900–1950* (Philadelphia: University of Pennsylvania Press, 1981), 90–91.

11. Jay S. Stowell, *Methodist Adventures in Negro Education* (Cincinnati, OH: Methodist Book Concern, 1922).

12. Du Bois, *The Souls of Black Folk*, 202.

13. Du Bois, 201–202.

14. Du Bois, 203.

15. Manning Marable, *W. E. B. Du Bois: Black Radical Democrat* (New York: Twayne, 1986). Deep insights into Du Bois's ideological dualism phase can be found in Shamoon Zamir's brilliant essay "The Sorrow Songs/Songs of Myself: Du Bois, the Crisis of Leadership, and Prophetic Imagination," in *The Black Columbiad*, ed. Werner Sollors (Cambridge, MA: Harvard University Press, 1995), 152–160.

16. See Lewis, *W. E. B. Du Bois*, 297–342.

17. Lewis, 341.

18. Kevin Gaines, *Uplifting the Race: Black Leadership, Politics, and Culture in the Twentieth Century* (Chapel Hill: University of North Carolina Press, 1996), 66.

19. Booker T. Washington, *The Future of the Race* (New York: Scribner & Son, 1902), 132.

20. Gunnar Myrdal, *An American Dilemma: The Negro Problem and Modern Democracy* (New York: Harcourt Brace, 1944), 2:739. Emphasis added.

21. Myrdal, *An American Dilemma*, 2:739.

22. For a keen case study of the sway of the Bookerite accommodationist leadership approach among the first-generation African American middle class, see Kenneth Kusmer, *A Ghetto Takes Shape: Black Cleveland, 1870–1930* (Urbana: University of Illinois Press, 1976).

23. Linda McMurray, *To Keep the Waters Troubled: The Life of Ida B. Wells* (New York: Oxford University Press, 1998), 263.

24. McMurray, *To Keep the Waters Troubled*, 263.

25. A'Lelia Bundles, *On Her Own Ground: The Life and Times of Madam C. J. Walker* (New York: Scribners, 2001), 242. Emphasis added.

26. Banks, *Black Intellectuals*, 55.

27. Banks, 56.

28. Ray Sprigle, *In the Land of Jim Crow* (New York: Alfred Knopf, 1949), 101.

29. Charles S. Johnson, *Growing Up in the Black Belt: Negro Youth in the Rural South* (Washington, DC: American Youth Commission, 1941), 277–278.

30. Myrdal, *An American Dilemma*, 1:485. Emphasis added.

31. James Weldon Johnson, *Along This Way: The Autobiography of James Weldon Johnson* (New York: Viking Press, 1933), 209. Emphasis added.

32. Lionel Trilling, "A Tragic Situation," *The Nation*, December–January 1945, 584.

33. See Kenneth Janken's biography of Walter White's leadership era in the NACCP: *The Biography of Walter White, Mr. NAACP* (New York: New Press, 2003).

34. Du Bois, *The Souls of Black Folk*, 9.

35. Du Bois, 29.

36. Frederick Douglass, "Looking the Republican Party Squarely in the Face," address delivered in Cincinnati, OH, June 14, 1876. Published in *The Frederick Douglass Papers*, ser. 1, *Speeches, Debates, and Interviews*, vol. 14, *1864–1880*, ed. John W. Blassingame and John R. McKivigan (New Haven, CT: Yale University Press, 1991), 442.

37. See Ishmael Reed, "Interview," *Emerge*, July 1998.

38. James M. McPherson, "Days of Wrath," *New York Review of Books*, May 12, 2005, 17.

39. Cornel West, "Black Strivings in a Twilight Civilization," in Henry Louis Gates Jr. and Cornel West, *The Future of the Race* (New York: Oxford University Press, 1996), 81.

1. Horace Mann Bond

I should point out that I had a close mentor-protégé relationship with Horace Mann Bond that commenced during my undergraduate years at Lincoln University (1949–1953) and continued until his death in 1972. Some of my understanding of Bond's intellectual odyssey stems from numerous conversations with him regarding his intellectual career. Furthermore, I am indebted to a host of exceptional studies on Bond, foremost among them Wayne J. Urban's *Black Scholar: Horace Mann Bond, 1904–1972*. Another study of Bond's professional career that proved indispensable to my research is Michael Fultz's Harvard University School of Education doctoral dissertation, a summary of which can be found in Fultz's "'A Quintessential American': Horace Mann Bond, 1924–1939," which was published in the *Harvard Educational Review* in 1985. Another student of Bond's career, William B. Thomas, probed Bond's pioneering research into IQ testing in his article "Black Intellectuals' Critique of Early Mental Testing: A Little-Known Saga of the 1920s," published in 1982 in the *American Journal of Education*. A useful contextual work relating to Bond's career, treating Bond's family background and social development, is Roger Williams's *The Bonds* (1971). Finally, Horace Mann Bond's papers are located at the University of Massachusetts Amherst and are on microfilm. I am indebted to the staff managing microfilm holdings of the Bond papers at Lincoln University's Langston Hughes Memorial Library.

1. Wayne Urban, *Black Scholar: Horace Mann Bond, 1904–1972* (Athens: University of Georgia Press, 1992), 2. Urban's biography proved to be an invaluable resource as I researched each phase of Bond's life and career.
2. John Gunther, *Inside U.S.A.* (New York: Harper & Brothers, 1947), 680–681.
3. One such scholar was William B. Thomas, who published a series of articles on Bond's IQ-testing research, including "Black Intellectuals' Critique of Early Mental Testing: A Little-Known Saga of the 1920s," *American Journal of Education* 90, no. 3 (1982): 258–292.
4. Clark Foreman, *Environmental Factors in Negro Elementary Education* (New York: Norton, 1932).
5. Horace Mann Bond, *Education of the Negro in the American Social Order* (New York: Prentice Hall, 1934).
6. Horace Mann Bond, *Negro Education in Alabama: A Study in Cotton and Steel* (Washington, DC: Associated Publishers, 1939).
7. Urban, *Black Scholar*, 87.
8. Bond, *Negro Education in Alabama*, 81.
9. Bond, 106.
10. Bond, 115.
11. Bond, 115–116.
12. Urban, *Black Scholar*, 85–86.
13. Urban, 85–86.
14. See Bond, *Negro Education in Alabama*, 258ff.
15. Bond, 256–257.
16. Bond, 257.
17. Bond, 257–258.
18. Bond, 257.
19. Bond, 258.
20. Bond, 203–204.
21. Bond, 204.
22. Bond, 204–205.
23. Bond, 204. Emphasis added.
24. Bond, 205.
25. Bond, 207.
26. Bond, 207–208.
27. Bond, 208.
28. Bond, 208.
29. Bond, 212.
30. Bond, 213–214.
31. Bond, 220.
32. Bond, 221.
33. Bond, 214.

34. Horace Mann Bond, "William Edward Burghardt Du Bois: A Portrait in Race Leadership," in Bond Papers, Part IV, Reel 12, 5.

35. Horace Mann Bond, "Negro Leadership Since Washington," *South Atlantic Quarterly* 24, no. 2 (1925): 116.

36. Bond, "Negro Leadership," 117–118.

37. While working under Bond's academic deanship, Allison Davis fashioned the ideas and pursued the research that resulted in his pathbreaking study of the southern racial caste system, a study on which St. Clair Drake was a primary fieldwork researcher and draftsman. The study was published as *Deep South: A Social Anthropological Study of Caste and Class* (Chicago: University of Chicago Press, 1941).

38. Author interviews with St. Clair Drake, April–May 1987.

39. Horace Mann Bond and Julia Washington Bond, *The Star Creek Papers*, ed. Adam Fairclough (Athens: University of Georgia Press, 1997).

40. See Bond Papers, Part I, Reel 5.

41. See Bond and Bond, *The Star Creek Papers*, 28.

42. Bond and Bond, 28–29.

43. Bond and Bond, 28–29.

44. Quoted in Urban, *Black Scholar*, 53.

45. Urban, 65. Accounts of the lynching of Jerome Wilson can be found in Bond and Bond, *The Star Creek Papers*.

46. Urban, *Black Scholar*, 65.

47. See Bond Papers, Part I, Reel 5.

48. Urban, *Black Scholar*, 103.

49. Author interviews with St. Clair Drake, April–May 1987.

50. Urban, *Black Scholar*, 108–109.

51. Urban, 109.

52. Urban, 110.

53. For Bond's Washington Parish Training College commencement address, May 5, 1935, titled "The Road to Freedom," see Bond Papers, Part IV, Reel 10.

54. Text of Bond's Gannon Theological Seminary lecture on May 19, 1942, can be found in Bond Papers, Part IV, Reel 10. Emphasis added.

55. Dennis Dickerson, "African American Religious Intellectuals and the Theological Foundations of the Civil Rights Movement, 1930–55," *Church History* 74, no. 2 (2005): 217–235.

56. Urban, *Black Scholar*, 111.

57. Linda Reed, *Simple Decency and Common Sense: The Southern Conference Movement, 1938–1963* (Bloomington: Indiana University Press, 1991), xx–xxi.

58. Reed, *Simple Decency*, 19. In addition to Foreman, newly elected officials included honorary president Louise Charlton, a federal judge who was a U.S. commissioner of the Northern District of Alabama; Frank Graham, a liberal

University of North Carolina professor and founding member of the Southern Policy Committee, a group formed in 1935 to combat poverty in the South; secretary Mollie Dowd, a board member of the Women's Trade Union League in Birmingham; and executive secretary H. C. Nixon, a fellow founding member of the Southern Policy Committee and a liberal Tulane University professor.

59. Reed, *Simple Decency*, 15–16. In addition to the aforementioned officers, the "who's who" included Joseph Gelders, a liberal physics professor at the University of Alabama; Lucy Randolph Mason, a field organizer in Atlanta for the Congress of Industrial Organizations; William Mitch, president of the Alabama Industrial Union Council; and H. L. Mitchell of the Southern Tenant Farmers Union. Other Black delegates were the Communist labor union organizer Hosea Hudson, the AME bishop J. A. Bragg, National Urban League regional director Jesse O. Thomas, and National Negro Congress secretary John P. Davis.

60. Reed, *Simple Decency*, 32. It is worth mentioning that in late 1942, when the SCHW's eighteen-member executive board was expanded to thirty-six, Black professionals were allocated twelve spots. All of those elected were squarely on the liberal and progressive side of the political spectrum; all of them, in Reed's view, "represented the [SCHW's] strongest black supporters." In addition to the aforementioned Bethune, Patterson, and Davis, board members included Charlotte Hawkins Brown, the president of Palmer Institute in North Carolina; Charles S. Johnson and Ira Reid of Fisk University; and Rufus Clement, president of Atlanta University and the brother-in-law of Horace Mann Bond's brother J. Max Bond.

61. See Nell Painter, *The Narrative of Hosea Hudson: His Life as a Negro Communist in the South* (Cambridge, MA: Harvard University Press, 1979).

62. Painter, *The Narrative of Hosea Hudson*, 149.

63. The text of the conference report can be found in Charles S. Johnson, "Southern Conference on Race Relations," *Journal of Negro Education* 12, no. 1 (1943): 134–138.

64. Roi Ottley, *New World A-Coming: Inside Black America* (Cambridge, MA: Riverside Press, 1943), 238.

65. Johnson, "Southern Conference on Race Relations," 135.

66. For example, there is no mention of the crucial 1942 Durham Southern Conference on Race Relations in Reed's major study of "the southern conference movement" from 1938 to 1963. Neither does Horace Mann Bond's biographer mention the 1942 Durham conference and thus its role in the rise of Bond's reform-leftist civil rights activism, following upon Bond's participation in the 1938 founding conference of the SCHW.

67. Richard Robbins, *Sidelines Activist: Charles S. Johnson and the Struggle for Civil Rights* (Jackson: University of Mississippi Press, 1996).

68. Reed, *Simple Decency*, 97, 180.

69. For a study of the Lincoln University village community's history, see Marianne H. Russo and Paul A. Russo, *Hinsonville, A Community at the Crossroads: The Story of a Nineteenth-Century African American Village* (Selingsgrove, PA: Susquehanna University Press, 2005).

70. This historic development is probed in Raymond Wolters, *The New Negro on Campus: Black Students' Protests in the 1920s* (Princeton, NJ: Princeton University Press, 1975).

71. Urban, *Black Scholar*, 125. Editor's note: Kilson tells the Grim story at length in his posthumously published autobiography, *A Black Intellectual's Odyssey: From a Pennsylvania Milltown to the Ivy League* (Durham, NC: Duke University Press, 2021).

72. Urban, *Black Scholar*, 125.

73. Urban, 126.

74. See Martin Kilson and Marion Kilson, "Portrait of the 50th Reunion of Lincoln University Class of 1953" (unpublished manuscript, Lincoln University Archives).

75. Urban, *Black Scholar*, 151.

76. Urban, 179–181.

77. Horace Mann Bond, *Education for Freedom: A History of Lincoln University, Pennsylvania* (Princeton, NJ: Princeton University Press, 1976), 59–60.

78. Urban, *Back Scholar*, 179–181.

79. Bond, *Education for Freedom*, 75–76.

80. In addition to Bond, others who felt Grimké's influence were Langston Hughes; the civic leader Monroe Dowling; Thurgood Marshall; the NAACP lawyers Robert L. Carter and Franklin Williams; the clergyman and founder of Operation Crossroads Africa James Robinson; the performer Roscoe Lee Browne; the actor, activist, and diplomat Horace Dawson; Jacques Wilmore; and Larry Neal.

81. Bond, *Education for Freedom*, 324.

82. Bond, 326

83. Bond, 326.

84. Quoted in Bond, 326–327.

85. See William M. Banks, *Black Intellectuals: Race and Responsibility in American Life* (New York: Norton, 1996), 56.

2. John Aubrey Davis

1. Michele F. Pacifico, "'Don't Buy Where You Can't Work': The New Negro Alliance of Washington," *Washington History* 6, no. 1 (Spring–Summer 1994): 67.

2. William H. Hastie, "The Way of the Alliance," in *The New Negro Alliance Year Book 1939* (Washington, DC: New Negro Alliance, 1939), 14.

3. John Aubrey Davis, "Notes for Dr. Martin Kilson" (n.d., ca. 1987).

4. Hastie, "The Way of the Alliance."

5. Davis, "Notes for Dr. Martin Kilson."

6. Pacifico, "'Don't Buy Where You Can't Work,'" 68–69.

7. Pacifico, 72.

8. Pacifico, 72.

9. Pacifico, 72–73.

10. Davis, "Notes for Dr. Martin Kilson."

11. Rolandus H. Cooper, "Notes from the Alliance Case Book," in *The New Negro Alliance Yearbook 1939*, 24.

12. Cooper, "Notes from the Alliance Case Book," 24.

13. Cooper, 25.

14. Davis, "Notes for Dr. Martin Kilson."

15. Among the pastors and their congregations in Nabrit's report were Walter Brooks, Nineteenth Street Baptist Church; R. W. Brooks, Lincoln Memorial Congregational Temple; E. C. Smith, Metropolitan Baptist Church; G. O. Bullock, Third Baptist Church; C. T. Murray, Vermont Avenue Baptist Church; R. Douglas Grimes, Salem Baptist Church; Josiah Elliott, St. Luke's Episcopal Church (the first all-Black Episcopal congregation organized by white Episcopalians); H. B. Taylor, Fifteenth Street Presbyterian Church; A. F. Elmes, People's Congregational Church; and W. Wallace, African Methodist Episcopal Zion Church. See James M. Nabrit, "Civil Rights Endorsers of the Alliance," in *New Negro Alliance Yearbook 1939*, 31–33.

16. Pacifico, "'Don't Buy Where You Can't Work,'" 82–83.

17. Pacifico, 82–84.

18. Summaries of the alliance's brief presented to the U.S. Supreme Court in March 1938 are found in R. Rhoden Coward, "The History of the Alliance," in *New Negro Alliance Yearbook 1939*, 15–16. See also Pacifico, "'Don't Buy Where You Can't Work.'"

19. Pacifico, "'Don't Buy Where You Can't Work,'" 84.

20. Leon A. Ransom, "The Supreme Court Speaks," in *New Negro Alliance Yearbook 1939*, 18.

21. Pacifico, "'Don't Buy Where You Can't Work,'" 84–85.

22. Davis, "Notes for Dr. Martin Kilson."

23. Davis.

24. Davis.

25. Davis.

26. John A. Davis, *How Management Can Integrate Negroes in War Industries* (New York: New York State War Council, 1942), 5.

27. Davis, *How Management Can Integrate Negroes*, 5.

28. Denton Watson, *Lion in the Lobby: Clarence Mitchell, Jr.'s Struggle for the Passage of Civil Rights Laws* (New York: William Morrow, 1990), 130.

29. John A. Davis, "Non-discrimination in the Federal Services," *Annals of the American Academy of Political and Social Science* 244 (March 1946): 66.

30. Watson, *Lion in the Lobby*, 132.

31. Quoted in Desmond King, *Separate and Unequal: Black Americans and the U.S. Federal Government* (Oxford: Clarendon Press, 1997), 75. Desmond King's work is the most complete study of FEPC operations available.

32. Malcolm Ross, "The President's Committee on Fair Employment Practices: Beginning and Growth" (memorandum, n.d.), National Archives RG 228 of FEPC box 64. Quoted in King, *Separate and Unequal*, 75.

33. Davis, "Non-discrimination in the Federal Services," 67.

34. Davis, 68.

35. Davis, 71–72.

36. Davis, 72.

37. Davis, 73

38. John A. Davis, C. L. Golightly, and I. W. Hemphill, "The Wartime Employment of Negroes in the Federal Government" (memorandum, n.d.), National Archives RG 228 of FEPC, box 358. Quoted in Davis, "Non-discrimination in the Federal Services," 75.

39. See Watson, *Lion in the Lobby*, 138ff.

40. Watson, 68–69.

41. Davis, "Non-discrimination in the Federal Services," 69.

42. Davis, 68.

43. Genna Rae McNeil, *Groundwork: Charles Hamilton Houston and the Struggle for Civil Rights* (Philadelphia: University of Pennsylvania Press, 1990).

44. See King, *Separate and Unequal*, 96–103, which treats the FEPC job training experience during World War II.

45. Quoted in King, 99–101.

46. Quoted in King, 101.

47. King, 101.

48. King, 101.

49. See King, 101.

50. Watson, *Lion in the Lobby*, 143–144. A thorough account of the violent resistance to the FEPC by white workers and their unions can be found in a keen portrayal of the FEPC's experience by its last chairman. See Malcolm Ross, *All Manner of Men* (New York: Reynal & Hitchcock, 1948), chaps. 5–6, 8.

51. Watson, *Lion in the Lobby*, 143–144.

52. Jonathan Holloway, *Confronting the Veil: Abram Harris, E. Franklin Frazier, Ralph J. Bunche, 1919–1940* (Chapel Hill: University of North Carolina Press, 2002).

53. There are two other similarly authoritative probes of the FEPC by Malcolm Ross, its former chairman, and Professor Desmond King.

54. Watson, *Lion in the Lobby*, 147–148.

55. See Jesse Parkhurst Guzman, ed., *Negro Year Book: A Review of Events Affecting Negro Life* (Tuskegee, AL: Tuskegee Institute Department of Records and Research, 1947), 136.

56. Davis, "Non-discrimination in the Federal Services," 65.

57. Davis, 65.

58. John Aubrey Davis, letter to Martin Kilson, October 26, 1992.

59. Joining Davis in this special category are, from his experience with the New Negro Alliance, Rolandus Cooper, Rhoden Coward, Eugene Davidson, Thurman Dodson, Naylor Fitzhugh, William Hastie, Belford Lawson, Thurgood Marshall, James Nabrit, George Rycraw, and Doxey Wilkerson. From the FEPC experience, deserving of recognition are George Crockett, Elmer Henderson, Charles Hamilton Houston, George Johnson, Theodore Jones, Marjorie Lawson, Clarence Mitchell, and Robert Weaver.

60. Davis, "Notes for Dr. Martin Kilson."

61. A. Philip Randolph, letter to Walter White (July 17, 1952), NAACP Papers—Part 14: Race Relations in the International Arena 1940–1945, reel 13.

62. Walter White, letter to Department of State (July 17, 1952), NAACP Papers—Part 14: Race Relations in the International Arena 1940–1945, reel 13.

63. The foregoing discussion of the outcomes of Davis's State Department consultancy is based on conversations with John Aubrey Davis. See also *Progress Report on the Employment of Colored Persons in the Department of State*, attached to E. N. Montague, letter to Clarence Mitchell (March 31, 1953), NAACP Papers—Part 14: Race in the International Arena 1940–1945, reel 13.

64. Penny Von Eschen, *Race Against Empire: Black Americans and Anti-colonialism, 1937–1957* (Ithaca, NY: Cornell University Press, 1997).

65. Martin Staniland, *American Intellectuals and African Nationalists, 1955–1970* (New Haven, CT: Yale University Press, 1999).

66. The best study of the cadre of francophone Black intellectuals who launched the First World Congress of Black Writers and Artists is Janet G. Vaillant, *Black, French, and African: A Life of Léopold Sédar Senghor* (Cambridge, MA: Harvard University Press, 1990).

67. Davis, "Notes for Dr. Martin Kilson."

68. Walter C. Carrington, "Black America and African Liberation," *Focus: Journal of the Joint Center for Political and Economic Studies* 19, no. 4 (1991): 8.

69. E. Franklin Frazier, "What Can the American Negro Contribute to the Social Development of Africa?," in *Africa Seen by American Negroes*, ed. John A. Davis (Paris: Editions Presence Africaine, 1958), 263–278.

70. E. Franklin Frazier, *Black Bourgeoisie* (Glencoe, IL: Free Press, 1956). Keen critiques of Frazier's discourse on the Black professional class can be found in James E. Teele, ed., *E. Franklin Frazier and the Black Bourgeoisie* (Columbia: University of Missouri Press, 2002).

71. Adelaide Cromwell and Martin Kilson, ed., *Apropos of Africa: Sentiments of American Negro Leadership Toward Africa, 1850–1950s* (London: Frank Cass, 1969); Okon Edet Uya, ed., *Black Brotherhood: Afro-Americans and Africa* (Lexington, MA: D. C. Heath, 1971); James H. Meriwether, *Proudly We Can Be Africans: Black Americans and Africa, 1935–1961* (Chapel Hill: University of North Carolina Press, 2002).

72. Kevin Gaines, *African Americans in Ghana: Black Expatriates and the Civil Rights Era* (Chapel Hill: University of North Carolina Press, 2006).

73. Jerry Watts, *Harold Cruse's The Crisis of the Negro Intellectual Reconsidered* (New York: Routledge, 2004).

74. Gerald Horne, *Black Liberation/Red Scare: Ben Davis and the Communist Party* (Newark, DE: Associated Press, 1994).

3. The Young Ralph Bunche and Africa

1. Raymond Leslie Buell, a young assistant professor in Harvard's Department of Government in the 1920s, preceded Bunche in conducting political science fieldwork research on European colonial governance in Africa, and he published his findings in a brilliant and monumental two-volume work titled *The Native Problem in Africa* (1927). I have speculated for some time that Assistant Professor Buell, who left Harvard around 1931 or 1932 to head up the Foreign Policy Association in New York City, made a contribution to the design of Bunche's doctoral research project in Dahomey and Togoland, but I have never been able to confirm this speculation.

2. Gunnar Myrdal, *An American Dilemma: The Negro Problem and American Democracy* (New York: Harper & Brothers, 1944).

3. W. E. B. Du Bois, *The Souls of Black Folk* (Chicago: A. C. McClurg, 1903).

4. Du Bois, *The Souls of Black Folk*.

5. W. E. B. Du Bois, *Dusk of Dawn: An Autobiography Toward a Race Concept* (New York: Harcourt Brace, 1940).

6. John Aubrey Davis, "Notes for Dr. Martin Kilson re Chapter on Dr. Aubrey Davis" (n.d., ca. 1987).

7. Ralph Bunche, *A World View of Race* (Washington, DC: Associates in Negro Folk Education, 1936), 1.

8. Bunche, *A World View of Race*, 1.

9. Bunche, 36.

10. Bunche, 38.

11. Bunche, 38.

12. Bunche, 40–42.

13. Ralph J. Bunche, "French Administration in Togoland and Dahomey" (PhD diss., Harvard University, 1934), 1–2.

14. Bunche, "French Administration in Togoland and Dahomey," 2ff.

15. Bunche, 388. Emphasis added.

16. Bunche, *A World View of Race*, 46.

17. Bunche, 47.

18. Bunche, 46.

19. Bunche, 47.

20. Bunche, 46–47.

21. Bunche, 46–65. These pages contain an extended discussion by Bunche of the embryonic African educated elite during the 1930s.

22. Bunche, "French Administration in Togoland and Dahomey," 96.

23. Bunche, 388.

24. Bunche, 129.

25. Bunche, *A World View of Race*, 52.

26. Bunche discusses African elite formation at several places in "French Administration in Togoland and Dahomey," 95ff, 103ff, 318ff, 388ff. See also Bunche, *A World View of Race*, 46–49, 50–56, 57–65.

   There is some overlap in the discussions in these two texts, since Bunche used some sections from his doctoral dissertation in writing *A World View of Race*. However, the analysis in the latter is more distinctly leftist-Marxist than it is in the dissertation.

27. Bunche, "French Administration in Togoland and Dahomey," 95–96.

28. Bunche, 97.

29. Bunche, 95–105, 131ff.

30. Bunche, 131.

31. Bunche, 389

32. Bunche, 315, 318.

33. Bunche, 392.

34. Bunche, 422. Emphasis added. For additional discussion, see Bunche, *A World View of Race*, 58–61.

35. Bunche, "French Administration in Togoland and Dahomey," 422. Emphasis added.

36. See Karl W. Deutsch, *Nationalism and Social Communication* (Cambridge, MA: MIT Press, 1953).

37. Bunche, "French Administration in Togoland and Dahomey," 128.

38. Bunche, *A World View of Race*, 63.

39. Bunche, 63. For Immanuel Wallerstein's perspective, see *The Political Economy of Contemporary Africa*, ed. Peter Gutkind and Immanuel Wallerstein (Beverly Hills, CA: Sage Publishing, 1986).

40. Bunche, "French Administration in Togoland and Dahomey," 421. For a comparative view of sources of resistance in British colonial territories during the era between the two world wars, see Martin Kilson, *Political Change in a West African State* (Cambridge, MA: Harvard University Press, 1966). See also Martin Kilson, "Anatomy of African Class Consciousness: Agrarian Populism in Ghana," in *Studies on Power and Class in Africa*, ed. Irving Markovitz (New York: Oxford University Press, 1986).

41. Bunche, "French Administration in Togoland and Dahomey," 423.

42. Bunche, *A World View of Race*, 82–96.

43. Bunche, 92.

44. Bunche, 95–96.

4. Harold Cruse Reconsidered

1. Harold W. Cruse, *The Crisis of the Negro Intellectual* (New York: William Morrow, 1967).

2. David R. Roediger, *The Wages of Whiteness* (New York: Verso, 1992); Noel Ignatiev, *How the Irish Became White* (New York: Routledge, 1995).

3. John Higham, *Strangers in the Land: Patterns of American Nativism* (New Brunswick, NJ: Rutgers University Press, 1955).

4. Cruse, *Crisis of the Negro Intellectual*, 363.

5. Cruse, 363–364.

6. Cruse, 364.

7. Cruse, 20.

8. Michael Rudolph West, *The Education of Booker T. Washington: American Democracy and the Idea of Race Relations* (New York: Columbia University Press, 2006).

9. West, *The Education of Booker T. Washington*, 58ff. See 196–204 for West's elaboration of this convoluted analytical perspective on the Bookerite accommodationist leadership paradigm.

10. Quoted in Horace Mann Bond, *Education for Freedom: A History of Lincoln University* (Princeton, NJ: Princeton University Press, 1976), 326–327.

11. Hazel V. Carby, "The New Auction Block: Blackness and the Marketplace," in *A Companion to African-American Studies*, ed. Lewis R. Gordon and Jane Anna Gordon (Oxford: Blackwell, 2006), 134.

12. Cruse, *Crisis of the Negro Intellectual*, 20.

13. Quoted in Cruse, 21.

14. Elliott M. Rudwick, *W. E. B. Du Bois: A Study in Minority Group Leadership* (Philadelphia: University of Pennsylvania Press, 1960); Henry Lee Moon, *The Emerging Thought of W. E. B. Du Bois* (New York: Simon and Schuster, 1972).

15. Cruse, *Crisis of the Negro Intellectual*, 20.

16. Cruse, 21.

17. Cruse, 21.

18. James Weldon Johnson, *Black Manhattan* (New York: Knopf, 1930), 149.

19. Johnson, *Black Manhattan*, 283.

20. Cruse, *Crisis of the Negro Intellectual*, 25.

21. Cruse, 25–26.

22. Cruse, 25–26.

23. Cruse, 363–364.

24. Cruse, 169,

25. Cruse, 117.

26. Cruse, 147.

27. Cruse, 372–373.

28. Cruse, 117–118.

29. See Winston James, *Holding Aloft the Banner of Ethiopia: Caribbean Radicalism in Early Twentieth-Century America* (New York: Verso, 1998), 262ff.

30. Cruse, *Crisis of the Negro Intellectual*, 45.

31. James, *Holding Aloft the Banner of Ethiopia*, 284.

32. Cruse, *Crisis of the Negro Intellectual*, 46–47.

33. Cruse, 19.

34. Martin Kilson, "From the Birth to a Mature Afro-American Studies at Harvard, 1969–2000," in Gordon and Gordon, *A Companion to African-American Studies*.

35. Cruse, *Crisis of the Negro Intellectual*, 26.

36. For analyses of the Harlem Renaissance era that contradict Cruse's observation, see, for example, Robert A. Bone, *The Negro Novel in America* (New York: Columbia University Press, 1965). See also Nathan I. Huggins, *Harlem Renaissance* (New York: Oxford University Press, 1971).

5. E. Franklin Frazier and *Black Bourgeoisie* Reconsidered

This chapter dates from 2001, and while revisions occurred over the next decade or more, some of the figures and terms used are reflective of an earlier time.

1. E. Franklin Frazier, *Black Bourgeoisie* (New York: Collier, 1962), 169–170, 176.

2. See, for example, Kenneth R. Manning, *Black Apollo of Science: The Life of Ernest Everett Just* (New York: Oxford University Press, 1983). I attempt to analytically contextualize the Frazierian issue of "play acting" and "make-believe"

behavior among the twentieth-century Black middle-class and professional sectors in this chapter. My purpose is to correct the imbalance in Frazier's "social pathology" argument in *Black Bourgeoisie*.

3. Data on the growth of white-collar jobs among African Americans from the 1960s to 1980s can be found in the following: Dan Cortz, "The Negro Middle Class," *Fortune*, November 1966; Richard Freeman, *Black Elite: The New Market for Highly Educated Black Americans* (New York: McGraw Hill, 1976); and Bart Landry, *The New Black Middle Class* (Berkeley: University of California Press, 1987).

4. These data can be found in Diane N. Westcott, "Blacks in the 1970s: Did They Scale the Job Ladder?," *Monthly Labor Review*, no. 105 (June 1982): 29–38.

5. For an evaluation of the politicization of the post-Frazier Black bourgeoisie, see Martin L. Kilson, "The State of African-American Politics," in *The State of Black America 1998*, ed. Lee Daniels (New York: National Urban League, 1998).

6. Adelaide M. Cromwell's Intellectual Odyssey

1. BA, Smith College, 1940; MA, University of Pennsylvania, 1931; certificate in social casework from Bryn Mawr College, 1943; PhD, Radcliffe College, 1952; faculty appointments at Hunter College, Smith College, and Boston University, 1951–1985. For a summary of Cromwell's career, see Barbara A. Burg, "Cromwell, Adelaide M.," in *African American National Biography*, vol. 2, ed. Henry Louis Gates Jr. and Evelyn Brooks Higginbotham (New York: Oxford University Press, 2008), 476–478.

2. Adelaide M. Cromwell, *Unveiled Voices, Unvarnished Memories: The Cromwell Family in Slavery and Segregation, 1692–1972* (Columbia: University of Missouri Press, 2007).

3. Adelaide M. Cromwell, *My Mothering Aunt: Otelia Cromwell* (Northampton, MA: Smith College, 2010).

4. Cromwell, *My Mothering Aunt*, 20.

5. The Seven Sisters were the elite women's colleges in the eastern United States: Barnard, Bryn Mawr, Mount Holyoke, Radcliffe, Smith, Vassar, and Wellesley.

6. Adelaide M. Cromwell, *The Other Brahmins: Boston's Black Upper Class 1750–1950* (Fayetteville: University of Arkansas Press, 1994).

7. A contemporary study of Black elites is Martin Kilson, *The Transformation of the African American Intelligentsia, 1880–2012* (Cambridge, MA: Harvard University Press, 2014).

8. Cromwell, *The Other Brahmins*, 83.

9. Adelaide Cromwell Hill and Martin Kilson, eds., *Apropos of Africa: Sentiments of American Negro Leaders on Africa from the 1800s to the 1950s* (London: Frank Cass, 1969).

10. W. E. B. Du Bois, "The American Negro Intelligentsia," in Cromwell Hill and Kilson, *Apropos of Africa*, 321.

11. Adelaide M. Cromwell, *Dynamics of the African/Afro-American Connection from Dependency to Self-Reliance* (Washington, DC: Howard University Press, 1987).

12. Adelaide M. Cromwell, *An African Victorian Feminist: The Life and Times of Adelaide Smith Casely Hayford 1868–1960* (London: F. Cass, 1986).

13. Cromwell, *An African Victorian Feminist*, xiii.

14. Cromwell, xv–xvi.

15. Cromwell, 29.

16. Cromwell, 204–205.

17. Adelaide M. Cromwell, "Afterword," in Dorothy West, *The Living Is Easy* (1948; New York: Feminist Press, 1982), 349–364; Adelaide M. Cromwell, "Introduction," in Mary Antoinette Brown Sherman, *Jellemoh: A Story of the Life and Times of Victoria Elizabeth Jellemoh Grimes, a Liberian Wife and Mother* (Northridge, CA: New World African Press, 2005), v–x.

18. "What Is Africa to Us?," in *The Black Power Revolt*, ed. Floyd B. Barbour (New York: Collier, 1969), 145–155; "Black Education in the Seventies: A Lesson from the Past," in *The Black Seventies,* ed. Floyd B. Barbour (Boston: Porter Sargent, 1970), 50–67; and "The Black Presence in the West End of Boston, 1800–1864: A Demographic Map," in *Courage and Conscience: Black and White Abolitionists in Boston*, ed. Donald M. Jacobs (Bloomington: Indiana University Press, 1993), 155–167.

19. "What Is Africa to Us?," 153, 155.

20. "Black Education," 55.

21. "Black Education," 61.

7. Ishmael Reed and Cornel West

1. Since this essay was written, Walter Williams died in 2020 at the age of eighty-four, having taught a class at George Mason University immediately before his death.

2. C. Wright Mills, *White Collar: The American Middle Classes* (New York: Oxford University Press, 1951), chap. 7.

3. R. J. M. Blackett, *Beating Against the Barrier: The Lives of Six Nineteenth-Century Afro-Americans* (Ithaca, NY: Cornell University Press, 1986).

4. Lionel Trilling, "A Tragic Situation," *The Nation,* January–December 1945, 584.

5. Toni Morrison, "Nobel Lecture," NobelPrize.org, December 7, 1993, https://www.nobelprize.org/prizes/literature/1993/morrison/lecture/.

6. Charles S. Johnson, *The Negro College Graduate* (Chapel Hill: University of North Carolina Press, 1932), 22.

7. See Adam Shatz, "About Face: A Leading Black Conservative, Glenn Loury, Has Switched Sides," *New York Times Magazine*, January 20, 2002.

8. Jerry Gafio Watts, *Amiri Baraka: The Politics and Art of a Black Intellectual* (New York: New York University Press, 2001).

9. See Jonathan Holloway, "The 'Crisis Canon' in the Twentieth Century," *Black Scholar* 31, no. 1 (2001): 2–13.

10. These figures derive from a 2020 listing of Reed's various works.

11. John Dilulio has converted recently to a liberal Catholic-evangelist outlook that is sympathetic to Black urban crises.

12. Ishmael Reed, *Airing Dirty Laundry* (New York: Addison-Wesley, 1993).

13. Pete Hamill, "Breaking the Silence," *Essence*, March 1988.

14. Reed, *Airing Dirty Laundry*, 20–22.

15. Reed, 5–6.

16. Reed, 26.

17. Reed, 26.

18. Jervis Anderson, "The Public Intellectual," *New Yorker*, January 17, 1992.

19. Cornel West, *The Ethical Dimensions of Marxist Thought* (New York: Monthly Review Press, 1991).

20. Cornel West, *Race Matters* (Boston: Beacon Press, 1993).

21. See Martin Kilson, "Anatomy of Black Conservatism," *Transition*, no. 59 (1993): 4–19. This article was the text of the first St. Clair Drake Memorial Lecture at Stanford University in 1992.

22. Nancy Cunard, *Negro Anthology* (London: Wishart, 1934).

23. Kenneth Manning, *Black Apollo of Science: The Life of Ernest Everett Just* (New York: Oxford University Press, 1983).

24. Kilson, "Anatomy of Black Conservatism."

Index

Page numbers in italics indicate illustrations; those with a *t* indicate tables.

Primus, Pearl, 26
professional class. *See under* social class
protest politics, 202–203
public intellectuals, 215–218, 242–246;
    debut of, 215, 218–222; function of,
    217–218; humanism and, 236–242;
    ideological issues of, 224–227;
    leadership issues of, 227–232; Lipset
    on, 2–3; populism and, 232–237;
    Tocqueville on, 217; types of,
    222–232. *See also* Black intelligentsia

Quakers, 64, 243
Queenan, Thomas Kilson, 230

"race etiquette," 20
race riots, 12–13, 156
racism, 23, 25, 155; by African-
    Americans, 21–22; capitalism and,
    87–91, 128–129; classism and, 153;
    Ellison on, 239–240; French versus
    British colonial, 145–147; Jim Crow
    laws and, 30–31, 35–36, 60–61; Ku
    Klux Klan and, 62, 150, 155;
    networking opportunities and, 195,
    197–198; in northern states, 60–61;
    residual, 200; social class and,
    187–188; studies of, 20–21; Trilling
    on, 219–220; West on, 239
Randolph, A. Philip, 86, 115–116, 137,
    177, 202
Ransom, Leon, 93
Ransom, Reverdy, 6, 54, 246
Rastafarians, 176
Reagan, Ronald, 239
Reconstruction, 71; Du Bois on, 182;
    educational policies of, 32–33, 35
Reddick, L. D., 46
Redding, J. Saunders, 46
Redfield, Robert, 47
Reed, Adolph, 225

Reed, Ishmael, 24, 232–237; works of:
    Airing Dirty Laundry, 234, 236;
    Japanese by Spring, 232–233
Reed, Linda, 55–56, 252n60
reform-leftist view, 224–226, 230, 232
Reid, Ira, 56, 61, 78, 252n60
Rendall, Isaac Norton, 69–70
Republican Party, 127, 162, 196–197;
    Douglass on, 249n36;
    neoconservative, 105, 239;
    Reconstruction policies of, 71
Retail Clerk Association, 92
Richards, Philip, 245
Richmond Race Relations Conference
    (1943), 59–60
Rivero, Manuel, 64
robber barons, 42, 154–155
Roberts, Owen Josephus, 93
Robeson, Paul, 61, 118, 159
Robinson, James, 122–123, 210, 253n80
Robinson, Randall, 125
Rockefeller Brothers Fund, 194
Rockefeller Foundation, 19, 194
Roediger, David, 155
Rogers, J. A., 177
Ronnick, Michelle Valerie, 7
Roosevelt, Franklin D.: Fair
    Employment Practices Committee
    of, 94–95, 98–113, 129–130, 137;
    NAACP and, 97; New Deal
    programs of, 56, 95, 207
Roosevelt, Theodore, 166
Rosenblatt, Roger, 235
Rosenwald, Julius, 46, 222
Rosenwald Foundation, 19, 78, 96
Rosenwald Fund, 47, 52
Ross, Malcolm, 130
Rudwick, Elliott, 21, 167
Ruffin, Nacy, 4
Rush, Benjamin, 68–69
Russian serfs, 23–24